Enjoy!!
Wendy

Best wishes

Sarah
AROC
2000

KU-331-262

The man who says it can't be done ought to get out of the way of the man who's doing it

THE BURGER KING

JIM MCLAMORE AND THE BUILDING OF AN EMPIRE

JAMES W. MCLAMORE

McGraw-Hill
New York San Francisco Washington, D.C. Auckland Bogotá
Caracas Lisbon London Madrid Mexico City Milan
Montreal New Delhi San Juan Singapore
Sydney Tokyo Toronto

Library of Congress Cataloging-in-Publication Data

McLamore, James W.
    The burger king : Jim McLamore and the building of an empire /
James W. McLamore.
        p.   cm.
    Includes index.
    ISBN 0-07-045255-5 (alk. paper)
    1. Burger King Corporation.   2. McLamore, James W.
3. Restaurateurs—United States—Biography.   I. Title.
TX945.5.B87M35   1997
338.7'6164795—dc21   97-22285
                                                                  CIP

McGraw-Hill

A Division of The McGraw-Hill Companies

Copyright © 1998 by The Estate of James W. McLamore. All rights
reserved. Printed in the United States of America. Except as permitted
under the United States Copyright Act of 1976, no part of this publication may be reproduced or distributed in any form or by any means, or
stored in a data base or retrieval system, without the prior written permission of the publisher.

Burger King Corporation is the exclusive licensee of the
following registered trademarks: *Burger King; Whopper;
Home of the Whopper; Have It Your Way; Make It
Special, Make It Burger King;* and the Burger King logo
shown at left. The Burger King® trademarks are used
and reproduced with permission of Burger King
Corporation, 1997, Miami, Florida.

2 3 4 5 6 7 8 9 0   DOC/DOC   9 0 2 1 0 9 8 7

ISBN 0-07-045255-5

Dad would have dedicated this book to his partner of forty-nine years, Nancy Nichol McLamore. For as long as I can remember, Dad always remembered to introduce Nancy during each of his speeches or at special functions. She was his partner in life and made sure he wanted for nothing throughout their marriage. Her dedication to him would have been returned with his book's dedication to her.

—Sterling Whitman McLamore

Contents

Preface

Jim McLamore, the businessman, was a true entrepreneur, one whose vision created a great American enterprise. He was dogmatic in his approach to his goals in business and in life. He was the ideal person to team up with Dave Edgerton and start the Burger King Empire. Jim was the perfect CEO whose strengths in planning, administration, and finance made an excellent partnership with Dave, who was the perfect operational and engineering expert. Together they created one of the greatest success stories of our times.

This book represents the bulk of my father's professional life. His accomplishments and achievements did not stop with his retirement from Burger King in 1972 at age 46, but continued as a board member for many corporations and carried through to his philanthropic work. His philosophy of giving back to his community and to the institutions that helped develop him along the way was paramount to his wishes for the McLamore Family Foundation. Fittingly, near the end of his life, the franchise community, together with Burger King Corporation, paid tribute to Dad by creating the Burger King/McLamore Foundation for supporting education throughout the United States.

Dad's greatest talent was his gentle approach to doing business. Whether a crew member, a manager, a franchisee, or a corporate executive, he always treated you with respect and was eager to learn more about you and your opinions. Many early franchisees have said, "His word was his bond and that's just the way we did business in the beginning." Trust, loyalty, devotion, and compassion were virtues deeply ingrained in his personality. Fortunately, he carried those traits into his philanthropic efforts. As chairman of the Board of Trustees of the University of Miami, Dad spearheaded the now famous $400 million five-year fund-raising plan, which far exceeded its goal by reaching over $500 million by its conclusion. Chuck Cobb, a family friend and fellow board member, said at Dad's memorial service, "He judged his ability to inspire a donation by how big a gulp they took when he asked for their contribution."

An article written after his death made mention of Dad as the "Master Gardner"—capable of growing people as well as plants. Clearly, he had talent at both, but he was best known for his tropical garden at home. Dad carried over his personal gardening interests to the Fairchild Tropical Garden after Hurricane Andrew took its toll. As the newly elected chairman of the board of the Garden, he took great pride in announcing a $5 million fund-raising plan to a shocked board of directors, throwing in the fact that he had already raised $1.5 million.

We are constantly reminded by others what a great inspiration Dad has been and how lucky they feel to have known him. Clearly, he was a hero to us all and will be missed.

Sterling Whitman McLamore

Introduction

I started my first fast-food restaurant at the ripe old age of 23, a few years before entering into the partnership that blossomed into Burger King.

What led me there? My early life holds some clues.

I would venture to say that personality traits are rather well-established long before we become teenagers. The influences that help develop a child's personality emerge early in life, and usually they stick like glue.

By the time I was 10 years old I had developed a pretty fair sense of some of the things I thought were important. Certainly my family was important to me. I lost my mother and maternal grandfather when I was 3 and my grandmother when I was 11. I never knew my paternal grandparents. My father died when I was 21, after a long illness, so the number of years I was able to benefit from parental care and guidance as a young boy was quite limited. Nevertheless, my experiences with family were all memorable and extremely influential in helping me determine a course in life.

One of the things I learned growing up in this situation was how to listen, which I think is almost a lost art today.

* * *

I was born on May 30, 1926, in New York City. My parents were Thomas Milton McLamore and Marian Floyd Whitman McLamore. Born in Texas and raised in Louisiana, Dad was an Army lieutenant in France during World War I. After his discharge and marriage, he worked in the Whitman family textile business in New York.

It is fair to say I was born to wealth and culture. However, the stock market crash of 1929 virtually wiped out the family fortune and drastically changed our lifestyle.

Although I was only a toddler, I have distinct memories of that frantic year. James Spurr Whitman, my industrialist grandfather, died then. I feel certain that what happened on Wall Street was largely responsible for his death. I can imagine that the realization of his losses devastated him.

In short order, the family sold our New York City townhouse and our suburban home in Montclair, New Jersey. We moved to Edgehill, the family farm in Central Valley, New York, which Grandfather Whitman had owned since the turn of the century. Just 50 miles north of New York City, Central Valley was still "the country" then. Edgehill, as we called our home, was a working farm and summer retreat. It became an important focus of life for the family.

My awakening really started a few years later, as the Great Depression deepened during the early 1930s. The shock of this time, and the loss of the family wealth, must have had a terrible effect on Mother. Committed to a sanitarium shortly after the birth of my brother, David Milton, in 1928, she died while still institutionalized in 1933. (I also had a sister, Claire, born in 1924.)

I never knew my mother except for a brief moment in 1928. I have a vague recollection of seeing David and Mother together, in her bedroom at our Montclair home, when David was just a few months old. I was just over two years old at the time. After she was committed to the institution, I never saw her again. We children were never permitted to visit there. She was 43 years old when she died.

* * *

Edgehill was a large, active dairy farm with three residences and many outbuildings that ran along a single road, just below the crest of the western slope of Central Valley. The view was spectacular. One building in the distance especially intrigued me: At the top of the mountain across the valley, above the town of Harriman, stood the impressive mansion of Edward Henry Harriman. This famous man had made a fortune in stock market speculations.

As a young boy growing up in Central Valley, I became fascinated in learning about Mr. Harriman and all that he had done. In 1897, he gained control of the then-bankrupt Union Pacific Railroad and soon built it into one of the country's leading railroads. Next to the Erie Railroad Station in the town that bore his name, he built a large warehouse, factory, and inclined railway to aid in the construction and maintenance of his mountaintop mansion. I remember the thrill of traveling up the "incline" with my grandmother in 1931 or 1932 to visit his widow for tea.

I became deeply attached to Edgehill and to the two young servants—Anna Smakel, from Czechoslovakia, and Katie O'Sullivan, from Ireland—who cared for and loved my sister, brother, and me.

Then, during the summer of 1933, as we reached the depth of the Depression and with the farm struggling to make a profit, the cow barn burned to the ground. Although the livestock was saved, Edgehill as a working farm suddenly ceased to exist. What the fire did not finish, the rising tide of the Depression did.

Grandmother Whitman needed to act quickly in order to provide income to support the family. She had to let Anna and Katie go. That loss was devastating to us children. About the same time, Dad lost his job at the Chase National Bank in New York. His salary, although meager, had been important to our survival.

To make ends meet, Grandmother parted with some of her most prized possessions—silverware, china, furniture, and jewelry. She was also forced to sell half of our 200 acres. She rented our home, the "Big House," and the farm's bungalow to vacationing city families. We moved to the "Farm House," where our farm manager and his family had lived.

Grandmother had kept a 1924 Cadillac and a 1926 Huppmobile. I remember the many trips we made in those two cars, hauling food, supplies, and pieces of furniture in the process of moving. I had just turned seven, and I vividly recall holding bowls and plates of food as we drove over the dirt road to our new home. Even to a little boy, it was evident that things would be different. Through it all, however, Grandmother was a tower of strength. She never let on that these were stressful times for her, or that she was worried about holding the family together.

In a reminiscence written 30 years later, my sister Claire beautifully reminded our family how vital "the little things" were then: "I don't think any child today would react the way Jim McLamore did at the age of seven when he came downstairs Christmas morning...and saw that football under the tree. I guess he's never forgotten it, and I guess his Dad, who loved him more than anything in the world, must have thought (before God took him away from us so soon) that life must have been worth it, if just to have seen the joy on that boy's face!"

Yes, I loved that football. I loved sports and played them throughout my youth.

My education began in the Central Valley Public Schools. Because there was no kindergarten, I started first grade at age five. Later in my school career, I was always a year younger than my classmates. Competing with older kids motivated me to be as good or better than they were. I always wanted to be the best student or best athlete in the class, and the challenge was heightened by the disparity in ages.

I enjoyed my public schooling and always thought of it as a fine learning experience. I was entrusted with valuable leadership roles and ultimately was elected president of our eighth grade class. I also gained some experience in public speaking at township events and various student gatherings. After one parade on Decoration Day—we'd call it Memorial Day now—I delivered the oration "O Captain, My Captain" at the public gazebo in town. I was eleven, and plenty nervous, but I had memorized the poem well enough to recite. I came to understand that being a good public speaker is a talent that encourages the development of other communication skills. I always recommend public speaking, and clear communication, as being of considerable value to people hoping to succeed in the world of business.

* * *

In 1933, my grandmother was 69 years old. Her doctors had warned her that she had a weak heart and should be careful about overexerting herself. Notwithstanding, she orchestrated our move to the farm house and took charge of family life. She had been accustomed to living a life of comfort and style, with domestic servants to cook, clean, and look after the children. Now, with only a single part-time helper, these jobs were hers to assume.

I loved her very much, and I remember her in so many ways. One day, when I was six or seven, I pulled up all of her prized asters and poppies, which I thought were weeds. When she witnessed the devastation, I could tell that she was terribly upset. But in realizing I had made an honest mistake, she remonstrated me rather gently, with a firm yet noble manner. This was typical of her. She had dignity, and she had class. I learned a little bit about the value of these qualities, and I made up my mind to emulate her in every way I could.

Grandmother was insistent that her three grandchildren should receive as fine an education as possible. In 1937, she found the perfect answer. She determined that Claire would go to the Northfield Academy for Girls in Massachusetts, the sister school of the Mount Hermon School for Boys where I would be sent two years later. Grandmother sold more of her personal assets to fund our education.

Dad helped as well. After a few years at a Works Progress Administration job, he set about reactivating Edgehill, this time as a turkey farm. My aunt, Theresa Baker, helped finance him in this risky venture. Later she followed my early business career closely, and she named me in her will as the trustee of her estate. Her confidence meant a great deal to me. I was learning the value of integrity and fair dealing as well as the reward for honesty and performance. It was another valuable lesson.

My family's sacrifices in the name of education served us very well. Already a fine pianist, thanks to Grandmother's own tutelage, Claire developed into one of Northfield's most outstanding musicians. Indeed, she went on to the Eastman School of Music in Rochester, New York, and eventually earned fame as one of the most famous and internationally recognized opera singers in the world.

Shortly before I went off to high school, however, another tragedy struck. Grandmother suffered a severe heart attack and died. To me at 11 years old, it was absolutely devastating. It didn't help to have her corpse lying in an open coffin in the living area of our home. Seeing her that way, in the room where we had spent so many wonderful moments, was difficult and emotionally trying.

Now, with only Dad left, I knew that I would be required more and more to rely on myself.

* * *

Looking back on my childhood years, I realize that I developed an urgent desire to be successful in life. I had no idea of what that would involve, of course, but I had no shortage of ambition. I felt pretty good about my chances.

First of all, I had an instinctive liking for people, and I wanted people to like me in return. Being quite gregarious, always reaching out to make friends, I was trying to learn how to get along in the world.

Secondly, I had a strong competitive drive. I wanted not only to be a good student, but to excel in athletics. I thought winning was important. I didn't play just to be a participant. What was important was winning the game or being on the winning team.

I didn't think much about it at the time, but later—especially in the Burger King years—I came to believe that the desire to win is an important factor in developing and exercising leadership.

I also found that becoming a leader was a rather complicated process. I remember a few fistfights with the leader of the gang of boys I belonged to. I lost quite a few times, but I also remember beating the school bully, which improved my status considerably. The lesson I ultimately learned was that leadership can be expressed with more effective tools than fists. The frustration in losing a good fistfight helps a person explore all the other options.

* * *

Being a former teacher and high school principal, Dad knew the advantages of having a good education and he wanted me to have the best, as did Grandmother. I'm sure that they thought I could develop a more worldly perspective at Mount Hermon School in Massachusetts than at home on the farm.

Like its sister institution, the Northfield Academy for Girls, Mount Hermon was founded by Dwight L. Moody, one of the most famous Christian evangelists who ever lived. Mr. Moody's idea was to provide an education for young people of very modest means, which he accomplished by keeping tuition affordable and operating expenses low. A work program required students to perform many of the chores, from operating the dairy to cleaning the dormitories. The school was non-denominational and made up mostly of Protestant kids, but there were also many Catholic and Jewish boys along with a number of black kids and foreign students of many different religious persuasions. Bible study was required, as was atten-dance at five chapel services each week—two on Sunday.

The morning that Dad and I left for the trip to Mount Hermon I had a deep feeling of apprehension. I was very close to my father, and the thought of leaving him for any length of time was very difficult. Nevertheless, I soon got caught up in the excitement of the new experience.

The first few action-packed days went by very quickly. I was doing just fine. Unfortunately, I wasn't prepared for my first Sunday, which was a quiet day on campus.

I went as required to the morning chapel service, then went back to my room in Cottage Four. With no planned activities, classes, or athletic contests, the day turned into a total disaster for me. With nothing to do but think, my thoughts turned to my father and how very much I missed him and my home. The more I thought about it, the more depressed I became.

I suppose that any 13-year-old boy away from home for the first time would miss home and family, but as the day wore on I turned into a real basket case. By lunchtime I was reduced to sobbing and crying.

This sadness and the deepening depression of homesick-ness stayed with me around the clock for the next several weeks. With each passing day it simply got worse. I could barely function. I was really one sick little boy. (My housepar-ents, Jimmy and Ompie Mirtz, recalled almost 50 years later that I was probably the most homesick kid they ever had to contend with.) I began to hide in a secluded area to cry in pri-vate; I was very embarrassed to be in such an emotional state. Things got so bad that the school officials called my father to attend to me.

I recall Dad's arrival vividly, because I was so pleased and relieved to see him. I tried to explain how I felt as I pleaded to go home with him.

Dad turned to me. "Jimmy, I'm not going to take you home. You are going to stay here and tough it out, so you had better prepare yourself to do that."

I knew his heart was breaking. He told me that Mount Hermon was the right experience for me. There was nothing to do but force myself to straighten up and get on with it.

During the next few days, I gradually came out of my terrible depression and began to get caught up in the excitement of school activities. I threw myself into athletics, classes, studying, meeting other boys, making friends, and eating good food. I began to think of Mount Hermon as my new home away from home, and this helped trigger a sense of independence and self-reliance I had never quite known. This newfound confidence and the wonderful opportunity to learn and grow were inspirational.

My competitive instinct intensified at Mount Hermon. Playing on the football, basketball, and baseball teams, I learned the significance of winning or losing, the value of team play, and the importance of striving to do your very best. I also continued in the leadership roles that had begun in grade school, being elected class president during my junior and senior years.

Getting good grades was important, and I made the honor roll on occasion, but certainly I was no academic superstar. I might have improved on that, if I had placed less emphasis on sports or extracurricular activities. When the United States entered World War II on December 7, 1941, after the sneak Japanese attack on Pearl Harbor, I was 15 years old. Thoughts of serving in the military began to enter my mind. Still, the war seemed a long way off.

As a senior, I took career aptitude tests. The results were revealing. I was advised to pursue a business career connected with sales or marketing. I didn't have any problem with that. In fact, I never gave any thought to pursuing any other career—and I think I decided on that even before I went to Mount Hermon. My leisure reading certainly reflected my interest in business: What interested me most were Horatio Alger stories and books about the great American fortunes and the men who made them.

My goal after leaving Mount Hermon and entering college was to ultimately build a successful business career. Quite candidly, I hoped to get rich in the process. I was determined to succeed.

Some people would argue that perhaps there is something wrong with someone making a lot of money. Some people believe that when a person becomes wealthy, he always does so at the expense of others. Nothing would be farther from the truth, of course, but it is hard to convince a great many people about that.

The unfortunate fact is that there are all too many greedy and dishonest businesspeople who take advantage of situations that enable them to profit at the expense of the public. There is no way to effectively and totally control that in a democratic free society.

I still believe that the pursuit of business success, and the accumulation of wealth that usually accompanies it, is a worthy personal goal, deserving of respect. Handling newfound wealth is a totally different matter, because quite a few people simply don't know how to deal with it.

When the accumulation of wealth becomes an obsession and a goal unto itself, it often causes personal misery and the loss of a worthwhile set of values. I have seen many people in this situation. The problem usually begins with establishing the wrong priorities and focusing on self rather than activities that help enrich the lives of others.

* * *

I had long-term goals in mind even as a teenager. But my short-term concern was to find an affordable college that would prepare me for my business career.

I decided on Cornell University for many reasons. As a New York State resident, I would benefit from lower tuition fees. Also, I wanted to play football on the powerhouse team known as "The Big Red." When I learned that the only school at

Cornell offering a business program was the School of Hotel Administration, it didn't faze me. I saw the program as an opportunity, even though I had no particular interest in the hospitality business yet.

World War II was still raging, of course. But I didn't expect to be called up until sometime in 1944. I felt I could spend at least a year at Cornell in the meantime. Colleges were on year-round schedules during wartime, so after high school graduation I had ten days to hitchhike to Ithaca, find a job, and register.

Believe it or not, I had no idea how I was going to raise the $200 tuition needed for my first trimester. My father, who had remarried, simply didn't have the money. The person who helped me was Professor Herbert H. Whetzel, chairman of the Department of Plant Pathology at the agriculture school. Each year he hired a live-in student to do chores in his home and tend his garden. I got the job—my farm experience came in handy there.

The Prof, as I came to call him, miraculously arranged a tuition loan and a $50 scholarship from the American Hotel Association. He and his daughter, Gertrude Grover, and her young son, Billy, became lifelong friends of mine. Gardening became an all-consuming, passionate, and fascinating hobby for the rest of my life, thanks to the months I spent tending the Prof's garden.

I had no way of knowing in 1943 how big the hospitality industry would become. I happened to be standing right in the path of progress, though I didn't realize it then. I did know I was fortunate to be receiving an excellent education and formal training in a field that interested me.

By June 1944, however, I was tired. I had attended classes for 12 straight months without a break. My extra jobs were depriving me of sleep, much less the chance to play football. On top of it all was the uncertainty about being called into the service.

With mixed emotions, I decided to leave Cornell temporarily. I tried to join the U.S. Merchant Marine, simply because the pay was so high. Looking back, it was fortunate that I wasn't accepted; the risks of being torpedoed were severe. I enlisted in the Navy instead, but had to wait a few months to be called. In the interim I worked at the Hotel Astor in New York City, gaining practical experience that was a prerequisite for graduation.

At last my orders came. Off to Sampson, New York, for boot camp! Navy barbers immediately turned us into "shave tails"—a tough experience for 18-year-old boys who valued their appearance and individuality, but our hair came off right down to the scalp.

Training was rigorous. As one of two platoon leaders, I had the job of seeing that orders were carried out. Three tough recruits from Brooklyn, all a year or two older than I, decided to test me. A confrontation was inevitable and when it came, I had to act or risk losing control.

The Navy's procedure for resolving disputes was to meet in the drill hall and settle the matter any way we saw fit. That often meant a good fistfight. I told the trio's leader to meet me with his buddies after mess. They never showed, but they never gave me any problems after that. The experience reinforced my opinion of the value of standing up for principle. As with the bullies in grade school, I let people know that as a leader I was prepared to enforce discipline, and I was never challenged after that.

After boot camp, I worked briefly at a Bureau of Ordnance testing facility in Dam Neck, Virginia, helping to test the Navy's newest radar tracking devices. Then I received orders to report to the Naval Reserve Officer's Training Corps...at Cornell! This was wonderful luck, although my mentor "Prof" Whetzel had passed away.

My NROTC training included not only naval courses but electives. Naturally, I took those at the Hotel School. What a break to have the Navy pay for part of my education.

I even had time to try out for and make the football team. But I never amounted to much there. Having a natural athletic ability isn't enough, I learned. To be a standout performer requires a passion, intensity, and commitment that I didn't possess.

Fortunately, I absorbed this lesson and took it into the world of commerce a few years later. To put it in business terms: Don't take on an assignment with success as its major objective unless you are passionate about succeeding. Passion is a key ingredient in building a successful pattern in life. It is the source of inspiration and creativity. It builds inner determination, hopes, and aspirations. Without passion, it is difficult to establish realistic goals and to develop plans to achieve those goals. I got the first inkling of that on the gridiron at Cornell.

I view myself as a passionate, even intense individual simply because I know that is part of what it takes—not only to be a leader, but also to succeed. I've known a lot of people who lacked this focus. Most of them never achieved the level of success that could have been theirs.

Sitting on the bench as a third-string quarterback, I didn't have the passion to elevate myself. But I vowed right there that I wouldn't let that happen again.

* * *

My Navy career continued smoothly, particularly after the war ended in the autumn of 1945. I was still in uniform on the Cornell campus when I met a very attractive young woman from Miami named Nancy Nichol. What impressed me most about her was her unusually upbeat, friendly, and enthusiastic manner. We began to date. Both of us were just 19, but I was already developing some serious thoughts about the future.

Life at home was terribly mixed up at that time. My stepmother had been devastated by the loss of her son at Iwo Jima. Dad had been diagnosed with cancer. At this difficult juncture, Nancy suggested that I spend the Christmas holidays with her and her family in Miami. It was a most gracious and welcome invitation.

Nancy took the train. I hitchhiked, as so many soldiers still safely did. I'll never forget my final ride: The driver was hauling a big Chris Craft boat, and he let me hop into it and take a sun bath as we rode south! I laid back, imagining myself a man of considerable leisure enjoying the warm weather, the blue water, and the marvelous Florida scenery. I felt like a king. This was a slice of life I wanted more of, and I determined right there to get it.

During my wonderful visit with Nancy's family, it didn't take long to convince myself that Miami was the place I wanted to live. I also reached the conclusion that Nancy was the woman I wanted to spend the rest of my life with. In the meantime, the thought of returning to the cold climate of Ithaca in January and the regimen of U.S. Navy life wasn't very exciting, but it had to be done.

My discharge from the Navy came midyear in 1946, but I couldn't resume classes at Cornell right away. I needed a job that would satisfy the Hotel School's requirements for more "practice credits." So I worked as an all-around handyman and desk clerk at the Boxwood Manor Inn in Old Lyme, Connecticut. It was a tenuous time: Nancy and I wanted to marry, but I had no money or permanent job in sight. Also, my Dad was gravely ill. At least he got to meet Nancy and her parents before his untimely death.

While working in Miami at the Hollywood Beach Hotel later that year, I told my future father-in-law of my intention to marry Nancy. With a twinkle in his eye, he asked me how I intended to support her "in the manner to which she had become accustomed." I gave Dr. Nichol a not-too-reassuring answer, but still he gave us his blessing.

When my Dad died, I was 21. My sister and brother were busy with their own lives. The rest of our immediate family had died years before. I was alone except for Nancy, who came to me like a powerful and refreshing breath of spring at precisely the time I needed someone close to remind me that life could be wonderful, worthwhile, and promising.

After laying Dad to rest and selling the farm, I returned to Cornell. Nancy and I decided to get married and tough it out together. We were wed on April 27, 1947. It was the best thing that ever happened to me.

* * *

If I were a young person today, I would use my credit card very cautiously. I think too many Americans have taken on too much debt and not enough of them have given the proper amount of thought to saving, budgeting expenses, or planning for retirement. The seeds of trouble are there—the sudden loss of income can seriously disrupt lives. Ours is the most debt-driven society in the world, and it is not the best situation for Americans to be in. A lot of personal despair can be avoided by using better sense and better planning.

I personally began to get that message right after Nancy and I were married. We were in such bad shape financially. My father-in-law had given us $300 and his Chrysler car. Luckily, he had paid for Nancy's room and board at Cornell through the end of the Spring trimester. I was able to earn a bit of money working at odd jobs, but I wasn't able to save much.

Those were hard times, to be sure, but things were going to work out. I felt sure of that, even as I expected my future in the business world to be full of tough times. I had come to the point of realizing that I would constantly be faced with problems and difficult situations. I knew that in order to become a success in life, I had better figure out a way to deal with unexpected reverses and disappointments. I was already looking at my first one: I had taken on a wife, I had no money, I was still in college while trying to pay for it, I had no job with no prospects of one, and I was looking at a bleak job market where millions of returning servicemen were among the competition.

It was obvious that I had done a pretty poor job of planning. I determined to do a better job in the future.

Based on this experience, I firmly believe that one of the cardinal rules of success is planning. Success begins in the planning process. As far as personal and business planning are concerned, these start with preparing a budget, itemizing assets and liabilities, and projecting income and expense. It is surprising to me how little thought is given to the simple listing of these numbers, but without them there is very little discipline on spending and the utilization of resources. In short, there is no plan at all.

I put myself on the verge of going broke four times in my life, mostly when I was young and starting out. I didn't have the benefit of knowing what I know today. I wasn't thinking straight or using my head. Looking back, I see that I was hasty, impetuous, and often guilty of jumping to conclusions. I utterly failed in terms of planning.

My advice to young people starting out today is to get really familiar and comfortable with numbers, and learn how to use them. We take that approach within the Burger King organization, as well, because this is a company that puts people from all walks of life into a business that few of them have experienced. We try to teach financial discipline and fiscal planning. Still, I have seen very smart people fail in a franchise that should have been enormously successful—simply because they didn't plan properly.

* * *

I'll always remember a job-hunting incident that occurred shortly after my graduation from Cornell in August 1947. Following every lead offered by the University's employment service, my wife and I eagerly traveled to a restaurant in a small town in central Pennsylvania. The place turned out to be nothing more than a saloon—a dirty old building where a disheveled old bartender was serving drinks to four drunk coal miners at three o'clock in the afternoon. We took off, shaken by the fact that we couldn't see any promising opportunities opening up anywhere in the hospitality field.

Yes, the restaurant business was especially tough in those days. It consisted almost entirely of independent "Mom-and-Pop" operators. Americans rarely ate out, and even then it was more out of necessity than pleasure. The failure rate in the field was staggering. Banks stayed clear of financing new restaurants; the risk was far too great. The outlook wasn't any more promising on the hotel side.

I sensed, in 1947, that this bleak outlook would no doubt change for the better, but in the future. At that time I was concerned with the present—and the picture before me was of a stalemated and very sick hospitality field.

Before the year ended, however, I found my first job in the field. Nancy and I rejoiced! My professional career was beginning at last. Little did I suspect that it would lead, within a few years, to my association with Burger King.

The job was hardly glamorous: The YMCA in Wilmington, Delaware, was looking for someone to take over as their director of food service. The position looked very challenging to me, despite the meager pay involved ($267 a month). This YMCA operated a cafeteria, one of the oldest and largest in the state, as well as a soda shop on the main floor. Above the cafeteria kitchen and bake shop were several floors of banquet rooms, each of which was equipped with a booster kitchen serviced by an elevator from the main kitchen below. A staff of about thirty employees was needed to operate this complex facility.

I needed and desperately wanted this job, but several things concerned me. First, the "Y" had never employed a man in the position; previous food service directors had been women with dietitian's training and a certain amount of food service background. Second, I was a very young 21-year-old male with absolutely no experience in managing a business of any kind. My only related experience had been limited to food preparation courses at Cornell.

The job itself was not intimidating, because I knew that given a chance, I could do it. I wanted an opportunity to prove myself.

When that opportunity came, I immediately had my hands full. The cafeteria operation was in a disastrous state of affairs when I got there. Although I had never worked in a restaurant before, it was obvious to me that the inventory was totally out of control and that the employees were uninspired and lacking in direction. The staff was not focused on providing the high standards of food quality and customer satisfaction that I thought we should be delivering. The menu was unimaginative. And there were no plans in effect to study costs, develop efficiencies, and target profitability.

Here is an example. The building manager had allocated two large areas for storing supplies. Both were stacked high with canned goods and paper supplies, and it took me three days to complete my first inventory, which was ridiculous given the size of the operation. Some of the supplies dated back over ten years. Cans were exploding in their cases because they had been stored for such a long time. It was a classic case of an ill-advised "Last In, First Out" inventory control process. Well, at least I wouldn't need to order much in the way of nonperishables for a few months.

My first job was to unload that bloated inventory. The best way to do that was to create appetizing meals and sell them as cheaply as I could. In so doing, I was able to offer our customers some great value. This had two advantages: We began to attract new business, and we reduced the inventory very fast. Within a few months I was able to return those two storerooms to the building manager, who couldn't believe we didn't need them anymore.

At the age of 21, I was also getting my first taste of being a manager. I took a hands-on approach, and believed others should as well. Certainly that belief later helped to shape Burger King. However, as we all know, getting some people to roll up their sleeves isn't easy.

I had quite a conflict at first with my assistant manager at the Wilmington YMCA, a proper and pleasant dietitian named Mrs. Kelley. She spent most of her day recording information in ledger books; she was proud of her records, which indicated how much the YMCA had paid for goods and supplies going back 25 years. As far as I was concerned, this was totally useless information. If we needed such data, we could get it from the bookkeeping department. I thought Mrs. Kelley should be spending more time in the kitchen and on the serving line.

I picked up the phone and had the building manager send over a big laundry truck. All of Mrs. Kelley's ledgers went into that truck, as did the contents of her desk drawers. The entire load was dispatched into the furnace.

We shared an office. Now nothing was left in it except our two desks and two chairs. Mrs. Kelley wouldn't speak to me for weeks. However, with no bookkeeping to do, she kept very busy in the kitchen, the bake shop, and at the counter, supervising food preparation and customer servicing. Soon the service on the cafeteria line and the quality of our food began to improve.

Several weeks after the initial incident, Mrs. Kelley finally came to me. "Mr. McLamore," she said, "I hated you when you burned all of my books. But I can see now that you were right—they weren't serving a useful purpose. I have the time now to do the things I was trained for and I'm enjoying my work much more." She also expressed pride in how our business was improving.

From that moment on, Mrs. Kelley and I were the very best of friends. In fact, she became almost like a mother to me. No doubt I had been too impetuous and abrupt in handling the matter, but dramatizing the problem got us focused on the right issues.

In short, we got our priorities straight. Together, we concentrated on building sales and profits. As it turned out, we made more profit during my first year than the operation had made in the thirty previous years combined.

So it was during my tenure as director of food service at the Wilmington YMCA that I began to think in terms of organizing people and developing operating systems. This seemed to me the necessary first step in building a profit-making enterprise. It was not only a thrill for me to have produced such impressive results, but it gave me a sense of other kinds of opportunities that might become available in the industry. At a young age and already successful in my first job, I began to believe that I was capable of achieving solid results in the restaurant business. I was learning how much fun it was to make a profit, and the pleasure and satisfaction of doing so would stay with me for the rest of my life.

* * *

Working at the YMCA, I made a point of meeting as many local businesspeople as possible, because I wanted to develop a profitable banquet business. Our facilities were such that it would be an easy matter to expand our business in this fashion. The idea caught on quickly, and banquet profits grew steadily. The management of the YMCA was impressed with our financial performance. I was making more money for them than they had ever dreamed possible.

I began to consider my own situation. My $267 per month salary was very low, even by 1947 standards. Our first child, Pamela, had arrived, and we had taken out a sizable mortgage ($9000!) to buy an old farmhouse on five acres outside Wilmington. It was difficult to think about raising a family and maintaining a home on such a small income.

One of the local restaurateurs in Wilmington had noted my success at the YMCA. After a number of meetings, he convinced me to quit my job and go to work for him. The results were nearly catastrophic. It turned out that we just didn't get along very well. After a few months, I was dismissed after a particularly difficult confrontation. I drove back to the farm and broke the news to Nancy. It was especially troubling because we had very little money left after making our investment in the farm. And Nancy was pregnant again.

While at the YMCA, I had noticed a restaurant across the

street that was busy 24 hours a day. Called the Toddle House, it was part of a trend toward quick-service, short-order restaurants that enjoyed significant growth in the 1930s and 1940s. The Toddle House chain was one of several regional ventures that piggybacked the styling and success of the original White Castle system, which began in 1921.

These regional chains were clean and efficient, and they delivered a great price-value package to their customers. They proved to be popular places to go for quick, affordable food at any time of the day or night. Run properly and in good locations, they were very profitable operations. Certainly, the ten seats at the Toddle House were full most of the time, and often there were people standing up waiting to be served.

It looked like a sound business opportunity to me. I felt that if I copied the Toddle House concept, I could operate a successful competing business of my own. I could even do it right next door to the Toddle House, where a vacant shop was up for rent at $300 a month.

I signed a lease for the building and designed a food service concept that was just a little bit fancier than the Toddle House, but essentially the same kind of operation.

I decided to make the interior of the restaurant much different, however. Instead of putting in a ten-seat, straight-line counter, which was standard at the time, I installed a horseshoe-shaped counter with 14 seats. And instead of having a small space for food preparation, I designed a much larger production area that may sound familiar to anyone who has ever worked at Burger King: stainless-steel tables, a fryer, gas grill, refrigerator, exhaust hood, coffee maker, and drink station.

I also felt that the larger area inside the restaurant could be made very attractive by using linoleum floor and wallpaper. This would give the customers a pleasant view of the food preparation processes and provide a certain amount of ambience. In the event that the seats were fully occupied when customers arrived, I had comfortable seating to accommodate the overflow. I also installed one of the first air-conditioning units that were just coming onto the commercial market. A distinct competitive advantage: The Toddle House didn't have one!

All of this scrambling to design, build, and open the restaurant took place in the summer and fall of 1949. It was a productive time in other ways too: Another beautiful daughter, Sara Lynne (always called Lynne), arrived on September 16.

During Christmas week I was busy putting the finishing touches on the restaurant: hiring a crew, setting up an inventory of food and supplies, and attending to a host of other details. I decided to call the restaurant The Colonial Inn, and planned to keep it open around the clock. I never even put a lock on the door. We opened for business on January 4, 1950, at 700 Delaware Avenue in the heart of Wilmington. The logo on our sign, lit on both sides, was a colonial lady stirring a pot over an open hearth.

Finding reliable help was always a problem, but I was fortunate to have several key employees from the YMCA join me. One was Audrey Reeder, my chief lieutenant. She and her husband even moved into the apartment above the restaurant. The drawback in having a 24-hour-a-day operation was that the telephone at the farm would occasionally ring with the disturbing news that someone had failed to show up for work. Then Audrey or I would have to pull the graveyard shift. I spent many nights cooking hamburgers and short orders.

The good news was that from the day we opened, The Colonial Inn was a success. Our hamburgers, french fries, waffles, eggs, pancakes, tenderloin steaks, and coffee became very popular items, and our reputation spread rapidly as a good place to eat. At one point we had the distinction of being recommended by Duncan Hines, one of the first food writers and restaurant critics.

Having developed and trained a staff I could rely on, I dared to take a break. In March 1950, I drove Nancy and the two babies to Miami for a ten-day holiday with her parents. I enjoyed going back to our favorite part of the world. Sunny

Miami always had a magical appeal, and we were hopeful that someday we could move there permanently.

Returning to the restaurant in Wilmington, we found that things had gone very smoothly in our absence. In fact, I was hardly missed. Sales had been good, and I was pleased with the results. Business was picking up faster than I anticipated and with profits picking up, it appeared that our financial crisis might be over. It felt good to begin paying off some of our debts.

My confidence level returned. Before long I was deeply involved in developing plans to open a second restaurant. These were pretty heady times for me! The Colonial Inn took in $90,000 in sales during its first year and out of that I was able to net $15,000, which seemed to be all the money there was in the world. These numbers don't seem like very much now, but in the 1950s this was big time!

The money part of it was great, but so was the sense of accomplishment. I was 23 years old when I opened for business, and the success I enjoyed simply reinforced my confidence and determination to become a very successful restaurateur. This was what I was trained for and this was the only business I knew anything about.

The Colonial Inn whetted my appetite for business growth. I was anxious to keep moving. I had no idea how far the restaurant business and my own ambition would take me, but I was ready and eager to find out.

Into the "Soup"

Life is a learning experience, and as a young person entering the world of business I always knew that I had an awful lot to learn. I have often looked back on my first few years in business and tried to make note of the mistakes I made and what I should have learned after making them. If I had to counsel young people taking the first tentative steps in a business venture or even starting a new job, here is what I would tell them.

First of all, try to acknowledge the possibility that you are not as smart as you think you are. I say this for two reasons: The first is that if you think of yourself as being real smart, you will probably make some mistakes you could otherwise avoid. The second reason is that if you sound off like you know it all, you will turn off a lot of people who know that you fall short. You may need their friendship someday, but you could lose it in an instant by being too overbearing, cocky, and arrogant. A little humility will go a long way. I never knew anyone who learned anything by listening to himself talk.

Another important piece of advice would be that given me by Harvey C. Fruehauf, who led the Fruehauf Trailer Company during its important years of expansion and who became a valued friend, business associate, and mentor. He would caution me with the reminder, "Act in haste and repent at leisure." I met Harvey when our business relationship began in 1956. His counsel and friendship meant a lot to me, and I often wished that I had known him a bit earlier, like in 1951 when I was making so many judgmental mistakes and paying the price.

I drove the family to Miami in February of 1951 and arrived at a time when my wife's father, Dr. E. Sterling Nichol, was moving his practice from the Huntington Building in downtown Miami to a new facility called the 550 Building, which was then under construction on Brickell Avenue. It was the first commercial office building to be built on the west side of the Miami River. Brickell Avenue was the continuation of U.S. Highway 1, and it went south from downtown Miami through an area that was solidly residential at the time. Dr. Nichol advised me that the new building was looking for a tenant to operate a restaurant on the ground floor. He suggested that I consider the possibilities of leasing this space. I looked at it, and I'm afraid I was a bit overanxious and careless in my evaluation of both the location and the South Florida restaurant market itself.

It was important for me to make a judgment about the potential of opening a restaurant at this location. To begin the process I ate in a number of busy restaurants that I had heard about. I was amazed at what I discovered. Most restaurants had long lines of people standing out front waiting to get in! After standing in a number of those lines and putting up with frustrating delays in getting seated, I often received poor service and mediocre food. I was quite unimpressed with the restaurant operations, but what did impress me was the thought that if these restaurants could attract so many customers, then I could make a fortune by engaging in the restaurant business in Miami. This was a case of quick, impetuous judgment. I had set myself up for the shock of my life.

I was looking for a good excuse to move the family to Miami and without carefully examining the situation, I signed a lease for half of the ground floor space in the 550 Building and committed myself to opening a restaurant there. The lease provided that I would occupy this space at a monthly rental of $884. I jumped into this deal without taking the time or trouble to draw up a business plan, work up a menu strategy, or consider the deployment of my limited financial resources.

I figured that I could attend to all those details later. Mine was a case of careless examination, arrogant overconfidence, and a lack of any judgment at all. I convinced myself of two things: The first was the conclusion that Miami was in desperate need of more good restaurants. The second was the conclusion that this was a good location. I was dead wrong on both counts. "Cocky" was the right word to describe my mindset. I had set myself up for a major surprise.

After signing the lease I began to think about what kind of a restaurant would be best suited to that location. I decided that the restaurant would serve breakfast, lunch, and dinner and stay open from 7 a.m. to 9 p.m., seven days a week. The layout would consist of a soda fountain designed to serve short orders during breakfast and luncheon hours. The remaining portion of the dining area would feature tables, booths, and waitress service. The restaurant would seat a total of 80 customers.

That plan seemed simple enough, but life was about to become complicated. When I returned to Wilmington, I faced the job of finding a manager to take over The Colonial Inn, the small restaurant I owned then. I needed to do this before I could move the family to Miami. I had decided to keep The Colonial Inn because I expected that it would help to pay our living expenses in Miami. Another problem involved selling our farm, and this meant that my wife Nancy and our two children would have to remain in Wilmington until we could find a buyer. This was deeply troubling to both of us. I planned to return to Miami in early May after finishing the design for the restaurant. This would give me time to order the equipment and get the business ready to open in the early fall.

It was when I returned to Miami in May that I received the shock of my life. The restaurant activity I had witnessed in February was practically nonexistent in May! It had never occurred to me that Miami was a seasonal city that practically shut down during the off season and summer months.

I realized then that I had made a serious mistake. Miami in the late forties and early fifties was a seasonally oriented destination resort city, heavily trafficked during the winter months and woefully quiet during the rest of the year.

February happened to be the peak of the winter season. Many of the restaurants I had eaten in at the time of my February visit were closed and boarded up for the summer. The locals would say that during the summer months a person could "fire a cannon down the middle of Flagler Street and not hit anybody." I developed a real fear about the chances for having a successful opening of my new restaurant. The thought of a possible failure weighed heavily on my mind. This considerable worry was aggravated by the fact that Nancy and the children weren't with me They were living at the farm trying to sell the place. I was very lonely, but I had to stay in Miami to attend to a lot of problems associated with opening the restaurant. I knew that it was an equally lonely experience for Nancy. I had put the whole family in a very difficult position. I was terribly annoyed with myself. The only good that came out of the situation was that it taught me a valuable lesson.

While living alone in Miami, I had plenty of time to think about the mistake I had made in acting so impulsively about this restaurant project. Long before the restaurant began to take shape I knew that I was going to have some real problems. The surrounding market and the location itself left a lot to be desired. I was located in a small building with fewer than 60 people employed there. Most of the tenants were doctors whose patients were generally older and not too interested in eating in a restaurant. The patients were sick and had other things on their mind. The building would be empty by the time the dinner hour came around, and it would be closed on Saturday and Sunday. The other problems were that I couldn't expect much business to come from the surrounding neighborhood, and there was a real question as to whether fast-moving traffic would stop at a commercial restaurant located in an office building. I was to learn later that these were valid concerns.

I missed my family, and I was very annoyed at myself for jumping into this difficult situation so quickly. This was a scary, difficult, and unpleasant time in my life, and I was fully aware that having these negative thoughts was no way to start out in a new business.

What I couldn't know or appreciate at the time was that I was learning a valuable lesson which would serve me well in later life. I determined that if I survived this crisis I would be more careful and analytical in making any business decisions in the future.

Fortunately, Nancy was able to sell the farm even though it took several months for her to do it. I flew to Wilmington and drove the four of us back to Miami in July after making arrangements with a moving company to transport our personal effects to Florida. The Rickenbacker Causeway leading to Key Biscayne had recently opened to vehicular traffic and by 1951 a housing development was well underway on this beautiful island paradise. Key Biscayne was originally an isolated coconut plantation owned by the Matheson family, who deeded a large portion of the island to Dade County for use as a public park. The county agreed to construct the causeway, which made the park available to the public and opened up remaining portions of the island to housing and commercial development.

By 1951 the Mackle Company was building new and inexpensive homes in the range of $12,000 to $13,500. Purchase of these modern, attractive homes required only a minimal down payment, with very attractive mortgage financing terms available to the purchaser. Nancy and I didn't have enough cash to make the low down payment but we were able to lease one of these new homes and moved into the Mackle's subdivision in July. We had only a few weeks to get settled before the Brickell Bridge Restaurant opened for business in August.

All of the fears and worries that had troubled me since May proved to be completely warranted. When the restaurant opened, there was very little business to be had and my early promotions were unsuccessful in attracting customers. The very high rental charge for the space and the fact that my sales were only averaging $3000 per month during August, September, October, and November were enough to keep me in a state of deep concern. I was seriously questioning whether I could make a go of the place. There wasn't much doubt that if business didn't pick up soon I was going to go broke. I remember one particular Sunday when we took in only $8 for breakfast, $12 for lunch, and $10 for dinner. It was a long ride home that night. I was burdened with paying the salaries of two cooks, two dishwashers, and six waitresses. With such a near hopeless feeling about the future prospects for the business, I felt devastated. I had made a mistake of monumental proportions, and this damaged my self-esteem and began to erode my self-confidence. I wasn't ready to give up, but I had a tarnished ego and was looking disaster in the face.

My typical day included getting up at 5 a.m. so that I could be in the restaurant by 6 a.m. I cooked the breakfast and typed the luncheon and dinner menus during the morning hours. Acting as the host, I would seat customers during meal hours. As manager, I ordered the food and trained the employees. After the restaurant closed at 9 p.m., I stayed alone to mop the floors and wash pots, pans, and kitchen utensils before driving home because I couldn't afford to hire anyone to do these jobs. The high point of my day was relaxing on the screened-in porch of our little house, enjoying a bottle of beer, and talking with Nancy about her day and the children, whom I rarely ever saw. I was able to relieve some of the pressure by talking to Nancy about anything that came to mind, but mainly sharing my concerns about the restaurant and the problems we were facing. Being in this together, and with our survival as a family business very much on the line, we needed to talk things out. These quiet but late evenings together gave us the chance to do that. Usually we were able to get to bed by 11 p.m.

It was the same routine every day, for seven days a week. I didn't take a day off for over a year and a half while I was struggling to make the restaurant a success. Nancy told me that our neighbors thought she was a young divorcée with two small children because they never saw a man around the house. The good news was that although the Brickell Bridge was losing money steadily, we still had The Colonial Inn making enough money to keep us going. Meanwhile, I was trying to figure out a strategy that would stimulate sales and get us on the road to profitability. Although our quality of food and service was always very good, and I was determined to maintain these high standards, it was difficult to attract new business to an office-building restaurant on evenings and weekends.

Every day we offered two luncheon specials—one we sold for 65 cents and the other for 90 cents. In each case the customer had a choice of soup or juice, an entrée, two vegetables, rolls and butter, and a beverage. I learned that price was a big factor in attracting new business, and I did my best to offer reasonable prices and innovative menu ideas. At dinner the menu contained appeals to try such items as "golden fried jumbo Key West shrimp," "succulent fresh Gulfstream pompano, broiled to perfection," which I insisted should be as good as these descriptions promised they would be. The restaurant was always kept immaculately clean, and I spent hours training waitresses in the subtleties of providing the right kind of service. I did all the purchasing and worked closely with the chef on all aspects of food preparation. The dinner menu was changed daily. The highest price for a complete dinner, which included dessert and beverage was only $1.80. A large fresh shrimp cocktail with four jumbo shrimps cost only 40 cents when it was ordered à la carte, and for only 15 cents extra it could be included when a customer ordered a complete dinner. The value was there, but new customers were slow in coming in.

The "season" arrived in late December of 1951 when the holidays brought in the first wave of our long and eagerly awaited tourist traffic. It lasted through the month of February and brought with it some badly needed sales and profits to help shore up my sagging balance sheet. This was just enough financial support to get me through the winter and into the spring and summer months. When April and May of 1952 arrived, I was faced with the same low sales and the same devastating results that I had experienced when I first opened. The summer business was simply terrible, and I began losing money all over again at a rate I could ill afford. I had to do something, and I had to do it soon!

That "something" arrived in the form of a little boy named Charlie. Since opening the restaurant in August of the previous year, I employed as a dishwasher a young boy named

Henry. Henry was about 14 or 15 years old, and I probably paid him no more than the minimum wage, which was around 50 cents an hour at the time. Henry was a very industrious and dedicated employee who had an 11- or 12-year-old kid brother named Charlie who accompanied him to work every night. Charlie had an engaging way of approaching me. He usually began with a big smile, tugging at my sleeve trying to coax me into giving him a job. My only response was usually, "I can hardly afford to pay your brother, Charlie. I'm terribly sorry but I just don't have anything for you to do." Invariably Charlie would come back the next day and every following day inquiring if I had found a job for him to do.

One evening when Charlie walked into the restaurant, I called him over and said, "Charlie, I think I have a job for you. I'm going to give you a clean starched white chef's uniform, a tall chef's hat to go with it and a dinner bell. I want you to get out on Brickell Avenue, right in front of this restaurant and ring this dinner bell." I didn't stop there. "Be sure to smile at everybody going by. I want you to ring that dinner bell as loud as you can. I want people to hear it ring." I told Charlie that I was going to shine two spotlights on him so that he would be seen by everyone passing by. This brought out a big grin which lit up his face. Charlie was delighted to get this job even though I could afford to pay him only 50 cents an hour.

He came every night, got into his white chef's uniform and with that wonderful smile of his, rang his dinner bell for several hours in front of the restaurant. "Dinner-Bell Charlie" became a "happening" in Miami. He was such a charming, delightful little personality and the concept was so unique that thousands of people going home at night took notice of the Brickell Bridge Restaurant and this wonderfully new and unique little boy with the big smile ringing the dinner bell. I had finally come up with a clever idea to get the public's attention, but the question was, would this build traffic? I decided to advertise a bargain steak dinner.

I ran a series of advertisements in the Miami Herald featuring a picture of Dinner-Bell Charlie ringing his bell outside the restaurant. The advertisement read:

JUST A REMINDER
Little Charlie is still ringing the Dinner Bell to wel-
come you to Miami's greatest steak value. A full
pound PRIME SIRLOIN STEAK for just $1.95.
Other Complete Dinners from $1.40.
Join the crowd—watch for
LITTLE CHARLIE WITH THE DINNER BELL
BRICKELL BRIDGE RESTAURANT
550 Building
550 Brickell Avenue
Dinner Served from 5 until 9, 7 days a week
PLENTY OF FREE PARKING SPACE
BEHIND BUILDING

The price of $1.95 for this tender-top quality steak served
with a baked Idaho potato, salad, and beverage represented just
my cost. I would be able to do nothing more than breakeven on
each sale. The steak was absolutely first-class, and although I
knew I couldn't make a profit selling it, I did feel that I could
build traffic, which was the most pressing problem. My plan
was to train our waitresses to suggest other items such as lobster thermidor, veal parmigiana, fried shrimp, calf's liver or
whatever else I had on the menu because these other menu
items were profitable. With Charlie and our advertising pitching
our big-value steak dinner, sales and traffic increased dramatically. Ultimately, this unique promotion created a phenomenon
in Miami. Even during the summer months, when many other
restaurants were closed and boarded up, often at dinner time
we would have lines of people standing outside our restaurant.
The success of this extraordinary promotion surprised even me!
The pressure came off when I realized for the first time that I
had a good chance of making it after all. I had turned a losing
proposition around by coming up with an innovative marketing
idea. Within a few months I was breathing a lot easier. I was on
the winning side once again, and it felt great!

The success of this marketing ploy was one of the great
learning experiences of my business career, and it served me

well in helping build the Burger King business. The lesson was a bit of marketing wisdom. You can read about things like this, but you really have to experience them if you want the learning to be indelible. The message and the lesson learned was very simple: When you bring a product or service to market, you need to attach a unique, highly individualistic message to that product or service. The great steak dinner at a rock-bottom price was appealing, but that wasn't enough to attract a big wave of new business. I had to attract the reader's attention to the advertisement itself. People needed to read what the advertising suggested. Dinner-Bell Charlie did that. He sold the steak, and he told people where they could get it. In addition to that he sent out an invitation for people to see for themselves what this new personality really amounted to. There would be similarities in building the success of Burger King's "Whopper."

Unfortunately, at the same time the Brickell Bridge Restaurant began to perform very well, The Colonial Inn was heading downhill. The manager I had put in charge had taken my very simple food-service concept and complicated it by adding all sorts of items to the menu. The result was that our quality had been compromised along with our image as a well-managed short-order restaurant specializing in hamburgers. Sales declined and so did the restaurant's profitability. During the early years of the Brickell Bridge Restaurant struggle, the profits from The Colonial Inn had kept the wolf away from the family door. Now that restaurant was in trouble, and I had to contend with the problems caused by the management I had left in charge.

I had the good fortune at the Brickell Bridge restaurant to meet a young man named Bill Bilohorka. Bill was a recent graduate of the Penn State School of Hotel and Restaurant Management, and one day he just walked in off the street and asked me for a job. With sales at the Brickell Bridge growing steadily, I was able to afford to take him on as an assistant manager. He did a terrific job right from the beginning. I turned to Bill when things at The Colonial Inn started to go downhill and asked him if he would be willing to go to

Wilmington, take over the restaurant and try to sell it for me. It was obvious that absentee ownership, a thousand miles away, was not working.

The urgent requirement to change management at The Colonial Inn occurred at a most inopportune time. Nancy was pregnant for the third time, and we were still living in our small rented Key Biscayne home. As July of 1953 approached and business at The Colonial Inn continued to deteriorate, I received ultimatums from my manager that I would have to sell the business to him on his terms or he would simply walk out on me. He obviously assumed I was in a situation where I had no other choice.

Just as we reached a critical period in our negotiations, Nancy went into labor and I rushed her to Jackson Memorial Hospital on July 14 where she delivered a wonderful healthy baby boy on her own birthday! We decided to call the baby Sterling Whitman McLamore. Pam, who was then six years old and Lynne, who was almost four, waited for me to bring Nancy and the baby back home. When I went to the hospital I told Nancy that the situation in Wilmington was such that I had to leave that night and that Bill Bilohorka had agreed to go with me and take over the restaurant.

Nancy has always been a strong and resourceful woman. She was already raising two small children with absolutely no help from me, and on this day she was returning home with a two-day-old baby in her arms and a whole new burden of responsibility on her hands. She did all of this with no complaints of any kind. I just had time to say good-bye and head for the airport with Bill. These kinds of memories of Nancy's strength and character will always remain closely fixed in my mind.

When Bill and I arrived in Wilmington, I fired the manager and put Bill in charge of the restaurant confident that The Colonial Inn was in good hands. I returned to Miami a few days later. Nancy took on the responsibilities of managing the home and looking after two young girls and a new baby boy as if nothing had happened. I went back to my 7-day-a-week, 16-hour-a-day schedule at the Brickell Bridge Restaurant. Business was good and getting better all the time. I kept my fingers crossed that Bill would be able to sell The Colonial Inn. I wanted to get rid of that worry in the worst way.

Of particular interest to me at the time was this new baby of ours. I had felt bad about leaving Nancy alone to look after things while I was in Delaware for a few days. Now I could hardly wait to see what this new little boy was all about. Ever since we were married, I had worked long hours in our restaurants struggling to make a success. Our growing family was very important to us, and I was looking forward to the time when I could spend more time with them.

Bill was fortunate enough to find a buyer who paid us a reasonable sum for The Colonial Inn. To close the deal I retained a young attorney, newly graduated from law school and just starting in practice, to draw up the papers and effect the sale.

Thirty-five years later, when as a director of The Pillsbury Company, I was right in the middle of a lawsuit involving a hostile bid by the Grand Metropolitan Company to take over The Pillsbury Company, this same attorney, Andrew J. Christie, was serving as the Chief Justice of the Delaware Supreme Court. (There were many lawsuits involving corporate takeover activity during the 1980s, and the Delaware courts were deeply involved in handing down decisions based on these cases because most of the large corporations in the United States, like Pillsbury, were domiciled in Delaware. These decisions created corporate law which affected the governing of such matters. Unsolicited and hostile business takeovers were the main business-news stories of the "decade of greed," and one of the major cases concerned the takeover of The Pillsbury Company by Grand Metropolitan. This situation was hotly contested in the Delaware courts during the time when Christie was serving as the Chief Justice.) Although our paths never crossed, I enjoyed reflecting on the fact that this respected jurist was an old friend and attorney some 40 years earlier at a time when the two of us were just starting out in our professional careers.

After Bill sold The Colonial Inn he returned to Miami and rejoined me at the Brickell Bridge Restaurant, where business was good and profits satisfactory. By early 1954 I began discussing the possibility of joining Dave Edgerton, whom I had recently met, in the Insta Burger King business. For some time I had been thinking about starting a chain of restaurants myself. Dave's enthusiasm for an idea to establish a chain of limited-menu restaurants intrigued me enough to investigate the matter. I liked what Dave showed me, but it was obvious that I needed to sell the Brickell Bridge Restaurant in order to come up with the capital necessary to get into this new business. It was Bill Bilohorka who came up with the money to buy the restaurant from me during the spring of that year. With the sale of both The Colonial Inn and the Brickell Bridge Restaurant, I was ready to take on a new and much different challenge. I didn't realize that the road ahead was full of potholes.

Starting Out

David R. Edgerton, Jr., was brought up in Wilmette, Illinois, a suburb of Chicago. He attended The School of Hotel Administration at Cornell University and later found his way into the Howard Johnson organization, where he worked his way up to manager status in the Miami area. When I met Dave, I was not aware of the fact that he had been a restaurant manager in the Howard Johnson organization. He told me that he had managed their restaurant in the DuPont Plaza area in downtown Miami at the same time I was operating the Brickell Bridge Restaurant a scant 250 yards away on the west side of the Miami River.

By 1953 Dave was considering the possibilities of opening a Dairy Queen franchise. He knew that the margins in soft ice cream sales were high, and he was attempting to learn more about the potential profitability of this business. One of his trips took him to Jacksonville, Florida, during the summer of 1953. Driving on Beach Boulevard in the community of Jacksonville Beach, he noticed a building under construction that looked very much like a Dairy Queen. He stopped in to have a closer look and met the owners Keith G. Cramer and Matthew L. Burns. They informed Dave that this new business was to be called *Insta Burger* and have a menu consisting of 18-cent hamburgers, 18-cent milk shakes, 10-cent french fries, and 10-cent Coca Cola, root beer, and orange soft drinks.

The concept would be called a *self-service drive-in* to distinguish the restaurant from a carhop operation, which was the usual kind of service offered by drive-ins during that era.

Cramer's previous experience was at Keith's Drive-In, a restaurant he operated in Daytona Beach. Both he and his father-in-law, Matthew Burns, were experienced food-service operators, who had recently visited the McDonald's "speedy service system" drive-in located in San Bernardino, California. The McDonald brothers were not new to the restaurant business. They had established their first carhop drive-in in 1937. After the war, they opened a single very successful carhop drive-in located at Fourteenth and E streets in San Bernardino. Although it was successful, it was turning into a teenage hangout, which tended to discourage quite a number of other would-be customers. Realizing that over three-fourths of their food sales were in hamburgers, the McDonalds decided to redesign the operation, eliminate the carhops, and introduce a new concept, which was the idea of self-service. Their focus was on speed of service and low prices. In their rebuilt, but much smaller restaurant, they served a grilled 10-to-the-pound hamburger patty on a bun for 15 cents. It was dressed with catsup, mustard, chopped onions, and two pickle slices. This was their prescribed way of serving a hamburger. Customers could order hamburgers another way at the same price, but they had to wait a long time for their order to be filled.

The McDonald brothers' new and innovative concept of food service caught on rapidly. The quick speed of service appealed to their new customers. Fresh french fries, milk shakes, and soft drinks rounded out the menu. It was an easy matter for the restaurants to deliver quality food along with very fast service, simply because they had such a limited menu. The customer was, in a sense, waiting on himself under the self-service system. This eliminated costly overhead and assured a high margin of profit.

The year 1948 was a watershed for what soon became known as the *fast-food business*. Richard and Maurice McDonald were the pioneers who conceptualized an idea which was to take America and the world by storm. Their innovative new food service also marked the beginning of the end for the carhop drive-in industry, which experienced such significant growth in the thirties and forties by catering to an increasingly mobile America. After the McDonald brothers' conception opened and became so obviously successful, the public became transfixed with limited-menu, self-service restaurants of all kinds. This was destined to forever change the character and style of the food-service industry in both the United States and abroad.

According to the U.S. Department of Commerce, total eating and drinking place sales for 1948 were $10.7 billion. Forty years later the McDonald system alone was generating annual food sales of over $14 billion.

The often-told story of Ray Kroc's introduction to McDonald's illustrates the phenomenal success of the concept. In 1954 Kroc was an equipment salesman selling a line of multimixer milk-shake machines. The multimixer was a machine with five rotary spindles which could make up to five milk shakes at a time. To make a milk shake special, stainless-steel containers were filled with several scoops of ice cream, some milk, flavoring, and malt. The containers were placed on the spindle assembly where the contents were blended by high-speed mixers to produce a fine-tasting milk shake. Kroc believed that it was most unlikely that a single restaurant operation would require more than one single multimixer machine. The McDonald's restaurant in San Bernardino had ordered ten of these machines. Kroc was curious about this order and wanted to see for himself why this single establishment needed ten machines with the capacity to whip up 50 milk shakes at a time. He traveled to California and witnessed the phenomenal business McDonald's was doing. He noted that there was always a steady line of people waiting for service, standing all the way out to the street. The food was good, and it was offered at low prices and served in a clean facility. McDonald's customers were served in a matter of seconds. Kroc probably decided right there and then that he had to be part of that.

After considerable discussions and negotiations with the two McDonald brothers, Kroc agreed to become the sole agent for the McDonald's franchising program. He entered into an exclusive contract with the brothers to perform that service.

Before Kroc arrived on the scene, the brothers had already issued a few franchises, most of which were located in California. Inasmuch as neither of the brothers liked to fly, they decided not to expand their business beyond the Southern California area. At the time Kroc arrived, they had reconsidered and were in the process of looking for an agent to take on responsibility for the franchises.

The success of the McDonald's restaurant in San Bernardino attracted the trade press, which began publishing numerous articles about this modern-day food-service phenomena. Restaurateurs from all over the country came to California to see what this remarkable new innovation looked like. Before long the McDonald's operation was copied by restaurant operators in many parts of the country who thought they could create a similar success on their own.

After signing an agreement with the McDonald brothers, Kroc returned to Chicago and opened his first McDonald's restaurant on Lee Street in Des Plaines, Illinois. That historic event occurred in April of 1955. The restaurant was successful right from the beginning.

Cramer and Burns heard about the phenomenal success of the McDonald's unit and like many others wanted to see for themselves. They were greatly impressed. While in California they heard about the Insta machines, which the inventor George Read described as machines capable of automating the production of hamburgers and milk shakes. Deciding to examine these machines while they were there, they met Read who demonstrated how the machines worked. They liked what they saw and ultimately entered into a contract with Read to purchase the machines under a licensing arrangement which required them to open restaurants somewhat similar to the innovative McDonald's concept. In collaboration with Read, Cramer and Burns designed a restaurant building similar to the one they had just visited. They felt that their concept would work and hoped that Read's Insta broiler and Insta shake machine would give them a competitive advantage in exploiting the opportunity.

The contract with Read established Cramer and Burns as the first territorial licensees and gave them the state of Florida to develop. The agreement gave them the exclusive right to use the Insta machines and the Insta name in their territory. The agreement also authorized them to license others to operate restaurants of a uniform design using the Insta machines and the name. For each restaurant opened Read was to receive a modest franchise fee, his profit on the sale of the Insta machines, and a share of the 2 percent royalty fee each of the franchisees were required to pay. Cramer and Burns decided that their first restaurant would be named Insta Burger, and the building was soon under construction. What they could not have imagined at the time was how much trouble the machines would give them. That would come later.

The Insta Hamburger Broiler was something that might have been dreamed up by Rube Goldberg. The machine was about 3 feet long, 1 foot wide, and 2.5 feet high. It had 12 baskets which when activated would permit the operator to place a 10-per-pound raw hamburger patty on it. After the patty was placed, another activating device positioned a wire screen against the patty to hold it in place while the patty, basket and all, entered the machine and traversed around the inside between two electric calrod heating units. This process essentially "broiled" the meat. As the basket completed its turn through the machine and came out in front of the operator, the hinged wire mesh on the basket lifted away from the top side of the cooked patty. The lower part of the basket meshed with a stainless-steel slide which consisted of 5 stainless-steel rods which lifted the cooked patty off the basket.

As the cooked patty slid down the slide, it fell into a pan of hamburger sauce. The sauce, concocted by Read, Cramer, and Burns, was a hot mixture of catsup, mustard, relish, and "special seasoning." The sauce pan sat on an electric hot plate that kept the mixture warm. The operator lifted the cooked patty from the pan of sauce and placed it on the bun, some of the sauce would linger on the patty giving it (hopefully) a special flavoring. The bun was toasted by placing it open side up into a slot properly sized to accommodate the bun on the lower part of the basket. As the basket journeyed through the machine, the patty was in a vertical position above the bun, being broiled as it passed between the calrods. The bun which was positioned directly under the patty, received the hamburger drippings which dropped onto the bun during the cooking process. The theory was that the drippings from the hamburger meat would add flavor to the bun and hence to the finished product. If the process itself wasn't bad enough, the machine often failed to mesh properly, and ground to a halt. Operations had to be shut down until repairs could be made.

The Insta shake machine used a process of flash freezing a liquid dairy mix into a thick milk shake that was really quite good. The shakes were so thick that they had to be eaten with a wooden spoon which was served with each milk shake. The Insta shake was an ice-milk product, which meant that it had slightly less butter fat than ice cream. The flash-freezing method was a fairly fast process which helped to justify the Insta name. The machine was built with two separate refrigerated tanks at the top. One tank contained a vanilla milk shake mix and the other one a chocolate mix. In the center of the machine was the freezing cylinder. Over the cylinder was a motor which drove an attached beater assembly. The beater had hinged blades extending down into the freezing cylinder. When a shake was ordered, the operator pulled a little lever at either the chocolate or vanilla tank. This activated a device which lifted a measured portion of mix and ladled it into an adjoining stainless-steel reservoir. From there the mix drained down a clear plastic tube directly into the freezing cylinder. At the precise moment the mix entered the cylinder, the shake machine operator threw a switch on the motor which activated the beater assembly. This had the effect of throwing the liquid mix against the stainless-steel freezer cylinder wall where the mix froze and thickened instantly while the beater blades scraped the product off the cylinder wall and extruded it into a paper cup which was positioned at the bottom of the assembly.

If the ladle had picked up the right amount of mix, the cup would be full. Unfortunately, it didn't always work out quite that way. If the ladle had picked up too much mix, the cup overflowed and left a mess to clean up. If too little mix entered the cylinder, there was a need to jostle just enough additional mix for another "run" in order to fill the cup. Usually that exercise resulted in drawing too much mix, which created still another mess. The slightly discolored vanilla shakes that were produced after a chocolate had been run were referred to internally by employees as *mochas*. It was to be hoped the customers wouldn't object. Notwithstanding all of the problems encountered in using the Insta shake machines, the product was really exceptionally good. It had a velvety smooth texture, and it was quite cold and never grainy. Thanks to the unique process, the shake was produced with a very small "overrun," which is a term used to describe the amount of air that is incorporated into a milk shake. Very little air was beaten into this product, which made it much more palatable than shakes made today on the modern batch-type milk-shake machines.

When Cramer and Burns were building their first Insta Burger restaurant in Jacksonville, they met with Dave on several occasions. Dave was in the Jacksonville area because he was planning to open a Dairy Queen. He had spoken to Dairy Queen's regional manager and obtained approval to serve hamburgers in his Dairy Queen store. At the time he met Cramer and Burns, the foundation had already been poured on the building he had in mind. After looking over the Insta System, which was to sell milk shakes, french fries, and hamburgers, he abandoned the Dairy Queen idea in favor of joining Cramer and Burns. Before the restaurant opened, Dave suggested that they change the name from Insta Burger to Insta Burger King. He also drew a picture of a king character sitting on a hamburger with his arms around a milk shake and gave the sketch to Cramer and Burns with the suggestion that they use it as a trademark.

The restaurant eventually opened as Insta Burger King, with a sign featuring the king on the bun sitting on top of a pylon that extended vertically 12 feet above the roof of the building. The Insta name was prominently displayed on the front facia of the building and the name Burger King appeared just beneath it. The agreement with George Read was changed to provide that the name of the restaurants that were to be opened in the future would bear the name Insta Burger King. It also provided that the king on the bun symbol, along with the name Insta Burger King would be used as trademarks and service marks. These were already registered in Washington by Cramer and Burns. Dave expected nothing in return, and he received nothing. This was the first use of the Burger King name, which was destined to become one of the most popular and widely known brand names in the world. Getting to that point would take some doing.

Dave contracted with Cramer and Burns to build the second Insta Burger King drive-in restaurant in Miami. In contemplating this he realized that he needed additional capital if he was ever to expand this business concept any further. He felt that operating just a single self-service drive-in wouldn't make economic sense. He set about attracting a partner who could help supply additional capital and assist him in building the business. Returning to Miami he went to see Harvey Fuller, who owned a restaurant on Flagler Street. Harvey was one of Miami's better-known restaurateurs whom I went to see when I was building the Brickell Bridge Restaurant. It was Harvey who encouraged me to join the Miami Restaurant Association, where I was later elected president. Harvey took a serious look at Dave's idea and although he was attracted by it and thought the idea had some promise, he wasn't inclined at his age to invest in an unproven business concept of this sort. He suggested that Dave talk to me about it. Dave took the suggestion and this resulted in the two of us getting together.

Dave opened his Insta Burger King on March 1, 1954, at 3090 NW 36th Street in Miami. The building and the paved parking lot cost $13,000, which gives some idea of the modest nature of the facility. Dave didn't have the means to construct this building himself, but he was able to convince the owner of the property to build it and lease it back to him. Dave's Insta Burger King was the second restaurant using that name; but it attracted only a modest amount of interest from the public, averaging sales of less than $100 a day. The Insta Burger King concept was a novel experiment in food service at that time and the public simply wasn't ready for it. Even so,

Dave felt confident that in time the public would become familiar with it and that business would ultimately pick up.

Prior to this time very few restaurants in the country offered self-service as a way of serving customers. This system required customers to come up to an ordering window, pay in advance, and wait for their order to be filled. Food was placed in paper trays or put in paper containers and paper bags. In the early 1950s this was a completely new and different style of service unfamiliar to restaurant patrons. After being served, customers had an option to eat in their cars or on seats provided on an open patio adjoining one side of the building. In 1954 in Miami that idea was unproven, unfamiliar, and unpopular. Business continued to be slow, but Dave was intrigued by the idea of a restaurant with a limited menu, fast service, and low prices. His enthusiasm was very evident on those occasions when we had dinner together at my Brickell Bridge Restaurant. He stopped by often during the time his new restaurant concept was getting ready to open.

As we came to know each other better, Dave stepped up the pressure to join him as a business partner. He had invested almost all of his available capital in opening this first store. I must admit that the idea did intrigue me. I had sold my first restaurant, The Colonial Inn, a few months earlier and for the first time in my life I had a little capital available. I thought carefully abut the implications of joining him as a business partner.

The Brickell Bridge Restaurant was doing quite well at the time, but it was obvious to me that this purely commercial type of restaurant could never be developed into a multiunit chain operation and that really was what I had in mind. With Dave continuing to insist that I come out to see his new Insta Burger King, I sensed that this might be an opportunity worth looking into. I accepted his invitation and agreed to take a look at it when he opened for business.

One evening in April, Nancy and I drove out to 36th Street to meet Dave and see what his new enterprise was all about. I was intrigued with the cleanliness and brightness of the place, but what attracted me the most was the simplicity of the operation. I couldn't help but agree with Dave that this idea had the potential of being developed into a chain of restaurants. After our initial visit, Dave stepped up his persuasive appeal to join him in this venture. I liked Dave and thought that we would make a good team and enjoy a compatible working relationship. My problem was one of coming up with the capital necessary to match Dave's investment. This would require that I sell the Brickell Bridge Restaurant, and this in turn would shut off my source of income. From the beginning we spoke in terms of making equal investments so the two of us would become equal partners. I thought this was a reasonable and fair approach, but first I needed to confirm what Dave had told me about his capital investment and the profitability of the business. I asked him to let me look over whatever financial records he had in this regard. I planned to match whatever investment he had made, so information of this sort was necessary before I reached a final decision.

One must understand Dave Edgerton a bit in order to appreciate the fact that here was a guy who never focused very much on details, particularly those concerning financial matters. Accounting, financial issues, and money matters simply didn't interest him. Dave was a highly creative and an extraordinarily bright person predisposed to think mostly in conceptual terms. He told me that the business, even with low sales, was making a respectable profit. He had only been open for six or seven weeks by that time and said, "Jim, I don't have a financial statement or a set of books. I have been accumulating sales information which shows how much money we have taken in each day, and I can show you what I have paid out and let you look at my checkbook, but I haven't got a profit and loss statement or a balance sheet to show you." I said, "Dave, why don't you just gather up whatever records you have and deliver them to my accountant, Hugh Shillington, who is a CPA. He can prepare a financial statement for you. This should affirm the level of investment you have made in the business, and it should also show you how profitable the business has been since you opened."

This solution was quite acceptable to Dave who had previously told me that the business was already profitable, although he didn't have the exact figures to prove that. Citing the restaurant's ability to deliver low labor costs, he speculated that the operation was producing a profit of close to 28 percent of sales. Although I could hardly believe that this small business could produce such a high margin of profit on such limited sales, I did accept the idea that this was a profitable business. Dave delivered his "books" which were papers of all kinds stuffed in a peach basket, a container he had picked up from the local produce market. He simply threw in his sales records, checkbook, and various invoices representing the purchase of his equipment, preopening expenses, and miscellaneous expenses he had incurred in opening and operating the business. Several weeks later Mr. Shillington presented a financial statement on David Edgerton—sole proprietor, owner of the Insta Burger King business located at 3090 NW 36th Street, Miami, Florida. The statement was at considerable variance from Dave's estimate of the operating results. Not only was he *not* making 28 percent profit on sales, the report stated that he had actually lost 56 percent on the sales he had been able to generate up to that point. I have often been asked why I was willing to invest in a business that was reporting such dismal results. The answer is that the financial statement covered only a very brief period of time and it included a lot of start-up expenses which tended to distort the picture.

I was willing to look at it that way, but I was really more interested in looking at the character of David Edgerton and asking myself if this fellow would make a good business partner. I was completely satisfied on that point, so I was quite willing to trust my instincts as far as Dave's integrity and his commitment to the business were concerned. My major focus was on the business concept itself, and I liked what I saw there. The Insta Burger King idea was a simple food-service concept that with adequate sales could easily be expanded into a multiunit chain of restaurants. This was exactly what I was looking for. I could see that there were a number of operational problems to iron out, but the simple menu, low prices, high margins, and fast service were all ideas that made a lot of sense to me. I was ready to put everything I had on the line and join up with this very intelligent and interesting individual.

The financial statement from Hugh Shillington showed that Edgerton had made an investment of approximately $20,000 in the business. This was consistent with what Dave had told me. I agreed to match that capital and on June 1, 1954, three months after Dave had opened his first Insta Burger King restaurant, we formed a corporation called Burger King of Miami, Inc. This new company took title to Dave's proprietary assets and assumed all of his business liabilities. We issued 50 percent of the stock to each of us. Our statement showed that we had invested $40,000 and owned one Insta Burger King restaurant. After my investment, we had enough cash, if levered properly, to open a few more restaurants. We had a record of losses on the books, but aside from that we had confidence in the prospects for growth and expansion. The two of us couldn't have been more enthused about the future, and yet more unprepared for the events which would soon take place.

More "Soup"

The decision to join Dave and invest in the Insta Burger King business was certainly among the most crucial business decisions I had ever made up to that time. I had no way of knowing whether this novel concept of food service would catch the public's fancy or be successful. To me it was starting out all over again with the same fears and anxieties that had attended the opening of both The Colonial Inn and the Brickell Bridge Restaurant. I believed the concept would work, but the nagging question was always "Could the business succeed?" Could the two of us make a success out of building a chain of restaurants using this novel self-service concept and two rather screwy and temperamental machines? This wacky idea had never been tested in the marketplace. Would it work? Like I had done so many other times in the past few years, I was putting all my available capital on the line, and risking everything on the assumption that we could make a success out of a completely new and still unproven business idea.

Looking back, I certainly had to question my judgment. At the time I had a net worth of just a little over $20,000, which was all I had been able to accumulate after being in business for almost five years. Now I was betting the whole bundle on something my instinct told me was okay even though I knew very little about this completely new and untested business. Nancy and I had just bought a new home, which was heavily mortgaged. With three small children to support, it was quite risky to take on such a heavy financial burden. I had very little backup capital; I was in a 50-50 partnership with a person I certainly liked and respected but about whom I knew very little. Would the business succeed and could we get along with each other? The bet I had just made said that it simply had to. As it turned out, Dave and I got along wonderfully well. At least on that score, my instincts were good. We had differences of opinion and a few disagreements from time to time, but we enjoyed an exceptionally fine relationship over the years and became close personal friends as a result of that.

Dave and I discussed how much each of us should draw from the business. We reached a decision that I would draw $12,500 per year, and he would draw $10,000. Dave could see that with a new home and a family of five to support my financial needs were greater than his. I genuinely appreciated his thoughtful, understanding, and unselfish attitude about this.

Soon after forming our corporate partnership, we arranged to build two more Burger Kings. Without the financial means to develop real estate, it was necessary for us to convince investors to acquire land and build our single-purpose building on lease-back arrangements. The early Burger King buildings looked similar to soft ice cream or root-beer stands. The buildings cost around $15,000 and the land averaged about $25,000, so a real estate developer willing to take a chance on us had to make an investment of $40,000. If the business failed, the building would be of little use to the lender, the developer, or anyone else. There was a good amount of risk involved for everyone, including us.

We convinced two different property owners to build two new restaurants for us in Miami. The first one at 6091 SW 8th Street and the second one at 8995 NW 7th Avenue. There was nothing spectacular about either opening, and this was very discouraging to us. Both restaurants had uncovered patio areas for customers, but most of them preferred to eat in their cars. We opened our fourth store on U.S. Highway 1 in Homestead. It was a long way from Miami, but the owner of this site was willing to have us build a Burger King store there.

Sales in all the newly opened stores turned out to be very disappointing. In addition, the exclusive Insta machines were continually breaking down and causing serious business interruptions. This put us face-to-face with some serious financial problems. Our monthly operating statements told the grim story that we were losing money and we were losing it fast. The public seemed to be completely indifferent to our new concept of food service, and we couldn't figure out the reason for it. It began to appear that we just weren't going to make it. I'd been there before, but this time it really started to hurt. Dave and I were plenty shaken as 1955 drew to a close. We were up against a financial wall, and we knew it. We needed to do something, and we needed to do it in a hurry.

Business may have been terribly discouraging, but there was a bright side in my personal life. 1955 was a special year for our family, and we had much to be thankful for. On September 3 Nancy delivered our fourth child, another little girl whom we named Susan Evans. Little Susie soon became the centerpiece in our home. She had three adoring siblings and two very proud parents to look after her. Pam was almost eight years old and was already in the third grade. On the day Nancy came home from the hospital with Susie, Lynne went off to school on her first day in the first grade. She would be six years old in just a few days. Our two-year-old son, Whit, was still at home requiring the constant attention that any active child of that age would demand. The family was in great shape, and the addition of little Susie brought us even closer together. I tried not to let my business disappointment affect our family life, and I do not believe that it did. That was the one thing I had to hang on to, and Nancy, as expected, led the way.

While I was facing the worries and fears of a business that was in real trouble, Nancy, in her typically energetic and positive fashion, continued to provide a happy and comfortable home for the six of us. How she managed to run a household on my meager salary of $12,500 less taxes is a real tribute to her common sense and frugal nature. She had no help, cooked all the meals, did the shopping, and looked after the house and the children. It was a monumental task for any person, and she accomplished all of it with an ease which was uncanny. I never once heard her complain. She always had a way of appearing happy, buoyant, and upbeat to anyone who was around her. This attitude of hers was particularly reassuring to me at a time when Dave and I were desperately trying to put the company on a profitable course.

We began calendar year 1956 in terrible financial condition. The opening of the first four Burger King units was driven by our ambitious optimism, but we had used very poor business judgment in a number of different ways. We had spent my entire $20,000 capital contribution and had assumed additional debt, which by this time was threatening to overwhelm us. We had simply overexpanded in the hope that the four restaurants would be profitable. Unfortunately, this wasn't the way it had worked out. All four of the restaurants were unprofitable, so we had big problems to deal with.

At this point we had to get out and find some capital to support the business. By the spring of 1956 Dave and I had been business partners for over 18 months, and we were going nowhere. We were simply dead in the water, and with losses piling up, our capital was practically gone. Sales were flat to negative, and we were struggling to find reasons why. We just couldn't figure it out. The good news was that our spirits remained undaunted. We believed that somehow and in some way a magical event would happen to lead us out of the trouble we were in. For the moment, our mission was to save the company. To do this we would need additional investment capital. We began our desperate search for that capital.

The Desperate Search for Capital

As 1955 drew to a close, it was clear to Dave and me that we were in serious financial trouble. Nancy's father, Dr. Nichol, tried to help us by investing $3750 for some stock in the company, and he loaned us an additional $10,000 at 6 percent interest. Six years before that he convinced me to make an investment in Pepsi Cola stock saying he was so confident about it that he would make good on it if I ever lost any money. I never asked him to make good when the investment soured and wound up costing me about $6000. We never talked about it, but I felt that perhaps his investment in Burger King had something to do with a sense of obligation he might have felt toward me. He might have also felt bad about encouraging me to make my near ruinous investment in the Brickell Bridge Restaurant, but he had no reason to be concerned about that. Whatever I had done was my decision and not his. I always felt responsible for my own actions and decisions. "Nick" had always tried to help Nancy and me as we struggled to establish our livelihood, and I was forever grateful for having such a fine man for a father-in-law. Later on, following a difficult period in Dr. Nichol's life, Dave and I borrowed enough money to retire the investment he had made in the company, even though at the time Burger King's future was still pretty much in doubt.

In later years Nick mentioned to me on several occasions that he wished he had been able to keep his investment in

Burger King. Out of appreciation for all he had done for us, our board of directors granted him an option to purchase Burger King stock at any time during a 10-year period into the future. When he finally exercised this option, he obtained, at no cost to himself, something in excess of $150,000 worth of Pillsbury stock at the time of our merger with this company in 1967. We were pleased that he finally received a significant benefit as a result of his confidence in us and in Burger King. One of his important contributions had been introducing Dave and me to Harvey Fruehauf in 1956. When Nick died in 1970, his Pillsbury stock was the principal asset in his estate. Had he lived another 20 years and kept his investment and the accumulated dividends, his stock would have been worth close to $1 million.

In 1956 with the opening of each new Burger King, we hoped that business would pick up and improve, but this never did happen. Things continued to get worse, and the prospect of failure loomed larger and more threatening. We tried everything in a desperate attempt to figure out what we were doing wrong. It was apparent that most of our problem involved the Burger King system which we had inherited from Jacksonville's Cramer and Burns. The Insta equipment was troublesome, inefficient, and undependable. As a result we were unable to serve our customers consistently and efficiently. We simply could not maintain the quality of our food and service on a regular basis. Things just were not right. Our menu was reasonably acceptable, but it was also a bit ordinary; very little about it was either unique, special, or noteworthy. In retrospect, I believe it is fair to say that at the time we were just run of the mill.

The major problem contributing to our low level of sales in South Florida was that we couldn't get people excited about our low prices and fast service when we were having so many problems with the food we were serving. I was aware that our competitors were generating much higher volumes in units they were operating in states outside of Florida. It was difficult to understand why they were so successful when we were having such a difficult time trying to do the same thing they were. Everything seemed to focus on production problems and the quality and delivery of our food. When Burger King units were opened in other parts of Florida, their disappointing sales were quite similar to our own. I attributed some of our problems to the fact that the Royal Castle organization in South Florida had won excellent public acceptance and top-notch customer loyalty largely as the result of an effective advertising strategy.

Later on I came to believe that our initial pricing strategy was never on target. Our competitors were selling a small hamburger for 15 cents, while we were charging 18 cents. In the markets we served 18 cents was not viewed as a particularly exceptional value. I believe that one of our biggest mistakes at the time was staying with our higher-priced hamburger rather than offering one that we could design and sell for 15 cents. Fifteen cents was a magic number in those days and Royal Castle and McDonald's were living proof of that.

It was small consolation, but the competition which followed us into the Florida market fared worse than we did. Golden Point, Henry's, Red Barn, Burger Castle, Biff Burger, and numerous others came into the market and lasted only a short time before going out of business. Even highly successful chains like Hardee's and White Castle made attempts to penetrate the market, but all of them were forced to withdraw. Florida was a tough, competitive market, and starting a business like ours was a difficult undertaking for anyone—even those who had the experience, capital, intelligence, and courage to give it a try.

Many families and customers of all ages perceived that inexpensive hamburger couldn't possibly be wholesome. We had to work hard to overcome that concern. Another problem was with our pay-as-you-order system. This troubled a lot of new customers and made many of them uncomfortable. In order to understand how customers responded to our self-service system, I often sat in my car, which I would park across the street, to observe their reactions.

I learned that our system of service, which was new at the time, confused and irritated a lot of our customers. They were very concerned as to whether our employees could remember their order once they had paid for it. The Insta ticket system contributed to the problem.

For control purposes we had set up a system where, after paying for their order, our customers received serially numbered tickets They would have to wait before receiving their food. Customers didn't seem to know what the tickets were all about. For example, a customer ordering two 18-cent hamburgers received two blue 18-cent tickets. An order for 10-cent fries was worth one white "fry" ticket; red "drink" tickets were issued for soft drinks, and so forth. Customers often stared in disbelief upon receiving tickets in exchange for their money. A typical reaction was an incredulous look which I interpreted to mean, "Look I paid for food, not tickets, what do I do with these tickets?" To add to the confusion, after paying and receiving tickets, the customer was directed to another window where an employee was supposedly ready to deliver the order. Often it was necessary to ask the customer to repeat the order. This added more pressure to an already difficult situation particularly when the customer couldn't remember what had been ordered in the first place.

The theater-ticket idea was simply a terrible creation, and it soon became obvious that the entire system had to be changed before frustration and confusion simply overwhelmed it. Unfortunately, we stayed with this Jacksonville system much longer than we should have. We eventually changed it, but not before we had alienated a lot of new, first-time customers.

It was becoming increasingly obvious that Cramer and Burns did not have a grip on either the service problems or food quality and production problems. We were not giving our customers what they expected, and we were paying a heavy price because of it.

Dave and I decided that if we were going to live with the system, we had to speed it up and eliminate the service confusion. We devised a system which enabled us to deliver the customers' food within seconds of their placing an order. We were very sensitive to our customers' demand for faster "speed of service," and this became our major focus in developing a more efficient product-delivery system. We believed strongly that speed of service was a major customer issue at the time and that it will forever be one of the most important concerns of people who like to eat out. The success of our business still depends to a very great extent upon how fast and accurately we can deliver food to our customers. One of the great concerns I expressed during the 1990s involved the matter of menu proliferations. When this threatened our ability to serve our customers as quickly and accurately as they demanded, we created a problem of major significance. Ultimately, we got back to the basics of speed and order accuracy, but not before we lost a lot of business. Speed was part of our basic problem in 1955 and 1956. Our system of customer service was unacceptable at the time, and if we wanted to stay in business, we needed to do something about it.

To emphasize the importance of speed of service, I coined an expression in the 1950s which I posted in the restaurants. It simply stated: "Our customers have two things to spend—time and money—and they would rather spend their money." I used that expression often in our early training sessions and in our attempts to emphasize the importance of fast service.

The Insta machines turned out to be a complete and utter disaster. I have previously described the temperamental nature of the machines, but one incident involving the Insta broiler was particularly instructive. On that occasion during our first year in business, Dave had just finished adjusting the temperamental Insta broiler before opening. After running smoothly for an hour or so the machine began to malfunction just at the moment Dave was standing directly in front of it. When he saw what was happening and heard the gnarling, grinding, and twisting sound of metal on metal as the machine ground to a halt, he went into a fit of rage. Acting more in frustration than anything else, he reached into his tool box and grabbed a hatchet which had been his as a Boy Scout. The name on the handle was "Davy Edgerton." With his face turning red, he drew the hatchet back and sunk the blade into the stainless-steel machine, destroying a good part of the working mechanism. In an emotional defense of his own actions, Dave yelled, "I can build a better machine than this pile of junk," which prompted my response, "Well you better get busy and build it because right now we are out of business until we get our only spare machine in operation."

Dave, true to his words, did build a better broiler. He took his idea to a Swedish-born mechanic named Karl Sundman, who had a well-equipped machine shop. Three weeks later the pair finished production of a continuous-chain broiler that was efficient, fast, productive, and trouble free. To this day that basic design principle still sets the standard for all Burger King broilers, and it has served as a model for the manufacture of restaurant equipment used in operations similar to our own. This incident is just one of many "Edgerton stories" that I always take delight in telling.

Cramer and Burns sold other franchises during the mid 1950s, opening stores in Hollywood, Fort Lauderdale, West Palm Beach, Melbourne, Fort Pierce, Tampa, Orlando, and, of course, in their own Jacksonville area. These new franchisees experienced the same sales problems and financial difficulty that we were having. All of us were trying to hold on until we could figure out some way to jump-start the business and put it on the road to higher sales and profitability. With stagnant sales and losses piling up, we began to think that all of us might have made a mistake to get into the Insta Burger King business.

Unfortunately, our financial commitment was such that we had no choice other than sticking with it and seeing it through. These were very discouraging times. With the constant and lingering threat of failure staring us in the face, we hoped that the future would bring in the new ideas and improvements which would lead us out of the woods. Something very fundamental and basic was wrong with this business, and we were getting killed. We needed to find out what the problem was and fix it in a hurry. Time was running out and the two of us were pretty desperate.

Both of us felt that by attracting additional capital we might be able to grow out of our four-store base and into profitability. Our plan was to build more restaurants so that we could advertise and promote the business in the Dade County area. Dr. Nichol understood our need to raise more capital, and he tried many times to introduce me to a number of friends and patients in the hope that one or more of them might become interested in an investment in our struggling business. Dave shared my enthusiasm for expanding the business even though we both knew that in attracting more capital we would have to dilute our own equity ownership position.

Early in 1956 with our capital almost totally depleted and the company at or near to insolvency, Dr. Nichol hosted a cocktail reception at his home so that I could meet Harvey C. Fruehauf, and his wife, Angela. Mr. Fruehauf had been the driving force behind the development of the modern-day Fruehauf Trailer Company in Detroit. He had retired from the company in 1950 and was living in Miami Beach recovering from a recent heart attack. We had a delightful visit that evening. Harvey was a man who loved to talk about business, and based on his reactions to our conversation, it was clear that my story about Burger King had piqued his interest. He asked some good questions about my background and my experience in the restaurant business. I told him the whole story.

During our conversation he put a direct question to me, "Well son, how are you doing?" I told him that we were doing very poorly at the time and explained the problems we had run up against. I offered to show him the company's balance sheet which I had in my pocket, saying that this would tell the whole disappointing story. Scanning our financial statement, he could see our grim situation immediately. Dave and I had invested $40,000 in the business, but our losses to date had just about wiped out all of that capital. He could see that we were practically broke. I told Mr. Fruehauf that we were having difficulty paying our bills but at least for the moment our suppliers were being patient. I explained that we needed more capital if we were going to survive. I emphasized that additional capital would help us strengthen our financial condition and enable us to build more restaurants. I spoke about building an advertising and marketing program to help turn the business around.

It was at this point in our conversation that Harvey said words to the effect, "Well son, you look like a young man who knows what you want to do. I might be willing to invest with you. What amount of capital do you suggest I put in?" I asked him to consider putting in $65,000 and suggested that in return we would give him a half interest in the business. Dave and I would hold the other half interest ourselves. Without hesitation Harvey stated his willingness to make an investment on the terms I outlined. I was overwhelmed by both his quick decision and the prospect of having this man as a partner. The additional capital would save the company from going under. That was our greatest concern at the time. We agreed to meet a week later at the office of Lon Worth Crow Co., a mortgage banking and real estate firm that had helped us secure some of our locations.

We met on April 30, 1956, to close our deal. Harvey, who had subsequently challenged himself on the wisdom of investing in a business he knew very little about with two young men he had only recently met, asked to examine our balance sheet once again. I passed the statement over to him and watched him intently. His eyes fixed on the lower-right-hand corner where the capital account verified that Burger King of Miami, Inc., was almost insolvent. Appearing a bit perplexed, he looked up at me and said something to the effect that although this was a pretty risky investment, he was willing to do this out of his sense of confidence in the two of us. After saying that, he signed a check for $65,000 and handed it to me. As far as I was concerned, this was a huge sum of money that could well be the break we were looking for.

This extraordinary happening began an important chapter in my personal life. From this point forward Harvey became my very good friend and mentor, and this lasted until his death in 1968 some 12 years later. His friendship, advice, and counsel were very important in the development, growth, expansion, and success of Burger King during those early but difficult, exciting, and challenging years. Harvey never played an active role in the business, but he always made himself available. His patience and understanding were the kind of qualities that helped us think through the strategic decisions which would later provide the basis for our extraordinary growth and prosperity.

This book will mention Harvey Fruehauf's many contributions to the success of the company. I like to believe that the personal relationship we shared was as important to him as it certainly was to me. He was a thoughtful and considerate man who was a good judge of character. He had exceptionally fine judgment, and his experience in handling business affairs proved to be very helpful to us. I was fortunate to have shared so many years with him and had the benefit of his wise counsel.

Harvey's investment in Burger King, like both Dave's and mine, nearly went on the rocks at one point, but ultimately all of us came out big winners. Harvey believed in "putting all his eggs in one basket and then watching the basket." He had lots of pithy sayings like that. He also had plenty of earthy and practical advice to go along with his philosophy about ethical and fair dealing in the business world. I learned a lot from him, not only about proper and acceptable business principles and practices, but also about the importance of proper and ethical conduct.

I'm sure that Harvey could have lost his $65,000 investment and never missed it. I'm also certain that he enjoyed seeing his investment in Burger King multiply to the extent that it did. By 1967, when we merged with The Pillsbury Company, his investment was worth close to $10 million; by including dividend accumulations, the intervening success of The Pillsbury Company, and later the investment of Grand Metropolitan in its acquisition of Pillsbury, his investment was worth more than $100 million. Harvey would have enjoyed that—not so much because it represented a lot of money and an extraordinary return on his investment, but because he had gambled his faith and judgment on his initial instincts. He had won! Of course he cared about being right, but I suspect that his real pleasure would have been in reflecting on our early growth and development, when the company was in its infancy and struggling to find its place in the world of commerce and industry. Some of my most pleasurable moments were spent with him discussing corporate strategy and thinking beyond to what the future might bring.

Using the capital contribution supplied by Mr. Fruehauf, Dave and I set out to build three more Burger King restaurants. We opened store 5 at 7995 NW 27th Avenue in the fall of 1956 and store 6 at 9201 South Federal Highway in December, 1956, followed by store 7 at 3051 Coral Way in March of 1957. The opening of Store 5 gave us a badly needed boost in morale because the volume of business at that location was superior to any of the original four stores we had opened. Unfortunately, our sales in Stores 6 and 7 proved to be very disappointing, and this added to our frustration. As hard as we tried, we just couldn't seem to increase the level of store sales. Now with seven restaurants open and operating at unacceptably low levels of sales, we began losing money again and there seemed to be no reason to expect that we could alter this situation unless we came up with a different and novel way to run the business. Nothing seemed to be working, and unless we could figure out some way to prop up our business and boost sales, we stood a good chance of going under. It sickened me to think that we had invested all of Harvey's capital and had come up with so little to show for it.

This was devastating to me personally. I had suffered the indignity of a number of failing experiences during my business career up to that point. These were ill-conceived business ideas which on three separate occasions had brought me close to bankruptcy. The way things were going now, it looked as though I might be faced with going broke the fourth time. I asked myself if I would ever learn! My confidence and self-esteem were both at a low ebb. Further aggravating the situation was the likelihood of disappointing a decent person like Harvey Fruehauf—a man who invested with us because he believed in me, my integrity, and my business judgment. I was letting him down.

Perhaps I was too arrogant and cocky. I had become a great success at age 21 during my first job at the YMCA—so much so that I decided to switch jobs and I didn't make it there. This was a humbling and near catastrophic experience, but I was able to recover. My success at The Colonial Inn restored my confidence, but I suffered new disappointments at the Brickell Bridge Restaurant and nearly failed again. It was my investment in Insta Burger King that brought me face-to-face with going broke a third time. Mr. Fruehauf saved me briefly, but it now appeared likely that I could fail once again. I was down, and I was down deep. I really didn't know what to do.

Throughout this difficult period of time, I kept Harvey informed about everything we were doing. I shared our disappointment about the health of the business and told him how bad things were going. I had failed to produce promised results and that was killing me. We invested Harvey's capital in three new stores in the belief that this would help our business turn the profit corner, but this was not the way things were working out.

Looking back on this situation and in hindsight, it is undeniable that we had exercised very poor business judgment. I had a long record of doing that. Optimism replaced good sense and instead of taking some of Harvey's capital and paying down our burdensome debt, we plowed everything into building three more stores. We felt so confident that business would improve that we gambled everything on expansion and even went so far as to take on additional debt. This sad development put us in deeper trouble than we ever were in before.

I look back on those years of impetuous decision making and the poor judgment I exercised. I recall those many occasions when it looked as though I was surely going broke. Often I wonder how I survived and how I kept going. It cost me a lot of self-confidence, but there was still enough of that left to keep the spark alive. In spite of my record of failure, I felt that things would improve and that somehow I'd get the break I was looking for. I had to believe that. I was determined not to give up.

Approaching insolvency again, our financial plight grew more serious with each passing day. Sharing my concern with Harvey one evening, I explained that my greatest disappointment was the possibility of losing the money he had invested. I valued the confidence he had placed in me, and it troubled me deeply that we might prove unworthy of his trust. When I expressed this to him, he told me that he was more worried about me than he was about himself, and he encouraged me to think positively about my life and the future prospects of the business. He made a point of telling me not to worry about him, suggesting that if I continued to think positively about the future and read the Bible and prayed a little for guidance that things would probably work out for the best. In the meantime he urged me to cheer up and not get too discouraged. It was in these moments of great personal dismay and discouragement that Harvey gave me the boost and support that I needed. I never forgot this side of the rewarding personal relationship I enjoyed with this fine gentleman.

The Break We Were Looking For

The Whopper Is Born

One of my messages to people searching for success is the need to maintain confidence in their own ability to deal with defeat and disappointments in life. Negative thoughts produce negative results. Life will produce its share of bad luck and things will not always go the way they are planned, but an old adage suggests an inherent truth, "Quitters never win and winners never quit." Be guided by that. You can still do a lot of dumb things, make a lot of mistakes, and get discouraged, but usually there is a solution out there somewhere. You've got to look for it, and that demands a constant search. You can find it if you look hard enough and long enough. I know. Read on.

Dave and I were constantly thinking about how we were going to turn our desperate situation around. The whole Burger King system was stalled out. Cramer and Burns had encountered plenty of difficulty on their own. The five franchised Burger King stores they had helped to establish in Hollywood, Fort Lauderdale, and Palm Beach were doing worse than we were, and the situation wasn't much different further north in Tampa and Orlando. Their own Jacksonville restaurant operations weren't doing any better either. Dave and I were forced to recognize that the Burger King system lacked any real "zip" at all. It certainly didn't have any significant customer appeal. We had tried everything we could think of to stimulate sales, but nothing seemed to work. Early in 1957 Cramer and Burns opened a prefabricated Burger King restaurant in Gainesville, Florida. It was located close to the University of Florida campus. Their idea was that a prefab building could be moved to another location if it wasn't successful in the original spot. This defensive experiment served no useful purpose in improving the overall system; however, it did lead to our making the most important decision we had made since we opened for business three years earlier. Here is what happened.

Shortly after this prefab unit was installed and opened, Dave and I stopped to see it during a return to Miami from one of our many visits with Cramer and Burns in Jacksonville. During the few hours we spent there neither of us saw a single customer enter the restaurant. This only served to reinforce our notion that the Burger King idea was in big trouble and going downhill. Looking for something to do, I walked out of the new Burger King and glanced a block or so up the street. Less than 100 yards away was a drive-in restaurant which had a line of customers standing out front waiting to get served. I noticed a sign advertising a big hamburger, so I decided to walk up the street, have a look, and get in the line. The restaurant was run down and dirty and the appearance of their serving personnel left a lot to be desired. The parking lot was unpaved so as cars drove in dust blew about, which made it unpleasant for the people who were either standing in line or sitting in their cars. The men's room door, which was located on the outside of the building, was barely hanging on one hinge. The place was a mess, but I kept looking at the long line of customers waiting to buy their food. I had to know why these people were crowding the place when 100 yards down the street at the new Burger King, we had absolutely no business at all.

Standing in line and inching toward the order window, I noticed that the customers who were just served were carrying out bags of large hamburgers. I ordered two of them, one for me and one for Dave who was still down the street. I unwrapped this big hamburger and saw that it consisted of a quarter-pound hamburger patty on a big five-inch bun served with lettuce, tomatoes, mayonnaise, pickles, onions, and catsup. After a few bites it wasn't hard to understand why these customers were carrying them out by the bagful. The hamburger was big, and it tasted great. I walked back down the street to the new Burger King still munching that big hamburger and carrying the other one for Dave to try. I was really impressed with how good it tasted, and I wanted to get Dave's opinion. The new Burger King still didn't have any customers. Dave, with nothing more important to do, unwrapped his hamburger and enjoyed it as much as I had. It was at that point that I began to get an idea that would have a most important effect on our business.

After Dave and I had seen enough of the new prefabricated Burger King, we got in the car and headed south toward Miami and home. Our plan was to have dinner in Ocala at the Brahma Restaurant before continuing on to Miami. Dave always did the driving on our many trips around the state, and because it was late in the afternoon, I decided that it was cocktail time. I had a small bottle of bourbon in the glove compartment, so I poured a little of it into a 7-Up I had just bought at the gas station. All I could think about was that big, good tasting hamburger I had just eaten, and the more I thought about it the more enthusiastic I became about an idea that was building up in my mind.

Feeling in an expansive mood as we were driving through the little community of Micanopy, it occurred to me that it might be a good idea to introduce a big garnished hamburger in our Miami restaurants. I expressed this opinion to Dave, who quickly agreed. I suggested that we call our product a *Whopper,* knowing that this would convey imagery of something *big.* I also suggested that we put signs reading, "Home of the Whopper" under our Burger King name to indicate that our new product was the specialty of the house. We both agreed that this made a lot of sense. During the remainder of our trip to Ocala we talked about how we would go about introducing the Whopper. This was the main point of conversation during dinner that evening and all through the night on our long drive back to Miami. The idea of introducing the Whopper was all we could talk about. We arrived in Miami long after midnight, tired but excited about our plans to add the Whopper to our menu.

As soon as we could, we arranged to change the roof signs on all seven of our restaurants. Within days we set wooden A-frame signs out in front of each store which read, "New, Whopper Hamburger 37 cents." Dave and I thought that the 37 cents along with a 2-cent sales tax would keep the Whopper priced just under 40 cents, which we believed might be close to the price-resistance level. We raised the price to 39 cents a few weeks later. At the time we couldn't possibly have imagined that some day into the future this product would become the most popular and best-known sandwich in the United States—perhaps in the world.

We wrote product specifications for the Whopper, and all seven of our restaurants began serving the new sandwich within a few days of our return. From that day forward our business began to improve. The Whopper was a stunning success from the moment it was introduced. We had come up with the right idea at a most opportune time. As conditions existed, we would have been hard-pressed to hold on much longer. Within a short time sales and profits began to improve, and our future seemed to be much brighter. This was the break we had been looking for. We had found the key to our future success. We just *knew* that.

The introduction of the Whopper came at about the same time that we replaced the unreliable Insta milk shake machines with a new batch-type Sani-Serve shake machine. Dave's new broiler invention not only increased the speed of our food production line, it enabled us to cook the Whopper patty right alongside our regular patty. Had he not invented this broiler, we would have been stymied in bringing out the Whopper. The two new machines helped us improve the over-all productivity of our employees, but what was most important was the customer approval of our much faster service. The introduction of the Whopper had an extraordinarily positive effect on our business, and our rapidly growing customer base gave repeated assurance that everything was going to work out just fine.

Even before the historic introduction of the Whopper, we no longer looked to Jacksonville for leadership. The few statewide franchises that were in existence had long since turned to us for guidance and direction. We were the only source of innovation and change which was so desperately needed in our struggle for survival. The introduction of the Whopper was just one of many creative ideas we had come up with in trying to improve our business, but this one would turn out to be our real salvation. Dave and I told Cramer and Burns that we were getting rid of the Insta machines and their notoriously ineffective ticket system and that from this point forward we would be writing our own specifications for food products and equipment. In addition we let them know that we would set our own standards for restaurant operations and that in the future we would design our own buildings as well. Our Manual of Operating Data created by Dave Edgerton became the bible for operating our restaurants. We concluded that we no longer needed support from Jacksonville, and we told them so. They understood this and even seemed grateful to have us assume this kind of leadership. With all the innovative changes we were making, it was clear to everyone concerned that from now on the Burger King direction would come from Miami. With our restaurants around the state now serving the Whopper, the Insta signs came down and we became known simply as Burger King—Home of the Whopper.

As the months passed, our business activity and sales picked up at an astonishing pace. Dave and I gained some much-needed confidence in our future. Unfortunately, we were totally unprepared for the next problem we would have to face, and it wasn't long in coming.

Early Franchising

After our introduction of the Whopper, the company became embroiled in a controversy with the State of Florida about our reporting of the sales tax we were collecting. With no way of knowing how much total tax we were collecting on individual customer transactions, we adopted a formula given to us by the Sales Tax Department. This formula instructed us how much to pay them every month, and we did this faithfully. Three years later they concluded that their formula had been faulty and told us that we owed them $8304, including interest and penalties. We didn't have the money, but after negotiating with them, they accepted 168 postdated checks in settlement of their claim. The problem was covering the seven checks they planned to deposit every month for the next 24 months. This added to our already burdened financial situation.

About this same time a fellow named Charlie Krebs, from Cincinnati, walked into our office and asked if our Burger King store 5 was for sale. We were still in desperate need of cash, and he made us a cash offer of $20,000 for the business. After discussing the matter at length, Dave and I accepted his offer and signed an agreement making him a franchisee. Until then Dave and I always thought in terms of operating all the restaurants as company units. Charlie agreed to pay us a royalty of 2.9 percent a month and an advertising charge of 2 percent of sales. Our contract required him to operate the restaurant according to the standards outlined in our Manual of

Operating Data, a copy of which was attached to his franchise agreement.

We were suddenly in the franchising business, but this time as franchisors. The sale of store 5 to Krebs was followed by a growing interest in the Burger King business, which we attributed largely to the increase in sales brought about by the introduction of the Whopper. Charlie did well with his store from the day he bought it, and he talked about his success to other people, a few of whom became interested in buying some of our remaining stores. With all the problems we were facing, selling our company-owned stores seemed to be the best way to resolve our financial dilemma. We felt this would enable us to meet our principal objective which was to increase the number of units in the South Florida area. We wanted to do this just as fast as we possibly could so that we could begin to advertise our business. We felt from the beginning that advertising would play a key role in building our future success. There were many other advantages. Additional restaurants would give us considerably more buying power. The royalty income we expected to receive would help us defray our administrative overhead, and the franchise fees we intended to charge would be a major source of income to the company.

After the sale of store 5 we made the strategic decision to put our full emphasis and focus on franchising. The sale of four of our remaining units followed in quick succession, and this was accomplished with little effort. After receiving payment for these units, we built additional Burger Kings with the intention of franchising these restaurants and growing the business as fast as we possibly could. The watershed year for our switch from being a restaurant operating company to an organization fully committed to the concept of restaurant franchising was 1957. It was the right decision at the right time, and I must say that it felt good to be doing a few smart things for a change. Our spirits and outlook were decidedly brighter.

Cramer and Burns had sold franchises in Fort Lauderdale, Hollywood, and West Palm Beach. These operators were still bearing a heavy load of operating and profit problems. They wanted to sell out and recover part of the investment they had made, so they came to us seeking assistance. These people were tired of the business because they had been losing money ever since they opened. We agreed to take over their territories, remodel and upgrade their stores, and try to find other franchisees to buy them out. Cramer and Burns were pleased to issue a new territorial license authorizing us to build and operate additional restaurants in Palm Beach, Broward, and Monroe counties on the east coast of Florida and several counties on the west coast of Florida. At the time we were actively engaged in building very successful businesses in Dade County. This new agreement gave us the exclusive rights to develop Burger King restaurants in the entire South Florida area.

This was a distinct advantage to Cramer and Burns because we were making them look good. Our growth and forward momentum was impressive and our Jacksonville colleagues paid close attention to everything we were doing. It was now clear to everyone concerned that all the crisp, new, and innovative ideas were coming from Miami. It was also clear that Cramer and Burns were falling far behind in living up to their responsibility to provide the right kind of leadership to the system.

Our Jacksonville colleagues paid particular attention to the fact that Harvey Fruehauf had put capital into our company, and they spoke to us about that on many occasions. They were also impressed with how much our restaurant sales had increased since we introduced the Whopper. They were even more impressed with our steadily increased rate of expansion. They decided to follow our lead, and they entered into a partnership agreement with Ben Stein, a highly respected local businessman in the Jacksonville area. Mr. Stein agreed to make a 50 percent equity investment in their company, Burger King of Florida, Inc. In addition to his equity investment, Mr. Stein loaned the company a substantial sum of money to help with the expansion of the business.

Following this infusion of capital Cramer and Burns built

six or seven additional Burger King restaurants in the Jacksonville area. Unfortunately, they selected a number of poor locations, which resulted in disappointingly low sales. This was further complicated by the fact that these new restaurants were very poorly managed. They had failed to build an organization of well-trained employees, managers, and supervisors. These new stores did not deliver good food or good service to the public. They had no idea about how to provide that. Before long the company found itself in an extremely precarious financial position.

Cramer, Burns, and Burger King of Florida found themselves in the uncomfortable position of being unable to make payments on Mr. Stein's loans, which forced Mr. Stein to take over the company in an attempt to salvage his investment. At this point Cramer and Burns were forced to exit the business. This change in leadership required that in the future Dave and I would deal directly with Mr. Stein and the rather flimsy organization that had been left in place.

As it turned out, we discovered that it was a pleasure to do business with Ben Stein. He was a very astute businessman, and I always found him to be fair-minded and straightforward with us. Ben's problem was that he had taken over a restaurant business that he knew very little about. Our operations in South Florida were obviously the largest, most promising, and progressive of the Burger King restaurants then in existence. There were a handful of stores in the Tampa and Orlando areas, but these restaurants were very poorly run and still very unprofitable.

There were only a handful of franchisees in other parts of Florida, and Burger King had yet to expand outside the state. Mr. Stein had a serious problem on his hands. His Burger King business was pretty much dead in the water. With a dim outlook for future growth and too many unprofitable restaurants to contend with, he had a lot of problems. Establishing the appropriate operating standards for the restaurants in the Burger King system should have been the responsibility of the parent Jacksonville company, but these standards and practices had never been written. Burger King franchisees were left to do pretty much as they pleased. The result was that the whole system was in a terrible state of disorganization and confusion.

Dave and I were aware that franchisees other than those we had established had been left to their own devices. They simply didn't know how to operate these restaurants efficiently and well. Most of them were bordering on failure. Ben Stein knew that he had taken over a company which lacked the ability or knowledge to adequately administer and develop the Burger King system. We met occasionally to talk about the future of Burger King, and these meetings invariably led to discussions about our taking over the national franchise development idea. With our hands quite full back home in South Florida, we had very little time to sit down with Mr. Stein and seriously pursue any concrete proposals in this regard.

On a bit of a sour note the Jacksonville-based Burger King of Florida, Inc., appropriated our name "Whopper" and "Home of the Whopper" by registering these trade names in Washington. We were not aware that they had done this. I think that had we known, we probably would have objected, although I doubt that we would have contested the matter inasmuch as we had no current intentions of moving out of our territory in South Florida. Our interest was focused on improving the entire Burger King system, which we felt would ultimately serve to help us at least for the time being. We concentrated almost exclusively on building our own business in South Florida.

We felt that if the Whopper and all of our other good ideas about operations, building design, and equipment procurement were of help to us, they would benefit the system as a whole. The problem was that franchisees who were outside our sphere of influence simply didn't know how to execute our ideas.

By 1959 we were growing rapidly, and our new, modern, and successful restaurants began to appear everywhere in South Florida. Our growing presence became increasingly noticeable to local residents and also to the many visitors who were traveling in the Miami area. This brought inquiries about the availability of franchises in other parts of the country. We were pleased to talk with these people and show them our restaurant operation in South Florida, but when they asked about franchising opportunities, we could only refer them to Mr. Stein.

Many of these prospects went to Jacksonville to tour those facilities and discuss their interest in franchising, but it was quite apparent to them that the Jacksonville stores were poorly operated and not nearly as sharp and attractive as the stores they had just seen in South Florida. Mr. Stein's problem was that neither he nor members of his organization could talk intelligently to these prospects about putting them in the Burger King business.

The poor image of the Jacksonville restaurants discouraged the prospects we referred to the Stein organization. They never sold a single franchise to the people we sent to them. In most cases, after looking at the Jacksonville operations, these prospects just kept on going. I'm sure they felt that having the Jacksonville people responsible for their future success was a risk they were unwilling to take.

Ben grew increasingly frustrated with his inability to convert the interest we were generating into the sale of franchises. Occasionally, after meeting a number of interested prospects, he called me to suggest that Dave and I should take charge of the franchising end of the business. He understood that we were the only ones with the restaurant experience and expertise to do this. He saw and envied how rapidly and successfully we were growing our business in South Florida.

During the period between 1958 and 1960, Ben and I had many talks about our taking over the national development of Burger King, but we could never agree on a plan of mutual interest. It wasn't an urgent matter of concern to us at the time because we had so much to accomplish where we were. We had a tiger by the tail in South Florida, and we had plenty of territory left to expand in. Our existing franchisees were doing well, and we had a heavy demand for additional franchises. What was most significant at the time was the fact that our company had finally turned the profit corner. After living through some scary times, we were not particularly anxious to take on any new risks.

Something of considerable significance took place in late 1959, although at the time we had no idea of its future impact on our growing business. The event was the inauguration of the first commercial jet passenger service in the United States. These Boeing 707 jets were owned and put into service by Pan American World Airways. At the time Pan American was an international carrier without authority to fly domestic routes in the United States. Seeking the maximum utilization of their new Boeing 707s, they entered into an exchange agreement with Miami-based National Airlines to fly the Pan Am jets from Idlewild Airport (now John F. Kennedy Airport) in New York to Miami, with a return flight to New York.

We didn't think much about it at the time, but this early domestic jet airline service was destined to have significant impact on the development of Burger King all across the country. This historic event opened an era of convenient non-stop jet service between Miami and major cities everywhere. Within a few years it was possible for Miami-based business-men to fly quickly, comfortably, and conveniently to cities all over the country. This opened the possibility of expanding our Burger King business into other parts of the country. It had been virtually impossible to base a national organization in Miami because the old piston-driven aircraft was too slow and inconvenient to make air travel feasible. In 1959 Miami was still considered a destination resort, catering largely to tourist traffic. The Jet Age allowed the Miami business community to envision the development of business opportunities of consid-erable significance. We were destined to become part of that new vision.

As the Miami airport grew and jet service expanded, Dave and I took much more interest in Ben Stein's suggestion that we take over the development of Burger King on a national basis. One of the major logistical blocks to our expansion was rapidly being removed. Soon we would be able to travel quick-ly and easily to the major markets in the United States and perhaps later on to many cities around the world. I had plans

to eventually negotiate and hammer out a contractual arrangement with Ben Stein, but I felt that there would be time to do
that. For the moment with the 1950s ending we began to con-
template what the 1960s held in store for us. Our major prior-
ity was to build a large chain of Burger King restaurants
around our home base in South Florida. Both Dave and I
knew that we needed a solid base of profitable operations at
home before we could consider the prospects of jumping into
unfamiliar markets outside the state of Florida. If we ultimately decided to take this kind of risk, we were going to give the
matter very careful consideration before plunging ahead.

We're on the Air

During the first few months of 1958 we began to sell franchises in South Florida, and this enabled us to start some small-scale advertising. Television was out of the question. It was still much too expensive, but we did decide to start an advertising program using radio. Dave and I asked our franchisees to take an interest in the process, and we all met with our advertising agency, Hume, Smith and Mickleberry, which had come up with a jingle that soon became quite well known in the Miami area. The jingle boasted, "There's a Burger King close to you, 60-second service, too. Best burger buy for miles around, broiled not fried. How does that sound? Burger King, Burger King, Burger King!" This jingle was sung to a catchy tune and became quite popular with the kids. This early strategy began the positioning of Burger King as a good place to go for hamburgers and french fries.

By late 1958 we had reached a size sufficient to launch our first television advertising campaign. Our strategy there was to keep taking the Burger King story directly to the kids. We had long witnessed the remarkable success of the Miami-based Royal Castle system, which was then operating several hundred restaurants in the Southeast, with many of them located in South Florida. Started by William D. Singer in Miami in 1938, Royal Castle was headquartered in Miami and had stores located as far away as Louisiana. They grew rapidly and became the largest restaurant chain in the southeastern part of the United States. This made them formidable competitors in the Miami area.

Royal Castle was one of the early clones of the White Castle system which started in Wichita, Kansas, in 1921. White Tower, Krystal Castle, and Toddle House were other examples of clones of this notable concept. These operations were generally quite successful around the country, and the concept grew impressively during the thirties, forties, and into the fifties. Their featured item was a small 18-to-the-pound hamburger, steam grilled, and served on a small soft bun with cooked onions. At Royal Castle "birch beer" was served in a frosted mug. These small counter-service restaurants seated 10 customers and were open 24 hours a day. They were located on key intersections throughout all of Dade and Broward counties. Their menu also included freshly squeezed orange juice and all kinds of short orders which made them popular for breakfast and late-night snacks. They were busy throughout the day and night. The company was extremely successful. If they had any problem at all, it was all wrapped up in a changing American scene, where consumers who were eating out more often were demanding a much different style of restaurant service. The question before the Royal Castle organization would be, Could they provide it?

When Burger King opened for business in 1954, Royal Castle was the dominant restaurant presence in our market. They had good, effective marketing people and much of their advertising was aimed directly at small children. During the 1950s Royal Castle was the key sponsor of the most popular children's television show in Miami, *Skipper Chuck's Popeye Playhouse*. The show was hosted by "Skipper Chuck" Zink, a very popular and talented television personality. The program aired at 5 p.m. weekdays on Channel 4, which was the CBS affiliate and Miami's first television station. Children made up a live audience. The show was so popular that parents had to make reservations over a year in advance to enable their children to attend as part of the audience. Royal Castle virtually owned the kids' market, and as much as we wanted to get a piece of it, we were pretty well blocked. We knew that it wouldn't be easy to reach the children on television and besides we had less than $1000 a month to spend! This wasn't nearly enough to get on television, let alone sponsor a show like *Popeye Playhouse*.

In 1958 we agreed to sponsor a competing children's show, called *The Jim Dooley Show*. Mr. Dooley also had a live audience of children. His show featured a chimpanzee named Mr. Moke, whose antics always delighted the viewers. We met with Mr. Dooley, liked him and agreed to become a sponsor. The only condition I laid down was that we would be permitted to deliver a bag full of freshly made Whoppers during every live broadcast. That was OK with Jim, so at a certain hour every weekday our delivery man would carry a paper bag full of Whoppers into the studio. A freshly made Whopper has a wonderful aroma. It smells as good as it tastes! Mr. Moke obviously agreed because as soon as the studio door opened and the bag of Whoppers arrived, Mr. Moke smelled them and would go slightly berserk in anticipation of his meal. His custom was to grab the bag, tear it open and devour the big hamburgers as fast as he could. The children were always delighted at the spectacle and so was Jim. I'm sure the home audience enjoyed it just as the studio audience did.

I think this daily event with the Whoppers was the high point of the show in many ways. It certainly was for all of us at headquarters. We received at least three minutes of advertising for every minute we paid for. Thanks to Jim Dooley and Channel 10, the name Burger King began to gain a bit of local recognition and start to mean something in South Florida. I had no way of knowing, but this might have put some pressure on Royal Castle. I thought Burger King products were better, our places were cleaner, and our employees were better trained and more courteous than our competition, but in the late 1950s Royal Castle was the premier restaurant chain in our market. Throughout our formative years they were very worthy and formidable competitors.

Late in 1959 I received a call from Mr. Singer and an invitation to join him for lunch at the new Royal Castle offices which adjoined their newly built bakery and commissary. Their impressive building was located very close to our newest Burger King restaurant 10 in Hialeah. I was honored to receive his invitation and gladly accepted. Mr. Singer had earned a well-deserved reputation as being one of Miami's leading and most respected citizens. He was an astute businessman who had distinguished himself in many ways. During lunch he told me the story of how he had built the Royal Castle system and how it had become such a remarkably successful chain of restaurants.

We exchanged views on the changes that were taking place in the food-service industry and had a very open and cordial discussion on a number of related issues. I told him what Dave and I were trying to accomplish with Burger King and of our aspirations for future growth. It was a very candid, open, and friendly discussion. Later in our conversation he asked me if Dave and I would consider selling our company. I thought that this might have been the reason for his invitation to join him for lunch, but I really didn't need to give the matter very much thought. I told him that we were not interested as politely as I could and explained that we had plans to grow rapidly, preferably as an independent company.

Apparently Mr. Singer believed that Burger King was a sound restaurant concept with a great deal of future potential. I thought at the time that Mr. Singer might have felt that Royal Castle had already reached the peak of its popularity and public acceptance. This was pure speculation on my part. I had no way of knowing what was really on his mind. I was of the opinion, however, that the Royal Castle concept which had worked so well in years gone by, might now be having difficulty competing in our rapidly changing food-service market.

A few years after our luncheon visit, Royal Castle had their initial public offering of common stock at which time Mr. Singer sold his entire financial investment in the company. Following the public offering, the company floundered a bit and began to go steadily downhill with the result that by the early 1970s it had virtually ceased to exist. Such a story is a strong reminder that conditions and markets change and that businesses must change in order to keep up with the times. It is not a happy thought that Royal Castle no longer exists, but I always regarded the demise of this once-proud, robust, and vital organization as a stern warning to businesspeople every-where to stay alert and responsive to the demands of con-sumers or suffer the indignity and embarrassment of going out of business.

Royal Castle's departure from the scene serves as a stark reminder that a similar fate awaits any company failing to respond to change. This is the constant challenge. In 1954 Burger King began its existence on the cutting edge of change. The current marketplace reminds all of us that there are plen-ty of challengers out there who are ready and willing to take on even the biggest and strongest of the lot.

After my visit with Mr. Singer, Royal Castle decided to drop its long-standing sponsorship of *Skipper Chuck's Popeye Playhouse*. Our advertising agency, Hume, Smith and Mickleberry, called me as soon as the word of this shocking news went out. This was a situation that represented a big opportunity for Burger King. Up until this point, Royal Castle had enjoyed a virtual lock on the children's market. They had built a strong allegiance among children and families because of the strength of Chuck Zink's popularity and his endorse-ment and recommendation of their products and services. Dave and I agreed that sponsoring this program was a once-in-a-lifetime opportunity to divert that loyalty to Burger King.

Our problem centered on the high cost of sponsoring this program. It would cost us much more than any advertising we had ever considered before. Nevertheless, the opportunity was simply too good to pass up. We told the agency to buy it while they were still on the telephone telling us what had happened. We would buy the show and figure out later how we were going to pay for it. That decision turned out to be one of the important decisions we made during our early years in busi-ness. Our goal was to try to position Burger King as number 1 in the kids' market for hamburgers in South Florida. Being the favorite children's restaurant was an enviable position to be in. McDonald's found this out many years later when they direct-ed their own advertising toward the kids' market with their famous clown, Ronald McDonald. This brilliant strategy helped launch their company to impressive new heights of customer acceptance. Kids' approval proved to be an important factor in developing the right kind of marketing strategies in the growing food-service marketplace. We were to find out about that when we entered the 1960s.

I always had great respect for Chuck Zink and his integrity. Before he would permit Channel 4 to accept Burger King as a new sponsor of his show, he insisted on having a meeting with Dave and me. He visited our restaurants and talked to a few of our managers in order to satisfy himself that the representations he planned to make on our behalf would be fair to his audience. I liked that kind of an ethical approach to advertising, and I convinced Chuck that we would regard ourselves as holders of that trust. I assured him that we would live up to our responsibility.

We sponsored the Skipper Chuck show until it went off the air 15 or more years later. When the show was terminated, I wrote a letter to Mitchell Wolfson the founder-chairman of Wometco Enterprises and owner of WTVJ, Channel 4, just to let him know how grateful we were for our enduring relationship with Chuck and his program over our many years of sponsorship. Mr. Wolfson shared my letter with Chuck, who told me many years later that this letter meant a great deal to him. I feel sure that he had been greatly disappointed by WTVJ's decision to cancel his show, which for so many years had been an institution in South Florida. Chuck Zink will always be a highly respected television personality. Integrity can take a man a long way in life, and it certainly did this for Chuck Zink. This important marketing experience and our experiment with children's television advertising served us well during the early years of our national expansion. It also taught us the value of supporting quality programming when directing the Burger King message to young kids.

The Race Begins

Our television advertising had a significant impact on public awareness in South Florida. With a steady growth in sales and profitability, we began to receive a sizable number of requests for franchises. These inquiries encouraged us to think more about the possibility of introducing Burger King into other parts of the country. Dave and I saw a great opportunity in all this, and we were confident of our ability to exploit it. We remained painfully aware that this was Ben Stein's challenge and opportunity, not ours. As had always been our practice in the past, we continued to refer prospective franchisees to Jacksonville even though nothing ever came of their visits there.

Ben called me in 1959 in an obvious state of frustration and said, "Jim, you know that we can't establish these people in the Burger King business. You are sending lots of people who are interested in the franchise program, but we don't know how to go about putting these people in business. Besides we don't have an organization capable of handling it even if we did have the necessary background and experience. Why don't you and Dave take it over and work with me on some basis that we can both live with." I asked him what kind of an arrangement he had in mind. His thoughts were that we could sell franchises to interested prospects, establish them in business, charge them a royalty and just share the royalty with him. When I asked him to be specific regarding the sharing of royalty payments, he suggested that they be split exactly in half, 50 percent for each of us. He would give us the entire country to develop in any manner we saw fit. I told him that we couldn't possibly enter into an agreement like that because our 50 percent of the royalties couldn't possibly cover our costs of servicing the system. I asked what he intended to contribute for his 50 percent of the royalties and his answer was simply, "Nothing." This was a ridiculous proposal and I told him so, adding that we didn't have any interest in entering into such a lopsided arrangement. It simply didn't make any business or economic sense at all. I tried to explain to him that without the necessary income to adequately service our franchisees, the system would be doomed to failure right from the beginning. I don't think he agreed with that or even bothered to understand it, but after making the point we simply dropped the idea.

Dave and I kept sending prospects to Jacksonville, and all of them turned away discouraged and disinterested after taking a good look at the poorly managed Jacksonville operations. They realized that the Stein organization was incapable of putting them successfully in business. They were quick to see that once established in business, they couldn't expect to be serviced. As Ben's frustration level grew he continued to call me in an attempt to work out a deal for us to take over the national development of Burger King. The problem was that he wouldn't back off from his position that he would receive 50 percent of the royalties. I persisted in refusing to consider such an unbalanced arrangement, but as the months passed with no progress in sight I received a call from him in early 1961. "Jim, I am coming to Miami tomorrow. Would you have lunch with me at the Fontainebleau Hotel? I would like to resolve this matter of your developing Burger King nationally. You and Dave are the only ones who have the organization and know-how to expand this business. I have some new thoughts on the matter, so we should have a lot to talk about." The meeting sounded like a good idea to me because by this time we were as anxious to take over the situation as he was to have us do so. All we needed was to come up with a mutually fair arrangement. We met the following day in Miami.

Even before we were seated, Ben got right to the point. "All right Jim, we've been unable to reach an understanding about this for years. What do you suggest that we do to get the national development of Burger King off the ground?" I'd given a lot of thought to that, and I had a quick response. "Ben, turn over all your rights, title, and interest in the use of the names Burger King, Whopper, and Home of the Whopper, together with your total interest in the trademarks and service marks. With that in hand, Dave and I will commit to make our best effort to develop Burger King restaurants all over the country and worldwide. I won't guarantee you a specific performance of any kind because I don't know how successful we will be, but with regard to the royalties, I'll send you 15 percent of anything we collect every month. I can't afford to do any more than that." With that he just leaned back in his chair and said, "You've got yourself a deal. You draw up the agreement and I'll sign it so that you boys can get on with it."

I don't know how I came up with the 15 percent figure. I knew that Ben couldn't contribute anything to the arrangement, and I wasn't about to agree to pay him a big sum to do nothing at all. This development was exciting. I thanked Ben for lunch and told him how pleased I was to arrive at such an understanding. The contract would be just a formality. I was sure of that. We had a deal and so far as I was concerned, we were now the parent company of Burger King. Just knowing that we were finally in the position of directing the national and international growth and expansion of a business we had worked so hard to develop was as stimulating as anything I had ever done up to this point. Confident about what lay ahead, I headed back to the office to tell Dave the good news.

Both of us had felt that someday and on some basis Ben Stein would have to turn to us to lead Burger King out of Florida and establish the brand as a national restaurant chain. He really had no other choice. It was shameful that in the past we had had to turn down interested prospects who wanted Burger King franchises in other parts of the country. With our franchising program running so successfully in South Florida, we had an organization in place that could easily start the same activity in other areas. Ben could see that, and it was a smart decision on his part to let us take charge of the situation.

I was quite excited in breaking the news to Dave, who was back at the office and anxiously waiting to hear from me. "Well, Dave, we've got it. Ben has agreed to accept our proposal!" I could see how pleased he was in the realization that finally we had the big opportunity we had waited and hoped for. "The first thing I've got to do is call Tom Wakefield [our attorney] and get him going on that agreement. We need to get this thing done as fast as we can." Dave agreed, and I could see he was already deep in thought on how we should go about organizing the big push.

I called Tom right away, and after explaining the deal we had just agreed to, I asked him to prepare a contract and get it back to me as soon as possible.

After I reviewed the contracts, I forwarded the agreement to Ben who signed it and returned an executed copy for our files. The agreement gave us the rights and authority to develop Burger King throughout the world, except for parts of Northern and Central Florida. At the time there were a few franchised units operating in Tampa and Orlando plus a handful in other parts of the state, including Stein's own stores in the Duval County (Jacksonville) market. A few years later we took over all of Florida, except for this Duval County territory. Ben's youngest son, David, became involved in the business at about that time, and it was a good thing that he did because the Jacksonville restaurants had been very poorly managed in the past. An improvement was of vital importance, and David proved to be a very effective manager. He drew heavily upon our advice concerning operations and marketing with the result that the Jacksonville business began to improve significantly. Within a few years David had these restaurants operating profitably, and in terms of cleanliness and quality of operations, they were a credit to the system. We were proud to welcome young David as an important addition to the team.

We now had total control over the future destiny of Burger King, and we faced the challenge of building a strong national organization with confidence and enthusiasm. After struggling for seven years to create a successful formula, we felt secure in the knowledge that the system we had developed was a good one that could easily succeed in the domestic market. Dave Edgerton and I had made plenty of mistakes and done a lot of impulsive and unwise things in the past, usually because we didn't stop long enough to think things through carefully enough. As Harvey Fruehauf often cautioned us, "Act in haste and repent at leisure." From this time forward we would be careful to exercise good judgment in planning our forward progress. We had been through a lot together and almost suffered the indignity of going broke on several different occasions. Now with size, experience, a workable system, and a stronger balance sheet, we were positioned to grow. With a successful track record already established and with a significant demand for our franchises, we felt we had the world on a string. We couldn't wait to pull on that string and get moving!

When we signed our contract with Ben Stein early in 1961, we had very little available capital to invest in expanding the business. We lacked the means to purchase the trademarks. Our only option was to enter into a contractual "best efforts" agreement which would give us the use of these rights on an exclusive basis. The consideration was paying a fee for the privilege. This was the best we could come up with at the time, but it was a convenient and practical way to begin to build a multiunit restaurant chain. This was exactly what Dave and I had in mind before the first store opened. With a national target in sight, we were anxious to begin. It all looked promising. We had a successful program firmly established in South Florida, we had momentum, the Whopper, franchisee prospects standing in line, a refined operational formula, and great confidence in our own ability. We had it all. We were ready to launch.

I knew that someday we would have to buy out Mr. Stein's contract. A few months later I asked him what he would sell it for. He told me $100,000. This was a lot of money! Our competition was up against the same problem. Ray Kroc no doubt knew that he couldn't live forever with the agreement he had signed with the McDonald brothers, but it was probably the best he could do at the time. We both had the same problem, but as I look back, he came up with the better solution.

In 1954, enamored by the prospects of expanding the McDonald's concept, Ray Kroc entered into an agreement with the McDonald brothers to be the exclusive distributor of franchises. This gave him the right to use the McDonald's name and their system of food service. He was given the right to expand the business, but was obligated to adhere to the McDonald's operational standards and obtain the McDonald brothers' approval before making any changes to the operational system. The contract specified that franchisees would pay a royalty of 1.9 percent of sales, and it placed a $950 limit on the amount that could be charged for a franchise. Out of the systemwide sales royalty, 0.5 percent was payable to the McDonald brothers monthly. The remaining royalty of 1.4 percent of sales could be used to service the system and hopefully make a profit. This was a bad deal both financially and operationally. The McDonald brothers were to receive almost 30 percent of the royalties that Mr. Kroc was entitled to charge, but what was left could hardly be expected to cover the expenses of adequately and properly servicing the business. The $950 limitation on the charge for individual franchises would be an outright gift to the franchisees, but it would be an absolute disaster for Mr. Kroc, who would find himself in the unenviable position of expanding his business only to experience a loss on each sale of a franchise.

By 1961, numerous conflicts between the parties made a buyout of the McDonald brothers mandatory. The brothers demanded $2.7 million to step out of the picture. This was a huge sum at the time. Kroc's new McDonald's Corporation earned only $77,330 in 1960, and the net worth of the company was only slightly in excess of $250,000.

By 1961 Harry Sonneborn was president of McDonald's and owned 20 percent of the company. Sonneborn had proved to be very capable in developing real estate. He joined Kroc in 1955 at the age of 39. Previously he served as a financial vice president of Tastee Freeze, which was a fairly sizable chain of soft ice cream shops. He knew the franchising business, and he conceived a real estate financing idea that would play a significant role in contributing to the extraordinary growth and success of the company.

In 1956 Sonneborn formed a subsidiary company called, Franchise Realty Corporation. Its only purpose was to either buy land and construct restaurant buildings or to lease land and restaurant buildings built by investors. Sonneborn's plan required franchisees to put up a security deposit on each lease, usually in the amount of a year's rental in advance. These funds were used in various but important ways. If McDonald's bought a vacant property, the security deposit was used to make a down payment on the purchase of the land. The owner was offered top dollar for his property, but in order to get this high price, he had to agree that the remaining balance due to him could be paid over a period of 10 years. In addition, the owner was required to subordinate his purchase-money mortgage so that a superior mortgage could be placed on the property. This enabled McDonald's to borrow the money needed to construct the building. The franchisee's future rental payments were calculated to cover the monthly payments of principal and interest.

In the event the land and building was built-to-suit by the property owner or developer, it was leased directly to McDonald's and then subleased to a franchisee. The terms of the franchisee's sublease assured McDonald's of a handsome markup on each leasing transaction. Rental charges to franchisees were often based on markups running as high as 40 percent above cost. On top of that the franchisee was required to pay the higher of his marked-up rental or a set percentage of his sales (usually 8.5 percent), whichever was greater. The franchisee-leasee paid all taxes, insurance, and maintenance on the property so that the lease was always "net-net" to McDonald's.

These creative financing schemes were the basis upon which McDonald's became the largest retail property owner in the world. Their highest percentage of corporate earnings comes from real estate operations. It was clear from the beginning that this ingenious real estate development formula was earmarked for success. Sonneborn, in addressing the New York Society of Security Analysts shortly after going public in 1965, made the statement that his company was "first and foremost in the real estate business." One investment banker later referred to his ingenious financing concept as "McDonald's exquisite use of debt." What was not mentioned was that the key to this success was based on the success of the individual restaurants. Were that not the case, the scheme would have fallen flat as many less capable imitators would soon find out. This was a high-leveraged game with only a thin margin for mistakes.

Sonneborn's Franchise Realty Corporation was a wholly owned subsidiary of McDonald's, and by the early 1960s it was bearing a crushing burden of debt as the result of engaging in all of this real estate financing. If it ever developed that a certain number of franchisees were unable to pay their rent, the scheme might easily have backfired. By 1961 the consolidated financial condition of McDonald's painted a grim picture of a company precariously overleveraged with leasing debt. It would be next to impossible for them to obtain additional financing on conventional terms.

Sonneborn's challenge in 1961 was to obtain the financing needed to buy out the McDonald brothers. The licensing agreement they had signed with the McDonald brothers created a burdensome, if not impossible, situation for the company to contend with. They simply had to buy out the contract. With the help of John Bristol, a money manager and financial consultant to a number of clients, including major colleges and universities, a $2.7 million loan was worked out. Among Bristol's clients at that time was Princeton University which took $1 million of the financing. Some 15 years later I worked with Bristol in my capacity as Chairman of the University of Miami's Investments Committee. We retained Mr. Bristol to manage a portion of our endowment funds. I found him to be a shrewd and capable money manager and investor. He had certainly proved the point in his dealings with Kroc and Sonneborn.

The Sonneborn-Bristol loan package was a high-risk proposition, but it came at a time when it was imperative for McDonald's to get the $2.7 million loan even on the most onerous of terms. It was also a risk for investors and Bristol insisted that the reward to the lenders had to match that risk. The loan agreement called for a 6 percent interest charge, and the schedule of repayment of principal and interest was set at 0.5 percent of systemwide sales. This schedule was exactly equal to the payments called for in the contract Kroc had signed with the McDonald brothers. The royalties that were collected in the future would determine how fast the loan could be paid off. This was simple enough, but there was an added provision that specified that when the loan was finally paid off, a bonus to the lenders would come into play. The bonus would be equal to 0.5 percent of systemwide sales for the exact period of time it took to pay off the original loan. Thus, if it took eight years to pay off the original loan, McDonald's had to agree to pay a bonus of 0.5 percent of the future systemwide sales to the lenders during the ensuing eight-year period of time. It was an ingenious arrangement that was very rewarding to the lenders and critically needed by the borrowers. As it turned out, it was extremely costly to Kroc to relieve his company of a stifling, if not impossible, contract with the founding McDonald brothers.

This $2.7 million buyout of the McDonald's name was in many ways similar to our buyout of the Burger King name several years later. In 1967 we paid $2,550,000 to Ben Stein in order to purchase the Burger King trademarks and the national franchising rights. We had been licensing these in an agreement we had signed in 1961. Stein owned the Burger King trademarks, and we had to have them in order to conclude the Pillsbury merger. It was simple, we had to pay his price, whatever it was. Kroc, no doubt, must have felt the same way in 1961 as we did in 1967. He had to own the McDonald's name outright in order to relieve himself of an onerous operating and financial obligation. This was our situation when we came up against a problem which was remarkably similar. Whatever the cost, it was necessary to pay it, if we were to relieve ourselves of a multiplicity of problems.

By 1961 Kroc was having great success in expanding his business, even though corporate profits were still very low and the net worth of the company was relatively insignificant.

McDonald's franchisees were very successful, and their enthusiasm and prosperity stimulated considerable additional interest in the McDonald's program. The following figures show the comparative financial performances of Burger King and McDonald's from 1960 to 1967. These were important start-up years for both companies. It is evident from the numbers that Burger King was making impressive percentage gains, but McDonald's had begun to pull out in front as far as profits were concerned. We were focused on the number of successful units we were opening and as far as I was concerned, we were tracking our competitor quite well. As small as these numbers might appear, they did reflect the status of the industry at the time. These were the birthing years of the fast-food business and we were at or near the head of the pack.

| | PROFIT AFTER TAX | | STORES OPENED DURING YEAR | |
YEAR	McDONALD'S	BURGER KING	McDONALD'S	BURGER KING
1960	$77,330	$28,386	N/A	7
1961	16,103	47,083	81	8
1962	439,315	73,058	107	7
1963	1,048,611	151,807	111	13
1964	2,017,178	225,112	116	30
1965	3,402,136	446,239	95	49
1966	4,511,734	758,008	124	64
1967	N/A	972,317	105	72

Kroc and Sonneborn were in constant need of funds to expand their business. The year before they borrowed $2.7 million to buy out the McDonald brothers, they borrowed $1.5 million on terms which today seem almost scandalous. They negotiated a $1.5 million loan with State Mutual Life and Paul Revere Life at 7 percent interest. Each of these life insurance companies loaned half of the $1.5 million or $750,000 and *each lender* received as a "kicker" (or bonus) 10 percent of McDonald's common stock. *This was 20 percent of the entire equity of the company!* The finder's fee cost an additional 2.5 percent of McDonald's stock. This 22.5 percent dilution of the founding stockholders' hard-earned equity must have been a hard pill to swallow. In 1996 a 22.5 percent interest in McDonald's had a market value in excess of $8 billion! In 1960 Kroc, in desperate need of additional capital, had to pay a bonus that by any modern-day standard seems unconscionable. The story only serves to amplify how investors viewed the risky nature of the failure-prone restaurant and fast-food business at the time. What Burger King and McDonald's were doing in 1960 was pioneering a new, relatively untried and untested concept in food service which was viewed as a terribly risky business by banks and lenders. We were able to attract a certain amount of financial assistance in those years, but it was understood that it would be extremely costly. If we wanted the financing, we would have to pay dearly for it. Kroc and his young McDonald's Corporation certainly proved the point when they agreed to pay such a high price to get a mere $1.5 million loan in 1960.

I tell the McDonald's story out of the great respect and admiration I have always had for Ray Kroc, including his vision, his struggles, and his uncompromisingly high standards for restaurant operations. He opened his first McDonald's restaurant in Des Plaines, Illinois, on April 15, 1955, which was 13 months after our first Burger King restaurant opened in Miami. In May of 1959, during a trip to Chicago, I called Ray and asked if I might stop in to introduce myself. His offices were in the downtown area of Chicago at the time. Our visit was brief but very cordial. At the time I had no intention of operating Burger King restaurants anywhere other than in South Florida. With our parent, Jacksonville-based Burger King of Florida in such shambles, I couldn't imagine that we would later be in charge of its national development. It was a fact that Dave Edgerton and I were doing exactly what Kroc and Sonneborn were doing. Both companies were pioneering a relatively unknown and untried business concept. Having met the man so early in our business careers and witnessed the extraordinary growth of his company since we had first met, I was pleased on May 18, 1975, to act as Master of Ceremonies at an impressive dinner at the Palmer House which honored Ray as the NRA Restaurateur of the Year. When he reached the podium to receive his award, he stated that we had known each other for the past 16 years and during that time he held me in great respect adding, "After all, I named my big sandwich after Jim by calling it the 'Big Mac.'" That thoughtful and humorous remark brought the house down. I was proud to show visitors to my office a picture taken of the two of us on that special occasion. One of the great things about the American free-enterprise system is that two people can be vigorous competitors in the marketplace and still enjoy a cordiality that grows out of a respect and appreciation for each others achievements in that marketplace.

Putting Franchising in Gear

The table in the previous chapter comparing the growth and profitability of McDonald's and Burger King during the early 1960s shows that the two companies were running pretty close to each other in terms of their respective rates of expansion.

During the 1950s and early 1960s it was necessary for Burger King to stimulate demand for its franchises because the company was so relatively unknown at the time. One way was to run newspaper advertisements and another way was to grant territorial agreements which gave certain exclusive rights to franchisees to develop Burger King restaurants within specified geographical areas. This was an attractive incentive at the time, but today we no longer have to do this. The only protected geographical areas offered to new franchisees is a street address or a description of an individual location. In the United States exclusive market areas are no longer reserved for development. In the beginning very few prospective franchisees were willing to commit their energy and resources to the business unless they had assurances of an opportunity to grow and expand. They were in a position to demand that kind of commitment because there was only a minimal demand for the franchises we were interested in selling. Burger King needed to expand the business more than the prospective franchisees needed to buy the franchises. It was a simple case of supply and demand.

Dave and I were more than willing to issue territorial agreements in those days. We felt that this was the best way to position the company as a large, growing, and profitable organization which had the capacity to compete and grow on a national basis. We felt it was important to expand the system rapidly in order to establish Burger King as a leader in our field. We picked the best franchisee prospects we could find, and if they were willing to commit to us, we were willing to grant them territorial rights to develop and open a specific number of Burger King restaurants according to a set timetable we both agreed on. The franchisees agreed to forfeit their territorial rights if they failed to meet the opening schedule. This acted as an incentive for them to meet our growth objectives. This in turn contributed to our becoming a leader in the world of restaurant franchising.

We felt this incentive would encourage franchisees to build more Burger King restaurants in different parts of the country, which is exactly what happened. During the 1960s when expansion of this kind was almost unheard of, we were setting growth records which were hard to believe. Without the early motivation, involvement, and determination of our franchisees, it would have been much more difficult, if not impossible, to have built such a strong company in such a short period of time. We did it because our franchisees helped us do it. It was our early 1960s ability to establish ourselves as a key player in the infant restaurant franchising business that gave us the momentum which was so important. With it, we gained the reputation of being one of the best and most dynamic franchising organizations in the country.

Territorial franchising and the rapid expansion which followed required that Dave and I spend a good part of our time traveling around the country. Our intention to become a leading national franchisor was an extremely ambitious goal at the time, and we were limited by the fact that we still had a very small staff. We concentrated on building a capable management team now that we had set our sights on such an aggressive undertaking.

Our challenge was to put together an organization qualified to develop real estate, sell franchises, and train personnel.

With such an organization in place we were able to equip and open new restaurants very quickly. Our development plans represented a very complex undertaking requiring the attention of a talented group of key managers.

As we initiated our national development strategy, H. Glenn Jones joined us as chief financial officer, J. Thomas Brown became our general counsel, and Bill Koenig was appointed as treasurer. In quick succession "Bud" Granger took charge of franchise sales, Dave Talty headed restaurant operations, Bill Bradford took over our real estate operations, and S.M. "Pete" Piotrowski was put in charge of construction projects, commissary operations, transportation, and manufacturing. "Bud" Wilson came in as head of personnel and training. Glenn Conger was put in charge of procurement, and Bill Sellers assumed responsibility as head of restaurant installations and later headed Davmor Industries, our equipment manufacturing subsidiary. Jack Calhoun joined us as head of marketing operations. William C. Murphy joined us as head of our architectural department.

With the assistance of this growing team of key managers along with our enthusiastic franchisees helping to lead the way, our rate of growth began to climb steadily. By 1965 we were opening Burger King restaurants at an average rate of one a week throughout the year. This was an extraordinary achievement at a time when the food-service industry was hardly aware that chain restaurants even existed. On the heels of our success, we fully expected to see many new restaurant franchising organizations come into being. We weren't long in waiting. We just hoped to be able to stay well out in front of them.

Our first out-of-state store was opened in Wilmington, Delaware. Granting a franchise to four people I had known during my Colonial Inn days during the late 1940s, we learned an important lesson which we never forgot. All four of these men were passive financial investors and as absentee owners, there was nobody willing to assume the responsibility of managing the business. When a manager was finally selected with no equity stake in the business, the result was that the restaurant never did very well. From that time on, we avoided issuing franchises to investors who were not deeply committed to operating the business.

Earl Brown was the franchisee who opened our second Burger King restaurant outside the state of Florida. This one was located in Winston-Salem, North Carolina. The enthusiastic response to this opening gave us a great deal of encouragement about the prospects for succeeding in new and unfamiliar markets. Many future prospects went to Winston-Salem to investigate the profit-making potential of the Burger King business. Earl and his financial partner, Bob Forcum, went on to develop restaurants in the tri-city area of Winston-Salem–Greensboro–High Point. Their extraordinary achievement in these markets was a significant factor in stimulating interest in our franchise program.

Additional interest came from word-of-mouth advertising, with most of it coming from our strong, visible, and growing presence in the Miami area. We also ran small advertisements in a few newspapers. Adolf Deschler, a naturalized American citizen from Germany, was one of our earliest prospects. Adolf lived on Long Island, worked for a dairy, and delivered bottled milk door-to-door. After reading one of our advertisements and calling me, he flew to Miami and liked what he saw. Shortly thereafter we opened our first Burger King restaurant in Atlanta. The year was 1962.

Earlier that year I went to San Juan, Puerto Rico, with Bill Gibson and opened another successful restaurant. Thirty years later we had over 100 restaurants on the island. In 1963 Pete McGuire opened our first Burger King restaurant in Dallas. Alfred D. "Pete" Peterson opened our first restaurant in Minneapolis.

Dave Edgerton helped Jimmy and Billy Trotter open their first Burger King unit in New Orleans. This was the first of many Burger King restaurants opened by these two talented brothers. Murray Evans, a young man with very little money, but a great deal of self-confidence, opened in Mobile and started building a profitable enterprise in portions of Alabama, Mississippi, and the Florida Panhandle. Dave spent considerable time with Harold Jeske, Pat Ryan, Bob Furman, Ed

Pendrys, and others in establishing the Burger King presence in the three different territories which made up the greater Chicago market.

Haywood Fox was so impressed with Earl Brown's extraordinary success in the tri-cities that he built several stores in Charlotte. Fred Wessel, a school teacher from Miami, developed successful franchises in Alabama. Dave Murray did well in New Hampshire, as did Nick Janikies in Rhode Island. Bill Hufnagel and Chuck Mund successfully established Burger King in important markets in the greater New York City area. Earl Martin, Larry Stokes, and Dick Sherwood were early pioneers in South Carolina. Ben Young and Ben Schuler pioneered the Detroit market. The three Henry brothers were important franchisees. Leroy opened in Flint, Michigan, Oscar went to Colorado Springs, and Harry to Las Vegas. Marvin Schuster pioneered our business in the Carolinas and Georgia; Harvey Levine in New Jersey; Bill Russell and Carl Ferris in Philadelphia; Tom Gaddes in Washington, D.C.; Tom Macon in Ashville; Joe Hawken and Willard Petersen in Charleston.

The list goes on and on. I will always remember the fun and excitement of working with so many fine men and women who helped us during the early years of developing our business. Other important names include Dan Treweiler, Vini St. Pierre, Al Trueblood, Norbert Lucas, Denver Hollabaugh, Raleigh Nelson, Joe Tagliente, Henry Hintermeister, Thomas McMillan, Ed Davis, Phil Hertz, Dick Edgerton, Bill Harrington, Manuel Garcia, Chuck Keidel, Dick Sloan, Nelson Fox, Joe Angel, Damon Crabtree, Dick Fors, Ed Poe, Art Lucksinger, and many others.

There were many other fine people among the early franchisees who helped pioneer the early national development of Burger King. They deserve much of the credit for establishing the company as a leader and major participant in the fast-growing field of chain-restaurant operations. People from all walks of life joined under the Burger King banner to build successful businesses. They all worked hard, and with that single purpose in mind we all got along famously. The most satisfying part of the story is that almost without exception, everyone of these people was successful. The Burger King system made a profit for the participants, and that was the important factor. We became a very successful company because we were able to help our franchisees do well. Many of them went on to build sizable personal fortunes. Dave and I viewed their success as our own success. They were a part of our family, and we regarded them as such. Our common goal was to find the basket with the golden eggs, and we succeeded in doing this.

Looking back to the 1950s and 1960s, the fast-food business and chain-restaurant operations were still virtually unknown. Our earliest franchisees were very much like Dave and me in the sense that they were pioneers of a completely new concept in food service. Like all business start-ups there were plenty of risks involved, but these were magnified because the concept was so completely untried and untested. We had spent many years developing a system which really worked when it was properly managed. This was the basic reason for our early success at the national level, and it helped to create an avalanche of requests for new franchises. We capitalized on America's growing acceptance of the economically priced meals being made available to customers who chose to eat away from home. Within a few decades, the food-service business in the United States had changed and was totally dominated by restaurant chains. The "Mom-and-Pop" restaurants which were common in the past gradually faded from the American scene as changing lifestyles demanded new innovations in food-service operations. I felt very fortunate to be on the cutting edge of the changes that were swiftly taking place in the country.

Sniffing Around?

The Booz Allen Visit

By 1965 I had gained a certain degree of recognition as a leading spokesman for the growing fast-food industry. I was not particularly surprised to receive a call from a representative of the well-known management consulting firm of Booz Allen & Hamilton. They asked if they could come by the office for a visit and discuss new developments then taking place in the food-service industry. I received calls like this often, and I was pleased to accommodate them. Interest in the fast-food business had picked up around the country. What I did not know at the time and what was not disclosed to me during their visit was that the Booz Allen people were on assignment from The Pillsbury Company in Minneapolis. Their mission was to report back on changes that were taking place in the overall food industry. Grocery-store sales were essentially flat, competition among manufacturers of consumer food products such as Pillsbury was intense, and Pillsbury wanted answers as to what was going on with consumers and where they should focus their attention in order to grow their business.

In 1966 the Burger King corporate headquarters was located in the rear of the Coral Way (number 7) store. We had acquired a 25-foot piece of adjoining property and built an addition to the building in order to increase the size of our offices. As the company grew, we leased additional space in a small 50-foot building located adjacent to the property. With these acquisitions we increased the size of our offices to keep pace with the rapid national expansion of our business.

The Burger King business was really booming by the time 1965 rolled around. We were opening an average of over one new Burger King restaurant every week in cities all over the country. The additional space was needed to accommodate a growing staff. Several years earlier we moved the commissary to an industrial site alongside the Palmetto Expressway, just south of Bird Road. The former commissary space at the Coral Way location was converted into additional office space and was used to accommodate our new and growing departments in advertising, accounting, personnel, franchise development, real estate, construction, architecture, equipment procurement, and the like. Also located in this space was our training facility, which we called *Whopper College*. This teaching school made it possible to train our new franchisees on the procedures they would be required to follow in operating their soon-to-be-opened Burger King restaurants. Even with all the new space we had converted into a new headquarters building, it was clear that we would soon be in need of an even larger freestanding office facility. For the years 1965 and 1966, however, we were able to manage, even though we were in terribly crowded quarters.

It was into this busy, cramped beehive of activity that the Booz Allen people walked. I'm sure they could see that Burger King was an organization that was growing rapidly and that we were very, very busy. On the wall of my office I had a framed picture with an important message. With our Burger King trademark on top (which was the king sitting on a hamburger), the message read: "THIS IS A PROFIT-MAKING ORGANIZATION. THAT'S THE WAY WE INTENDED IT—AND THAT'S THE WAY IT IS!" I remember the two men looked at that statement intently for some time and made some comments about it. I thought this message was a perfect expression of our corporate resolve, and I used it often to let our franchisees, suppliers, bankers, and employees know that we had our sights set on becoming the best and most profitable company in the industry.

All of our Burger King associates knew that we were headed for the top, and we weren't ashamed to let our intentions be known to anyone who would care to listen. I think we all saw ourselves as a lean, mean, and hard-charging group of managers, highly focused on our mission of becoming the very best company in our field. At least among ourselves there was no doubt about the integrity of our corporate resolve. We set out to be the best in the business—and we expected to remain a very profitable company while we were attempting to reach that goal. Dreams and aspirations were guiding and directing us toward that objective.

I spent several hours with the Booz Allen people that day. Since my Cornell days, I had been interested in the history of the restaurant industry, its evolution, and the changes that had taken place over the years. I knew how the industry had come into existence, and I had my own ideas on where it was headed. Thanks to my past and current affiliation with various trade associations, I knew many of the men and women who were industry leaders at the time. I think the Booz Allen people saw me as a fountain of information on the subject. We talked for quite a while.

They seemed to be keying in on how fast the "away-from-home eating market" was growing. They were anxious to learn something about that particular market's potential. Specifically they were interested in getting some ideas about the impact this growth might have on the "at-home eating market." Pillsbury, after all, was in the consumer foods business and was engaged in selling its products to the nation's grocery stores. That business was flat and going nowhere. The Booz Allen people were looking for answers.

They knew that the food service business was growing rapidly, and they might have presumed that this was largely responsible for the flattening of sales in grocery stores. Since the opening of The Colonial Inn 15 years earlier, food-service sales in the United States had more than doubled to over $23 billion. By the 1990s food-service sales would grow to over $250 billion, but even the most optimistic among us could not have predicted anything quite like that. We knew in 1965 that a lot of people liked the food and service we were offering. The public was rushing out to eat in new Burger King restaurants and seemed to like the many new fast-food restaurants which were beginning to open in other parts of the country. For us these were good times! Eating out was becoming an American lifestyle and a way of life.

Statistical data was available from government and industry sources regarding changes that were taking place in both the food industry and the food-service industry. What was not readily available was information about which segments of the away-from-home market had the best long-term prospects for growth. The real focus of Booz Allen's investigation was on the companies and segments of the industry which would most likely be the major participants in the growth that was certain to occur.

During the past few years, I had been traveling extensively around the country visiting franchisees, picking out new locations, and selling franchises. So was Dave. Everywhere we went we noticed new limited-menu restaurants springing up. Dave was particularly aware of what was going on, and we shared information on what we saw during our trips. We made it our business to learn all we could about national marketing trends, and we made a particular point of studying each individual market in as much detail as we possibly could. We were well aware of the markets where local chains were strong, and we knew where the regional chains were doing well. Both of us felt that we knew quite a bit about their strong points and their weaknesses and hence where they were vulnerable. Dave and I had very firm opinions about where industry growth would occur and how new growth could be stimulated. I gave Booz Allen freely whatever knowledge and opinions I had in that regard.

McDonald's highly successful public offering in 1965 focused national attention on the phenomena and growth of limited-menu chain restaurants. Theirs was such an important retailing success story at the time that it was featured on the cover of *Time* magazine. This publicity and much which followed created a good deal of public awareness about the potential profitability of franchised restaurants. Booz Allen wanted to know more about this kind of business. What was its potential? How profitable was it? What were the hazards and pitfalls? Which companies were successful? What situations should be avoided? Was franchising a viable method for fueling growth within the industry? What uses of advertising and mass-marketing methods would come into play? These and many other related questions dominated our conversation.

Although I had no idea about their underlying purpose in calling on me, I had no doubt that they left with the feeling that limited-menu restaurants were going to enjoy substantial growth in the future. That message came through loud and clear. I also felt certain that by the time their visit was over, they must have concluded that I was fairly well-informed on the subject.

A short time after their visit, I received a call thanking me for the time I had given them. They asked a few follow-up questions, but the conversation was brief. I don't recall seeing either one of them again.

I learned many months later that in their report to Pillsbury, they attributed the flat growth in institutional food sales to be largely the result of the explosive growth taking place in the away-from-home market. They concluded their report by advising Pillsbury that if they wanted to participate in the overall food business, they should consider taking a position in the restaurant business. Pillsbury's response was to charge them with a new assignment, which was to identify the best way to gain access to that industry. They wanted to know how they might get into the business. Booz Allen came back after conducting another study that analyzed the strengths and weaknesses of most of the major independent chains. Their recommendation to Pillsbury was that they should consider the acquisition of Burger King Corporation as the best way to access the opportunity. Soon afterwards representatives of The Pillsbury Company made contact with us.

Removing Obstacles

We called it the *Burger King Commissary* and later changed its name to *Distron*. This was the humble beginning of a food production and delivery service which ensured the timely arrival of food and supplies into our restaurants. When we opened our second Miami Burger King, we delivered supplies to it from stock we kept in inventory at store 1 on 36th Street, and we continued doing this through the opening of our store 6. My personal station wagon served as our first delivery vehicle.

When we opened store 5, it became painfully obvious that we could no longer continue operating this way. We were in need of a business office and room to expand our commissary operation. We provided this space when we designed and built our Burger King store 7 at 3051 Coral Way in March of 1957. This building included a large warehouse and office space which adjoined the restaurant. We bought a used 1947 International panel truck for $100 which became our sole commissary delivery vehicle, replacing the station wagon. This beat-up old truck had a rear-end with a decided list or tilt to it due to a faulty rear end suspension. We had to struggle to keep it running. It was a wreck, but it was all we could afford at the time. Six months later we bought a brand-new Chevrolet panel truck for $2600. This upgrade in delivery equipment helped us provide more reliable service to our restaurants. We began to see the advantages and importance of centralizing our procurement and delivery operations.

By 1962 our commissary business had increased substantially. With our South Florida franchising program in full swing and new restaurants opening at a steady basis, we needed to accommodate the significant increase in our commissary business. We acquired an industrial property on the newly opened Palmetto Expressway and built a large freestanding warehouse and production facility. Being located on a railroad spur, we were in position to buy and receive supplies in carload lots at considerable savings. Daily deliveries by a growing fleet of trucks enabled us to provide greater efficiency and convenience to our restaurants. As we continued to open new restaurants in South Florida the new commissary helped call attention to Burger King's growing market presence. With an ever-increasing number of restaurants to serve, we established a distribution business that was destined to become the model for modern-day distribution services to chain restaurants.

The rapid growth of the Burger King system created some frustrating logistical problems about timely and reliable delivery of equipment to job sites. Our equipment and signs were manufactured by independent suppliers located in many different parts of the country. This required us to negotiate with individual purveyors about costs and delivery schedules. This took up a lot of time and energy. It was next to impossible to coordinate the exact arrival time of the equipment. This totally frustrated the installation process. Our practice was to send our installation people from Miami to see that everything was installed properly and functioning as it should. These installers simply couldn't complete their task on a timely basis because of delays in receiving so many different items from so many different sources. We were ordering delivery of walk-in coolers, sinks, shelving, signs, counters, shake machines, fryers, broilers, refrigerators, seating, drink stations, or other important items that needed to be installed before we could open for business. It seemed that nothing arrived when it was supposed to. It was a logistical nightmare.

By late 1962 we found ourselves in the position of opening as many as two or more restaurants in any given week. In handling this kind of activity, we were contending with an inefficient and unreliable delivery situation which constantly disrupted our store-opening schedules. To solve the problem, we ordered that all restaurant equipment be shipped directly to the Miami commissary, where we kept it in inventory. This enabled us to ship everything we needed to a particular job site all in one load. This ensured that the equipment would arrive at the exact time our Miami-based installation people appeared at the job site. When we implemented this plan, installation time was cut from several weeks to as little as three days at significant savings in cost and convenience. An added advantage was our ability to buy equipment in quantity at greatly reduced prices.

Finding storage space for this equipment presented another logistical problem. The Miami commissary was built to process and supply our South Florida restaurants with food, paper, and various other items. We didn't have room in the original 15,000-square-foot facility to do much more than that. When the need arose to provide space for storing restaurant equipment, we built a 15,000-square-foot addition to the building. This doubled the size of the plant.

To expedite matters even further, we contracted with a local sheet-metal firm to build some of our stainless-steel equipment. We contracted with a local sign company to build our neon signs. This even included the large pole sign which we installed in front of all the new restaurants. The counters, tables, and dining room furniture were manufactured in South Florida and shipped directly to the job sites. We could control deliveries of this kind. The rest of the equipment was shipped directly to Miami by specialty manufacturers located in many different parts of the country. This included fryers, milk-shake machines, drink stations, ice makers, and so forth. We found that it was less expensive and more convenient to inventory this equipment in Miami so that we could ship it directly to job sites ourselves.

The cost of shipping this equipment to the job sites was really very reasonable. Truckers delivering cargo to Miami had considerable difficulty obtaining backhauls, and this usually required them to deadhead north with an empty rig. It took the capacity of two 40-foot tractor trailers to hold the equipment we shipped to each location. This was the kind of business the truckers were anxious to get. It was actively solicited and made available to us at very low cost.

We took pride in pointing to the fact that two truckloads of equipment would arrive on a job site at a specified time and would contain everything from the huge neon pole sign and walk-in cooler to the pencils and paper clips in the manager's desk drawer. This unique and convenient system worked very smoothly and saved us a lot of money. It was the first delivery system of its kind in the infant fast-food industry, and it set a standard for the future.

The centralizing of equipment procurement and delivery became so efficient that within months we decided to build our own hamburger broilers. This was a means of protecting our technology and lowering our costs. These broilers were patterned after the initial design that David Edgerton conceived and built in 1955. We had enough extra space in the newly constructed commissary addition to enable us to build a better-quality broiler at substantial savings. This put us in the equipment-manufacturing business, albeit on a modest scale.

The broiler was made from parts cut from sheets of stainless steel. We bought the heavy-duty equipment which was designed to cut and form these steel panels. In starting the manufacturing process, we hired experienced sheet-metal workers and machinists. Once established as a manufacturer, we decided to effect additional cost savings by producing our own stainless-steel refrigerators, counters, sinks, shelving, walk-in coolers, fry stations, and other items. This created another space problem which required us to build a 15,000-square-foot addition to the existing building. When finished this gave us a total of 45,000 square feet of industrial warehousing and production space. Even this wouldn't be enough. With our national expansion growing so rapidly, we could see that more space would be needed in the future. Accordingly, we made a decision to build a full-scale equipment-manufacturing plant at a site located only a short distance from our expanded commissary facility.

We named our equipment-manufacturing division Davmor Industries, which was an acronym using the names of *Dave* and *McLamore*. We expected to be building and supplying much of the equipment that would be needed in the hundreds of new Burger King restaurants we planned to open every year into the future. We were convinced that we could build better-quality equipment than we were able to buy and that we could lower our costs at the same time.

In 1966 we built a completely new 50,000-square-foot plant and offices for Davmor Industries on a 20-acre site. Within a few years this business grew to the point of employing 325 machinists, sheet-metal workers, and furniture makers. Annual sales reached a high of $27,500,000 with pretax profits exceeding $4 million a year. Within a short time Davmor Industries positioned itself as one of the largest fabricators of restaurant equipment in the United States.

This was a unique start-up company with profitable operations from the day it opened for business. We demonstrated an ability to supply franchisees with equipment at a lower cost and higher quality than they could obtain from the outside. This was important, but the real contribution to the Burger King system was the reliable and timely delivery of our restaurant equipment. The company was so successful that we had to build two separate additions to the original plant. One of the additions came with six tractor-trailer loading bays. The plant needed to run three shifts around the clock at maximum capacity in order to keep up with the huge demand for the equipment we produced. On one occasion I invited Steve Clark, the mayor of Dade County, to visit with me and tour the plant. He couldn't believe the size and scope of the business we were doing. Very few people knew of the existence of Davmor Industries even though it was one of the largest equipment-manufacturing facilities in the state of Florida at the time. To us, it was just a company subsidiary that went about its work quietly and efficiently. We had no reason to seek notoriety and publicity. Davmor had only one customer and that was us!

Dave and I were so impressed with Davmor's early success and the continuing success of Distron, our rapidly expanding commissary business, that we formed a 50-50 joint venture with the Miami-based general contracting firm of Shafer and Miller. During the 1950s and into the early 1960s, this company had built many of our Burger King buildings; they had done a very good job. Dave and I felt that it would be much to our benefit to have this firm take over the job of constructing our restaurant buildings on a national level. Ron Shafer and Bill Miller liked the idea, but they were concerned about expanding their business without having adequate assurance that we would continue to use their construction services. I couldn't fault that. It was obvious that they would need to make a significant capital investment in their business. This would be at considerable risk if something went wrong with us as their sole customer.

We decided to form a 50-50 joint venture which resulted in the creation of a new general contracting firm, First Florida Building Corporation. This new company gave Burger King the benefit of having the services of a general contractor who was experienced in building our restaurants on a cost-efficient and timely basis. Under the leadership of Bill Miller, First Florida became one of the largest general contracting firms of its kind in the United States. Initially its sole specialty was the construction of Burger King restaurant buildings. The repetitive nature of this activity resulted in major cost and time efficiencies, which were of considerable benefit to Burger King and its franchisees. The company became so efficient that it was able to deliver restaurant buildings within 45 to 60 days of breaking ground. The decision to create First Florida was based on our need to provide the reliable delivery of Burger King restaurant buildings. This played a vital role in helping us reach our overall corporate objectives regarding growth and expansion.

We hired William C. Murphy, a graduate of the School of Architecture at the University of Miami. His job was to design and draw up plans for all our new restaurants. Over an extended period of time he took the exams necessary to become licensed in practically every state in the country. There was barely enough space on his office walls to hang all the framed certificates which bore witness to this young man's extraordinary status as an architect engaged in national construction projects. We were very proud of Bill, and with him as a valuable member of our management team, we expanded the Burger King business into cities and towns all over the country. These were great years filled with fun, excitement, and anticipation. We were on a successful mission, and we were enjoying it.

First Florida quickly demonstrated its talents as a low-cost producer of restaurant buildings. The company became so efficient in constructing quality buildings for Burger King that it took on construction responsibilities for many other fast-food chains. They faced the same problem we had, which was to find a building contractor able to consistently deliver quality construction on a timely, reliable, and cost-effective basis. First Florida served us and its many other customers very well. At any given time it might have 50 or more restaurants under construction all the way from Maine to California. Our First Florida venture was another innovative industry first in the rapidly expanding field of chain restaurants.

Within the short space of a few years, Burger King had three in-house quality distributors and producers in Distron (food and supplies), Davmor (equipment and furnishings), and First Florida (restaurant construction). These three companies shared in our success and rendered considerable assistance in helping the Burger King organization grow steadily and predictably during the early years of our national expansion.

Davmor Industries served the company for over a dozen years, but with the rapid growth of chain-restaurant organizations, other manufacturers came forth with a willingness to invest capital and compete for this business.

Davmor and Distron were created when there were few, if any, suppliers who were interested in or capable of providing the kind of services we had to have. Each restaurant needed a one-truck, one-stop, daily delivery of our complete line of food and supplies. There wasn't enough business of this kind to attract purveyors during the early years, so we had to do it ourselves. Many years later, when multiunit restaurant chains came into being, highly specialized companies were organized to supply this kind of service. They became hugely successful as a result. Out of necessity we created and pioneered a completely original concept in the distribution and manufacturing fields. We sold Distron in 1992 to Pro Source. In 1996, their CEO, David Parker, told me they were operating in every state from 33 strategically located distribution centers utilizing 2.3 million square feet of space. Sales were running at an annual rate of $4 billion. They had 593 tractors and 831 refrigerated trailers in operation and 3500 employees on the payroll. Pro Source purchased the Distron business from us for slightly over $100 million. That certainly represented a big jump from the days when my 1956 Ford station wagon was the sole delivery vehicle. Pro Source rendered a valuable and much needed service to the Burger King system. Their one-stop daily service became an industry standard. The magnitude of this operation has attracted stiff competition, but the efficiencies which were brought about have been of great benefit to chain restaurants everywhere.

With the growth and expansion of the 1960s and 1970s, independent suppliers came into existence intent upon capitalizing on the opportunities of doing business in such a lucrative market. We always knew that our three start-up companies would attract competition. Many franchisees, who started out very slowly and modestly during the late 1950s and early 1960s, had no previous experience in purchasing, procurement, or construction. Over time they grew into much larger businesses. As they gained experience, sophistication, and financial independence, they were able to contract for services and supplies from a number of different organizations, all of which were organized and anxious to serve them. Our franchisees began to challenge the idea of purchasing supplies and services from companies owned by or affiliated with the parent Burger King organization.

Franchisees value their independence and usually prefer to do business with outside contractors. Our franchisees were not obligated to purchase supplies from us, and we expected that they would ultimately try to seek sources of procurement on the outside. A gradual withdrawal of their support for Davmor Industries and First Florida Building Corporation might have been heavily influenced by the desire to be more independent in their search for value. The substantial increase and growth within the chain-restaurant industry attracted many new specialty vendors who actively solicited this kind of business.

Davmor Industries and Distron were sold, and First Florida entered new and different fields of construction activity. All of these affiliated companies played key roles during the early years of Burger King's national expansion. Without their support and the timely services they provided, we would have had a much more difficult time expanding the business. We knew that growing and staying on top was a matter of critical concern if we were ever to become a nationally recognized restaurant chain. These three companies helped us to do that.

Scrambling to Stay in the Lead

By 1965 the rapidly expanding food-service industry was a topic of considerable discussion in the financial world and in the trade press. People who invested in restaurant franchises were making a lot of money. This was big news. Stories about this kind of success were reported in newspaper and magazine articles. The newly conceived fast-food business was the talk of the day. The country woke up to the fact that this restaurant business phenomena was a field ripe with opportunity. It gradually began to lose its image as a failure-prone business. The increasing use of television advertising by leading companies such as McDonald's and Burger King contributed to building a national awareness about the advantages of eating out. The compelling message was that consumers could get good food, served quickly at low prices in clean restaurants. This is what the public was looking for. The restaurant industry's sales and profits grew impressively while sales in the nation's grocery stores began to flatten. Fast-food was suddenly the hot ticket and so was the restaurant business itself.

On April 15, 1965, McDonald's Corporation went public. This event stimulated growth and expansion within the fast-food industry like nothing that had ever happened before that time. Exactly 10 years earlier Ray Kroc opened his first McDonald's restaurant in Des Plaines, Illinois, a community in the Greater Chicago Area. Both events were historic. This public offering was one of the most extraordinarily successful underwritings of all time. The stock was issued at $22.50 per share, and by the end of the first day of trading, it was selling for $30 per share. Within a few weeks it had more than doubled to $49 per share. The public was well aware of McDonald's rapid growth during the past few years, and they were anxious to share in this great success. Investors clamored for the stock, feeling that they were looking at "a good thing." They were quite right about that. One hundred dollars invested in McDonald's stock in April of 1965 was worth well over one-half million dollars in 1996. By then the market value of this extraordinary company had reached $35 billion. This was phenomenal growth—unparalleled in the history of the restaurant industry. I doubt that we will ever again witness such a remarkable accomplishment.

The investing public's fascination and attraction to McDonald's focused public attention on the growth opportunities which might be available in the food-service field. Within a two-year span several other restaurant chains followed the McDonald's initiative by coming out with their own public offerings. These issues were snapped up by investors who were hoping to find the next McDonald's. Jack Massey, an astute businessman in Nashville and John Y. Brown, a young entrepreneur who later become Governor of Kentucky, bought Colonel Harland Sander's interest in his Kentucky Fried Chicken business for a meager $2 million in cash. Reorganizing the business concept and launching a professionally conceived franchising program, they brought out a public offering of Kentucky Fried Chicken. It was an instant success. Royal Castle in Miami and the Howard Johnson Company followed, with their own offerings of stock a short time after that. These events were met with success and strong public acceptance. Restaurant stocks were suddenly very much in demand, and this brought about a frenzy of activity on the part of a new breed of opportunistic restaurant-company stock promoters.

I wasn't particularly concerned about the competition that had come to life during the 1960s and early 1970s. It seemed to me that most of these newly formed restaurant companies were organized by promoters who had an eye out to make a quick dollar on the sale of franchises. They weren't restaurant operators. Their lack of experience in the restaurant business led them to downplay the need to develop a long-term approach toward running their businesses. Most of them paid but a minimal amount of attention to restaurant operations once their franchisees opened for business. They either abandoned them completely or failed to assist them in focusing on the basic fundamentals of running good restaurants. With this kind of organizational chaos and lack of experience, it was predictable that their franchisees would have a tough time making a success out of their new businesses. As far as I was concerned, these people were on a certain road to failure. It was just common sense that if enough franchisees failed, the franchisor couldn't be very far behind.

A company called Minnie Pearl Fried Chicken was a perfect example of this kind of a doomed-to-failure business promotion. Minnie Pearl was a well-known and respected Grand Ole Opry headliner who lent her name to a restaurant scheme that turned out to be one of the most notorious restaurant franchising fiascoes in the history of the food-service industry.

The promoter of this enterprise planned to duplicate the success of the Kentucky Fried Chicken concept by copying their franchising and operating format. Laying claim to become "the Pepsi Cola of the fried chicken business," he began to sell large "exclusive territories" to gullible investors, along with the promise of vast riches to be earned selling Minnie Pearl's fried chicken. In each franchising agreement the promoter obtained a commitment from territorial franchisees to open a specific number of Minnie Pearl Fried Chicken stores within a specified time frame. Each territorial agreement called for a specific fixed dollar payment to the franchisor. This charge was calculated on the number of stores which were planned to be opened in the territory. The actual cash payment to the parent Minnie Pearl company was minimal. The promoter accepted the franchisee's note for the rather substantial balance of the purchase price. For example, if a franchise contract called for the development of 20 stores in a particular territory, the agreement called for the payment of $5000 per store, or a total purchase price of $100,000 for the territory. A typical arrangement for the purchase of a $100,000 territory required a cash payment of $10,000 and the delivery of $90,000 in notes. The notes were payable at the rate of $5000 per store, whenever the stores were opened. As incredible as it sounds, the company reported the entire $100,000 as *earned income* as of the date the contract was signed. Reporting that this constituted "earnings" was justified by the reasoning that this was what the territory had been "sold" for. Just as surprisingly, this very misleading and absurd accounting treatment was deemed acceptable by Minnie Pearl's external auditors and accountants. The result was that investors were given a grossly distorted view of the company's true earnings and financial condition.

Initially this didn't seem to matter to investors because suddenly Minnie Pearl was a big hit on Wall Street. The company went public in 1968 at $20 a share and by the end of the first day's trading, the stock had more than doubled to over $40 per share. Within a short period of time, the market value of the company, based on its stock price was $81 million, yet it had assets of only $2.2 million and only five restaurants in actual operation, none of which were doing very well. Apparently investors never bothered to consider whether the notes the company had received could ever be paid off or whether the restaurants would ever be operated at a profit. As it turned out, neither happened. Very few payments were ever received on the notes, and before long the company was bankrupt and declared a colossal failure. Investors lost millions. The scam artists walked away with plenty.

Dozens of similar stock and franchising promotions came and went in the days following the McDonald's and KFC offerings. Lums was a Miami-based restaurant franchising company which featured hot dogs and beer. This company operated in a manner similar to the Minnie Pearl organization. Profits were reported based on the sale of franchises. The company earned a minimal profit on the actual operation of its restaurants. Going public with assets of only $5 million, the market valuation of Lums reached $91 million. Simple market euphoria drove up the price of the stock to a ridiculous level. Events like this helped to coin the phrase "Minnie Pearling it" when describing such stock promotions in the restaurant field. During the 1960s the public witnessed quite a few schemes of this sort. The promoters usually got rich, but investors invariably got clobbered.

With well-operated restaurant companies it was a different picture. McDonald's public offering in 1965 was an extraordinary success. Kentucky Fried Chicken followed soon afterwards, and it, too, was well received. After their public offering, Kentucky Fried Chicken reached a market capitalization of $364 million, which, at one point, was over 100 times their reported earnings, but even these earnings were based more on profit gained on franchising rather than on operations. Fortunes were made on two public sales of KFC stock. It was small wonder that "the suede-shoes boys" (as I often called the franchising promoters of the era) wanted to participate in an industry with this kind of action.

By the late 1960s there were dozens of restaurant franchising schemes afloat, and investment bankers were clamoring to take profitable restaurant companies public. I often thought that if we had maintained our corporate independence for just a few more years that the ultimate fortunes of Burger King Corporation might have turned out differently. We were one of the solid companies in the field, but the timing of our intentions to become a public company couldn't have been worse.

The sudden and extraordinary public interest in the restaurant business did not go unnoticed by our multiunit franchisees. We had issued a number of territorial franchise agreements in the early 1960s to stimulate the rapid growth and development of our national development program. This was a key strategy in building Burger King's national presence. This produced the desired effect in a number of key markets. By 1967 we had helped to create several small chains operating within the Burger King system. There was good and bad in all of this.

By 1967 many of our territorial franchisees had been in business long enough to post impressive earnings records. They had built successful companies within the Burger King system. Their success attracted many prospects seeking franchises of their own. This is what we were looking for. Our successful territorial franchisees provided bedrock support for the Burger King system when it was relatively unknown.

Our New Orleans–based franchisees, Jimmy and Billy Trotter, formed a company called Self Service Restaurants. They were successful operators of Burger King restaurants in Louisiana and parts of the Gulf Coast. They took their company public in the late 1960s. Mallory Restaurants, our Long Island franchisees, went public a year or so after that. It was when our three territorial franchisees in the Chicago area joined together with the intention to go public as one entity that I had to draw the line. We hadn't counted on having a number of public companies as franchisees.

On February 5, 1969, I delivered a memorandum to all franchisees entitled "Respecting the Assignment, Sale or Disposition of Restaurant Licenses," which had the effect of restricting franchisees from going public and which at least for the time being put an end to this practice. Having the general public as franchisees could have created some nasty problems.

Dave and I were keeping our eye on McDonald's and tracking their growth. Our rate of expansion was about the same as theirs during the early 1960s, even though they were opening many more restaurants than we were. We estimated that we were trailing them by approximately 40 months. We believed that if we handled things properly, we had a reasonable chance of catching up to them.

I was troubled by the fact that McDonald's, as a result of their public offering in 1965, was able to tap the financial markets and that we had been unable to do that. This gave them a clear advantage. Their real estate strategy was not only masterful, it was downright brilliant. They kept buying or leasing land and constructing their buildings using their franchisees' lease deposits as down payments. They relied on franchisees' rental payments to help retire any real estate obligations they assumed. Their investment banker observed at the time that McDonald's strategy to go the leveraged route rather than the equity route in its real estate dealings was "an exquisite decision." I liked the use of the word "exquisite" to describe their business strategy because it seemed to be such an appropriate and apt description. By the mid-1960s, we were trying to develop a similar strategy, but the risks involved appeared to be too great that early in our national development program.

As we opened new restaurants in cities and towns all over the country, our confidence grew. All of these restaurants were successful, which gave us the encouragement to gamble a bit more. Accordingly, we adopted a strategy of buying land and constructing our own buildings, which we then leased to franchisees. We also entered into lease arrangements for land and buildings built-to-suit by outside investors after which we offered them to our franchisees on sublease arrangements. We weren't smart enough or financially strong enough to do things the McDonald's way, but our real estate operations did play a profitable role in our overall business strategy. We began a search for long-term financing in order to increase our investments in real estate. It was easy to see that this side of our business could become a very profitable business strategy.

The high price-earnings ratio or "multiple" that the public placed on McDonald's stock often exceeded 40 times their earnings. This highly valued stock gave them a reason and an opportunity to buy out franchisees. By valuing the franchisee's businesses on the basis of a lower multiple of earnings, they could pay for it by issuing their own highly valued shares. This practice went on to a certain extent and had the effect of steadily increasing McDonald's earnings per share. This helped to drive up the price of their stock even further and, in turn, enabled them to continue their aggressive expansion into the real estate business. During the next 30 years or more after McDonald's original public offering in 1965, the company never reported a "down" quarter. This extraordinary performance of over 125 straight calendar quarters of increased earnings per share certainly is an enviable record and a tribute to the company's strength, vibrancy, and leadership.

Our concern at the time centered on McDonald's access to the debt and equity markets. They had pulled out in front of us in terms of profitability and the number of restaurants opened. It was obvious that it would be difficult to keep up with their future growth without a financial infusion of some kind. What were we going to do? We needed capital to stay in the race, and we needed to find it rather quickly.

In 1964 Dave and I reviewed our own situation. We concluded that we should try to purchase some additional equity in the company. Harvey Fruehauf owned close to 50 percent of our stock. He acquired this interest eight years earlier when he first invested in the company. Dave and I each owned a bit less than 25 percent apiece. A very small percentage of shares were owned by our other two directors, George Storer and Tom Wakefield. Tom had been our attorney and general counsel during the past 10 years. Recently we had issued stock options to employees, including one which we gave to Dr. Nichol.

Dave and I talked to Harvey about our purchasing an additional interest in the company based on whatever the fair market price of the stock might be at the time. This seemed to us to be a fair and reasonable proposal, so I was a bit surprised when our suggestion appeared to upset him. I thought it would make sense for the stockholders to encourage us to make a larger investment in the company.

Although this rejection on Harvey's part was disappointing to both of us, I soon forgot about it. As far as I was concerned, we had made a business proposal that was unacceptable to our partner and major stockholder, and I didn't think any more about it after that. The episode did, however, force me to consider my own situation, which was becoming a bit more difficult. Evaluating my own equity position in the business was complicated by the fact that the company was now considering the eventuality of an equity offering of its own. Doing that would dilute my equity position even further. A decision needed to be made, and the public offering by McDonald's

raised the level of urgency. In the event of a public offering of
Burger King stock, I would find myself in the position of owning less than a 20 percent interest in the company. This would
be further reduced as we made acquisitions, issued more
stock, or granted additional stock options. Dave and I had
never asked the board to grant us stock options, and as president of the company I never put a proposal of that kind on the
board's agenda. I was prepared to remain a minority stockholder as long as Burger King remained an independent company. However, it was clear to me that if Burger King were to
become a public company, Dave and I, with a shrinking equity
position, would have little assurance of having a strong voice
in determining corporate policy and directing the company's
future affairs. This was but one of many questions and concerns that were on my mind at the time.

When a call came from The Pillsbury Company a year or
so later asking if we would be interested in discussing the possibility of a merger, it seemed to be an idea at least worthy of
consideration. Before receiving that call, we were thinking in
terms of having an equity offering of our own. Harvey
Fruehauf proposed that we talk to Blyth and Company about
this and suggested that he and I go to New York City to look
into that possibility.

Harvey was a director of Georgia Pacific Corporation at
the time. Serving with him on the board was Stuart Hawes,
the current chairman and CEO of Blyth and Company.
Harvey's suggestion that we discuss a Burger King equity
offering with Blyth seemed like a good idea at the time, even
though I was totally unfamiliar with matters of this kind.
Having no prior experience dealing with investment bankers, I
was on foreign turf, but I thought it might be high time for me
to learn something about it.

Dave and I had spent a considerable amount of time developing Burger King's strategic business plans. Both of us were
completely familiar with the company's extraordinary profit-
making potential. From a personal standpoint I felt that a public offering of Burger King stock would be very well received.
Going public, in spite of certain disadvantages, was clearly our

preferred route to grow the business, and we approached the idea with a determination to make it happen.

Harvey and I flew to New York and checked into the Regency Hotel on Park Avenue. We went out to dinner at one of New York's nice restaurants and spent the evening talking about our situation and what we might encounter in the morning. Our appointment with Mr. Hawes was set for 10 a.m.

After breakfast we took a cab to the offices of Blyth and Company. I couldn't help but be impressed by the elegance of their office with its huge mahogany doors, thick carpets, and polished antique furnishings. The impression projected visions of wealth and prosperity. With only a limited knowledge about the stock market, I was unfamiliar with the process and implications of going public. I reminded myself that the only course I had failed at Cornell was Corporation Finance. In my business career up to this point, I had never crafted a complicated financial scenario designed to structure a large business organization. Being a real "numbers guy," I felt comfortable and confident about my planning ability to strategize a business plan. This was a bit different. My business background was attuned to building restaurants and operating them. I began to regret that I had never been exposed to more complex financial experiences. It might have been better for the company if we had brought in a knowledgeable and experienced financial adviser to guide us through these complexities. It occurred to me that this was hardly the best time or place to be learning all about the world of high finance.

I presented a package of financial information which included our business plan, earnings history, and balance sheet along with some information explaining what Burger King was all about. Mr. Hawes invited Edward Glassmeyer, a senior vice president of the firm to join us. Glassmeyer had been involved with Blyth's underwriting of the initial public offering of Ryder System, Inc., the Miami-based truck-leasing firm. It seemed to me that Glassmeyer's experience with Ryder System and his knowledge about the Miami market would have enabled him to recognize the potential of a Burger King offering, inasmuch as we were a well-established Florida-based company at the time. The two men examined our balance sheet and income statements, our cash-flow projections, our record of previous earnings, and the growth of our business in terms of new restaurants we had opened over the years. Our after-tax earnings for the year ending May 31, 1965, were $446,239, and our projection for the current year was in excess of $750,000. Considering where we had come from, I thought that this was a noteworthy achievement. As it turned out, Blyth and Company didn't seem to be nearly as impressed, even after considering our projections for future growth.

We may have been standing in the center of financial power in New York City, but at the time we were talking to the wrong people. I learned later that Blyth and Company was a banker for older, well-established companies and institutions. The company was mainly in the business of marketing bonds, rather than underwriting equity offerings of small companies such as our own. We ended the day with a cordial, pleasant meeting with Blyth, but after discussing our financing goals and objectives and listening to their reactions, I concluded that Burger King would probably not prove to be a very exciting prospect for them. It turned out that I was right about that.

We left our package of information for them to study. Mr. Hawes thanked us for coming, and Harvey and I flew back to Miami. We were optimistic and hopeful that our visit would produce the desired result, and we left New York with the feeling that we stood a reasonable chance that Blyth would assist us in taking Burger King public. I couldn't see how they could help but recognize that a public offering of our stock would be a success. Such a conclusion was an indication of how little I really understood about the world of investment banking.

We returned to New York a short time later only to be greeted with some disappointing news. Blyth told us that even though we had a rapidly growing business with impressive earnings growth and optimistic prospects for the future, we were too young, inexperienced, and undercapitalized to think about going public at this time. I asked what kind of a record they thought we would need to position the company for a public offering. The answer was vague and indefinite. On the basis of their response, I could no longer imagine that Blyth and Company would ever become our bell cow.

This was discouraging and disappointing news. If I had been more familiar with the many different ways investment bankers served their clients, I would have suggested that we take our proposal to a more aggressive firm that specialized in small entrepreneurial situations like ours. Being on such unfamiliar turf at the time, I didn't know which way to turn.

Many months later I was in New York visiting Ed Glassmeyer. We were walking down Park Avenue when he spotted Howard B. Johnson, the founder's son, headed our way. Blyth and Company had recently served as a lead banker in the Howard Johnson Company's public offering. Glassmeyer introduced me to young Johnson, who was then the CEO of the company, but he seemed aloof and disinterested in our conversation, so there was very little exchange between us.

I thought back to my impression of the Howard Johnson Company 30 years earlier. In 1937 I was 11 years old and my grandmother took me on a trip to New York City. We stopped at a recently opened Howard Johnson restaurant, located on the New Jersey side of the George Washington Bridge. It was an attractive place, sparkling clean, with a distinctive orange roof and lots of customers. The menu consisted of "frankforts" and 28 flavors of ice cream. The menu was simple and well-presented. I thought it was a terrific place. For years after that I followed the growth and development of their business. By 1967 the Howard Johnson Company had grown like Topsy, and with 800 restaurants in operation, they were acknowledged to be the largest restaurant chain in the United States, if not in the world. Nevertheless, at the time of our discussion with Blyth and Company, I was already convinced that the Howard Johnson organization was a company in big trouble. Throughout all the years I had spent building the Burger King business, I had never been impressed with the company, its management, or the way they had been running their business. I couldn't understand why Blyth and Company had underwritten this public offering. I remember a story which appeared 20 years later in the *Boston Globe*. The headline was in bold type, and it read: "The Rise and Fall of Howard Johnson's. The father built an American institution; the son will be remembered for its demise!"

I had an unpleasant recollection resulting from my encounter with the founder, Howard D. Johnson, in 1958. Mr. Johnson learned about the hamburger broiler which Dave had recently built and was curious about it. His general manager for the Florida division was a tennis-playing friend of mine who asked if I would demonstrate the machine to the old man. I was encouraged to believe that if Mr. Johnson liked it, he might order a number of these machines for use in his existing restaurants. Since there were 800 Howard Johnson restaurants in operation, I thought this could be an important piece of business for us. I agreed to demonstrate the broiler and delivered it to the Howard Johnson commissary in Miami one Saturday morning in order to give Mr. Johnson the demonstration he had asked for.

I later discovered that he had no intention of equipping his existing restaurants with the broiler. He had another purpose. His real intention was to buy just one broiler and put it in a new restaurant concept he was about to launch. It was already under construction in Massachusetts. His design was a close copy of our Burger King operation. He was obviously planning to compete with us, using our service concept as a base. I thought it was entirely unethical of him to deal with us like this. He bought the broiler, used it in his new restaurant, but the restaurant failed and he closed it. I heard nothing more from him or the Howard Johnson people after that. I lost any respect I might have had for the man after that, thinking that he should have leveled with me as to his real intentions. I just thought of him as a tough old bird who was callous enough to do business like that.

I've come to learn that people like that have a hard time succeeding in life. Many years later, when I was the master of ceremonies at a large gathering of restaurateurs, I introduced

Mr. Johnson as a "Pioneer of the Year." By that time his company was in a free fall. His restaurants were no longer competitive with the new chains, which were far more attuned to the changing consumer market. He didn't look well. I believe he was ill at the time, and I felt saddened that his career was ending like that. He died a few years later.

I was fascinated by the history of the Howard Johnson restaurants. In 1925 when Mr. Johnson was 27 years old and working in his father's drug store in Quincy, Massachusetts, he developed a quality ice cream product. He opened a few small places featuring frankfurters, hamburgers, ice cream, and other popular items. By 1935 there were 25 Howard Johnson restaurants in Massachusetts, and by 1940 there were over 100 restaurants along the Atlantic Coast, all the way to Florida. During the post-war era the chain grew rapidly, and by the early 1960s there were over 400 units in operation. This ranked the Howard Johnson Company as one of the largest full-service restaurant chains in the country. According to *Institution Magazine* the company grew to over 800 units by 1967, which in their rankings placed Howard Johnson as the largest chain of its kind in the United States.

During the 1960s, lifestyles began to change rather fast and so did the eating preferences of the American people. It was obvious to me at the time that the Howard Johnson Company was having difficulty keeping up with all of this change. What had worked so well for them in the thirties, forties, and fifties, was no longer acceptable in a changing consumer market. Their management organization seemed totally oblivious to the fact. As business declined, their restaurants fell in varying degrees of disrepair. By 1966 I couldn't help but believe that this company was doomed to failure. I was reminded of the old expression, "The pack will run as fast as the lead dog." In my view the lead dog in this case wasn't up to the job. Within 15 years of my meeting with the younger Mr. Johnson on Park Avenue, his company had been sold, split up, and essentially put out of business. The British firm, Imperial Group PLC, bought the company in 1980 and with $700 million invested, sold it five years later to the Marriott

Corporation at the fire-sale price of $162 million and the assumption of $138 million in debt.

Efforts to salvage what was left of the company led to the conversion of many Howard Johnson restaurants into other franchises more acceptable to the American public than the outdated food-service relics with the orange roofs, which had once been so highly successful. Howard Johnson franchisees bailed out by the hundreds. Quite a few of their turnpike facilities were converted into Burger King restaurants. By 1985 we had witnessed a major restaurant chain's demise. It was happening because there was no leadership. For years this management never listened to anyone. They didn't have a clue about what was happening in the marketplace. I knew that because I knew a lot of their top managers and key executives. They never sought opinions or advice from anyone. The public could have told them all they needed to know. Their customers left in droves and took their business elsewhere. A once great company stumbled and fell, and this couldn't help but remind me again how vulnerable any successful business can be once it loses touch with consumers and the market it serves.

At the time of my last visit to Blyth and Company, I had been operating my own restaurants for over 19 years. Adding in my years of hospitality training at Cornell, my total food-service experience came to over 23 years. When I first visited Blyth, I was 39 years old, but I was no novice in the restaurant business. I was well informed about its history and the growth and development which had taken place over the years. It was this kind of knowledge, experience, and understanding that helped me focus on what was needed if we wanted to establish Burger King as one of the outstanding restaurant chains in the country. I had a good partner in Dave Edgerton, who was just as informed and knowledgeable as I was. We both felt that we could achieve our ambitious goals if we worked hard and followed certain basic operating fundamentals in running our business. We believed that adopting a corporate strategy which consistently recognized the preferences of the American public meant we had to succeed. With our energy, commitment, and faith in what we were doing, there was no way to fail.

When we were talking with Blyth, Burger King was at a critical time in its history. With 206 restaurants in operation in May of 1966, we were ranked as one of the largest restaurant chains in the country. The fledgling fast-food industry was still in its infancy, but very few chains could lay claim to having more restaurants in operation or to be expanding at a faster clip than we were. The question before us in 1966 concerned how we were going to finance the company. We needed to grow the business at a rate which would ensure and maintain our leadership position. We had a huge opportunity before us, but despite our impressive record of growth, earnings, and momentum, we were still lacking the capital we needed to expand our business like we knew we should. Staying in the lead was critically important.

Disappointed with our continuing discussions with Blyth and knowing that we would have to find another way to keep Burger King in its leadership position, I hailed a cab for La Guardia airport and headed home to Miami. There was a lot of work to do. If we were going to keep pace with the leaders and the thundering herd of newcomers who were right on our heels, we had to make some important decisions about corporate strategy, and we had to do that in a hurry. There wasn't any time to lose.

The Decision to Join Pillsbury

The Pillsbury Company contacted us on March 26, 1966. Prior to that they had retained the services of JMB Consultants of Chicago for the purpose of opening discussions with us about a possible merger. I didn't realize at the time that this was the by-product of my visit a few months earlier with the Booz Allen & Hamilton consultants.

I thought we had a pretty good record to show. In the fiscal year ended May 31, 1965, we reported earnings of $446,239 after-tax and showed a net worth of $1,056,612 according to our independent accountants and external auditors Peat, Marwick, Mitchell & Co. When we reported results for fiscal year 1966 a few months later, we showed an after-tax profit of $758,008 and a net worth which had increased to $1,789,620. The business was growing very rapidly by this time, and few companies in our field could match our consistent annual returns of 50 to 70 percent on equity.

Halfway through the fiscal year which ended in May of 1966, it became increasingly evident that McDonald's was growing much faster than we were. The gap was widening. They had real financial strength, a proven real estate development formula, and ready access to the financial markets. These were advantages that we did not have. With the tremendous momentum they had received from the success of their recent public offering, I didn't see how we could catch up to them unless we could strengthen our own financial position. It was my judgment that we had to do that and do it in a hurry. Even though we were lagging behind the leader in terms of size and earnings, we were still regarded as the number 2 company in the hamburger segment of the fast-food industry. Our challenge was to stay in that position by getting the capital we needed to expand the business. Our ability to develop real estate would be the key to our future success and that would require either a lot of new capital or a clever way to finance our property acquisitions. Throughout 1965 and 1966 we had been exploring our strategic options because we knew that we were sitting on top of an extraordinary opportunity.

On a personal basis many things concerned me in 1965, all of which would have a decided impact in determining the future direction of the company. The dream about Burger King becoming the premier restaurant chain in the United States was my main driving force. But it was clear that we lacked the financial tools necessary to get the job done. First, I was particularly discouraged after our disappointing initial talks with Blyth and Company. Second, there wasn't much comfort in the realization that I was unable to increase my equity position in Burger King. I had hoped to be able to purchase a larger interest in the company, but with that opportunity unavailable, I had to consider the alternatives. Third, and perhaps most important of all, this was the point in my life when I needed to cash in some chips and start to enjoy the fruits of my labors. In the calendar year 1965, my Burger King salary was $32,500. After taxes were taken out I had less than $27,500 to support my family. I had no other source of income nor did I have any other liquid assets.

Nancy was trying to run a decent household on my salary while I was trying to provide for Pam, aged 19, Lynne aged 17, Whit aged 13, and little Susie aged 11. It wasn't easy. These children needed clothes, money for college, and many other things that I couldn't provide. I was desperate enough to ask Harvey Fruehauf for a personal loan just to see us through. Looking back on it, this entire situation was just a bit crazy. Even though the company was making a substantial profit, I wasn't able to provide Nancy and the family with a decent living.

I'm sure that if I had asked the board to increase my salary, they would have done it. My reluctance to make such a request was more a matter of pride than anything else. I felt as Harvey did that our best strategy was to plow all our profits back into the business. I was a tight-fisted manager when it came to controlling costs. Dave, Harvey, and I were strongly motivated to build our corporate reputation by reporting an impressive record of steadily increasing earnings while focusing on adding to the net worth of the company. Our board of directors never thought twice about declaring dividends, and we never got to the point of paying out bonuses based on individual job performances. Our strategy was to concentrate on building the capital floor of the company and expanding the business as fast as we possibly could.

When the Pillsbury proposal to consider a merger was put before us, I was inclined to open discussions with them. I explained my position to Dave, who indicated that he was willing to consider the matter, even though at the time he did not appear overly enthusiastic about the idea. Dave was a close and valued friend, associate, and confidant. He was always supportive of me and my family throughout our long-standing relationship. He was willing to go along with my wishes, even though I'm sure that he preferred to see the company remain independent. Dave was considerate enough to understand that I had a wife and four children to support. With expenses for college coming up, I just couldn't make it on my present income. I told Dave that I thought we could negotiate a satisfactory selling price and that my personal situation was heavily influencing my preference for selling the company. Dave told me that he was willing to look over the Pillsbury proposal.

We took the idea to Harvey who seemed less enthusiastic about it, but he sensed that it was Dave's and my desire to take a serious look at it and never strongly objected. I believe he would have preferred to go along as we were, tough it out and remain independent, but neither he nor his son Bud (Harvey, Jr.) ever suggested that we reject Pillsbury's overture.

Our discussions with Blyth and Company, which began in the early months of 1965, produced nothing tangible. We were told that a public offering was not in the cards. Throughout 1965 I kept in touch with Ed Glassmeyer of Blyth trying to work out some sort of a plan to finance Burger King's growth. In March of 1966 he proposed a stock purchase plan with a repurchase agreement. This had a significant "kicker" included for Blyth which none of us liked at all. After I reviewed the plan with our board of directors, we rejected the idea.

We tried everything else we could think of to beef up our finances. Bob McDonald, who was executive vice president of The First National Bank of Miami, supported us by increasing our revolving line of credit, and he tried without success to help us secure better arrangements for long-term financing, which we desperately needed to expand the business. If there were any creative financing schemes that might have been available, we were unable to come up with them.

During a trip to New York I called on Walter Dennis, an executive vice president of The Chase Manhattan Bank. I had met Walter at Harvey Fruehauf's ranch in Texas, when Harvey asked me to spend a few days with him so I could meet the directors of Georgia Pacific Corporation. They were having a board meeting in nearby Fort Worth. Harvey had invited the directors to a barbecue dinner at his ranch. This gave me the opportunity to meet and talk to a number of them including Mr. Dennis, who seemed quite interested in my story about Burger King. After several meetings with Walter in New York City, the disappointing news was that he couldn't come up with an acceptable financing plan. We kept on trying, but nothing seemed to work.

In the next few months I met with key executives of leading financial firms in New York City, including Stone and Webster, Eastman Dillon–Union Securities, Francis I. DuPont, Carl M. Loeb Rhodes, Irving Trust, John Hancock Life, and Mass Mutual. On one occasion I talked with the president of John Hancock about their becoming a financial backer. After looking at our situation, they offered to consider a loan, but they asked for a big percentage of our stock as a bonus for making it. I told them that we were not interested in that. It reminded me of the expensive financing arrangement that McDonald's was forced to accept during their earlier years. McDonald's recent public offering and its phenomenal

THE DECISION TO JOIN PILLSBURY

success increased the pressure to come up with some creative financing, but the year 1965 ended with nothing in sight. We had a growing demand for our franchises, but we lacked the ability to finance our expansion as rapidly as we wanted to.

In 1966 Kentucky Fried Chicken became a public company and immediately following that, our major competitor in Miami, Royal Castle, went public. The pressure continued to mount. On February 2, 1966, Harvey and I met again with Blyth and Company to discuss the possibility of going public. On February 4 I had a long talk with Harvey about our already high debt to equity ratio and the need to obtain additional working capital. We were constantly dealing with questions related to financing the growth of our business.

On March 26 I received a call from Jim Moore, who identified himself as president of JMB Consultants in Chicago. He said that The Pillsbury Company was interested in talking to us about the possibility of a merger and asked if I would be willing to meet and discuss the matter. I agreed and we met for lunch on March 30 along with Ted Judge, a Pillsbury vice president, who was then head of their mergers and acquisition department. During the luncheon I learned that Pillsbury's interest in Burger King had been aroused by reports they had received from the consultants from Booz Allen & Hamilton, who had interviewed me earlier.

I gave Judge a general overview of Burger King—our history and recent growth, together with a general assessment of the company's growth opportunity as we saw it. I asked him to fill me in on Pillsbury, and he provided some pertinent information in that regard. He asked what I thought Burger King might be worth. I told him that we had used $20 million as a value in contemplating a public offering, and I thought that this was a figure that our board might be willing to discuss. I based this on 20 times the after-tax earnings we expected to make in our next fiscal year. The meeting produced nothing conclusive, but both of us had enough to think over. I needed time to inform our board about these discussions, and I asked Judge to provide me with some information about Pillsbury to pass on to our directors.

On April 1, two days after the meeting with Judge and Moore, the Burger King board met for a meeting that had been scheduled well in advance. I informed the board about the interest that Pillsbury had expressed and about my discussion a few days earlier with Moore and Judge. I also presented a proposal from Blyth and Company suggesting that we revisit the idea of considering a public offering of our stock. The board decided that for the moment at least, we would delay any further discussions with Blyth. I waited a few weeks before informing Glassmeyer of this decision.

During the next two weeks we continued to meet with commercial bankers and investment bankers hoping to come up with a workable financing plan. On April 14, I informed Glassmeyer of our decision not to go public. The following day we received a $1.5 million long-term loan commitment from Mass Mutual. This was our first Burger King real estate financing package using straight debt, which became the format of many future financing arrangements. However, as far as our overall financial needs were concerned, this package fell far short of what we were looking for. By mid-April we were negotiating to acquire or enter into lease-back arrangements on 76 store sites in different cities all over the country. Most of these deals involved developers who built our units to specification and then leased the property directly to us. In these situations we could sublease the restaurant directly to our franchisees. Little or no cash was required under this kind of arrangement, so for a while we were able to continue our growth on this basis. What we were missing, of course, was a bigger infusion of capital and the opportunity to own and develop real estate for our own account.

A call from JMB Consultants on April 30 advised us that Pillsbury was having some difficulty putting a proposal together. We heard from them only occasionally during the summer months which followed. I put the matter in the back of my mind because we had other important matters to consider. At the time we were busy firming up a number of real estate financing packages with several large life insurance companies.

Pillsbury's interest heightened again in late August of 1966. I went to Minneapolis on August 24 with our chief financial officer, H. Glenn Jones, and met for dinner with Pillsbury's Ted Judge and Walter Gregory, the JMB representative assigned to the negotiations. On the 25th and 26th we met with Pillsbury executives and toured some of their facilities. Discussions with the top executives of Pillsbury were interesting and focused on the subject of a possible merger.

On September 7, Walter Gregory called me from his Chicago office to ask if Paul Gerot, Pillsbury's chairman and CEO, Terry Hanold, their chief financial officer, and Ted Judge could meet with our board of directors in Detroit at a meeting we had scheduled for September 15. This was acceptable, and the meeting took place in Harvey's office in the Guardian Building at 10 o'clock that morning. They came to propose a merger consisting of a package of Pillsbury common and preferred stock. We looked it over, asked a few questions, and agreed to meet again within two weeks, after we had an opportunity to consider their proposal in more detail.

On September 28 Dave and I flew to Minneapolis with our general counsel and board member, Tom Wakefield. We met Harvey and Bud Fruehauf, both of whom had flown in from Detroit. The five of us discussed the Pillsbury proposal before and during dinner. The following day, after a long meeting with Pillsbury management, we worked out a tentative understanding and ended the day with dinner at the Minnekada Club hosted by Pillsbury president, Bob Keith, and Paul Gerot. After a brief wrap-up conference the following morning, we flew back to Miami, and the Fruehauf's returned to Detroit. There was one thing missing. Gerot had made it clear that unless Pillsbury owned the Burger King trademarks we had no deal.

The 1961 contract with Ben Stein gave us worldwide rights to develop Burger King. In that contract we obtained the exclusive use of the trade names, service marks, and trademarks and assumed the responsibility to police and protect them. The only consideration we offered to Mr. Stein was the monthly payment of 15 percent of any royalties we collected.

By 1963, royalties were coming to Miami in ever-increasing amounts. At the time we signed our contract with Mr. Stein, I instructed our bookkeeper to write a check every month for his 15 percent share and to provide a record of the restaurants which had paid the royalties. We kept him totally informed about our new store openings. This enabled him to develop a greater sense of the future income he might expect to receive. I'm sure that he could see that something of considerable financial significance was taking place. Each month our check to him was larger and larger.

Of course we could see what was happening, too! I knew that someday we were going to pay Ben Stein a huge sum of money to buy him out. I remember giving him a call during the summer of 1962 saying, "Ben, I'd like to buy out that national development contract. What will it cost me?" Obviously, he had anticipated my call and responded without hesitation: "Jim, I'm willing to sell it to you for $100,000." Of course, that was only a year into our contract.

In 1962 such a payment on our part was completely out of the question. I didn't even take time to consider his offer. I doubt that I could have raised $10,000 at that point. My only response was "Ben, I don't believe there is any possibility of our raising $100,000, but I'd like to think it over and get back to you at a later date." He said that would be fine and that he was pleased to see the progress we were making. We had enjoyed a very good personal and business relationship over the years based on mutual respect and the fact that our business arrangement was meeting all of our expectations. We always looked forward to our conversations and occasional visits. I figured I'd get back to him later as soon as I could raise the money.

Things continued to go well, in fact they were going extraordinarily well. Our franchisees were expanding, everyone of them operating successfully, and we had a backlog of franchise demand. Royalties were coming in at a rapidly increasing rate, and our future outlook was most encouraging. Profits were also coming in at a good clip, and we were plowing them back into the business. Things were quite rosy. With increased profits coming in, we were generating enough cash flow from operations to keep our modest rate of expansion alive.

About six months later, when I thought I could come up with $100,000, I called Ben and said, "About our conversation a few months ago, I've been able to come up with the $100,000 you mentioned. I'd like to go ahead with a buyout of our contract." His response was as quick as it always was. He just said "Jim, I've been giving that some additional thought. You boys are doing a fine job of building your business, and I think you are going to do much better in the future. Your royalties will increase substantially and so will my share. I think that the value of my interest is worth $300,000 today, and it will probably be worth much more later. I'm prepared to deal with you on the basis of $300,000. Why don't you think it over and let me know what you want to do." This was as much out of the question as $100,000 was the first time we talked. Ben always kept a giant step in front of me, and I came to expect that he would probably stay in that position. I doubted that I could ever catch up, so I decided to let the matter stand. We would grow the business, pay out the 15 percent every month, and let it go at that. Without obtaining the financing we needed so badly, I didn't see any other alternative.

When negotiations with Pillsbury were under way during the latter part of 1966 and early 1967, we were paying Ben a substantial sum of money every month and it was still growing. Pillsbury could see that if the business grew anywhere near my projections that we would be paying Ben Stein a king's ransom every year. Then there was the matter of the trademarks themselves. Pillsbury Chairman Paul Gerot called me and said, "Jim, we must have ownership of the Burger King trademarks. This acquisition won't work without them. Would you try to obtain them for us?" I said, "Sure, Paul—I'll just put the matter directly to Mr. Stein and get back to you. I'm sure he won't stand in the way of the acquisition, but I expect his price will be high."

I called Ben and told him what was taking place, noting that Pillsbury had offered to acquire our company, but conditioned upon acquiring the trademarks and canceling our contractual royalty-sharing agreement. I asked him to give Pillsbury and me a price. He didn't need much time to think about that. He simply said, "Jim, I believe it is worth $2.5 million today, and I would be willing to sell it for that." I just said, "Let me present that to the Pillsbury people," and hung up. I called Gerot, who agreed to pay it. The contracts were drawn up and the closing was set at the same time as our own.

In addition to the $2.5 million Pillsbury agreed to pay, Ben Stein asked for an extra $50,000 for his attorney's fees. Pillsbury agreed to do this too, thereby resolving the trademark-royalty issue that could have prevented the merger from taking place.

I was disappointed and a little annoyed when Stein reneged on the original deal and extracted the extra $50,000. It made no financial difference to Dave, Harvey, or me because the terms of our deal were agreed upon and understood by all parties. What bothered me was that Ben had changed his deal with Pillsbury at the last minute. I wasn't used to doing business that way.

I thought Pillsbury was getting jerked around on this, and I told Ben that I was upset about it. Aside from allowing me to vent a bit of anger, my strong objection counted for very little. Ben would receive a check for $2,550,000 when the closing took place, and if Pillsbury or Paul Gerot were upset about the extra $50,000, they never mentioned it to me. I was glad to see the matter resolved, and I soon forgot the whole episode.

Was our acquisition of Ben Stein's contract a good one? Perhaps the answer lies in the fact that by 1996, Burger King's systemwide sales were over $8 billion annually and royalty income would have been calculated at a rate approximating $240 million a year. If the contract and the 15 percent clause had been in effect at that time, Ben Stein's Jacksonville company would have been receiving over $35 million a year. Of course it is doubtful that the agreement would have stayed in place that long before a settlement of some kind was arranged.

Meanwhile our office in Miami was busy accommodating Pillsbury's accountants and lawyers who were engaged in a due-diligence process in an effort to verify all that we had represented to them.

On October 20 Nancy and I hosted a dinner party at our home in Miami to introduce Paul Gerot and Bob Keith to members of our management team and their spouses. Paul and Bob left the next morning in their company plane to visit and talk with several of our franchisees, including Harold Jeske and Pat Ryan in Chicago, Jimmy and Billy Trotter in New Orleans, and Earl Brown in North Carolina. I tagged along with my golf clubs in tow and got off in Winston-Salem, where Earl and I enjoyed three days of golf at Pinehurst.

Gerot and Hanold returned to Miami on October 27 with the Pillsbury corporate secretary, Bob Hauer, to discuss remaining problems and reach final accord on a merger agreement. Harvey, Dave, and I finished our discussions with Gerot and Hanold and resolved all the major issues that were raised. We concluded our meeting with a luncheon at the Riviera Country Club in Coral Gables.

Gerot presented his recommendation to the Pillsbury board on November 1. On November 2 I received two calls—one from Gerot who advised that his board had considered the matter and would meet again one week later to make a final decision. The other call was from Harvey Fruehauf, who said he thought we made a poor deal with Pillsbury. Harvey seemed to be quite upset about the proposed merger. I was disappointed that at this late date he felt that way.

The following day I met with Ben Stein and his lawyers from 9 a.m. until 2:30 p.m. He agreed to give us an option to close on the $2,550,000 trademark-licensing acquisition until May 31, 1967. The option cost us $5000.

The next day Harvey and I met and resolved his concerns; I advised Gerot that we were all in accord. The Pillsbury board met the following week and approved the merger arrangement except for certain terms involving the Pillsbury preferred stock. I talked with Harvey in Texas a few days later, and he agreed to the changes that Gerot had proposed.

I flew to Dallas on November 20. Harvey met me at Love Field with his Lockheed Lodestar, and we flew out to his ranch near Stephensville. He was in great spirits and seemed quite pleased to see me. He had a bar all set up inside his plane, and even as we were heading down the runway for take-off, Harvey was standing up at the bar making me a martini, much to the pilot's dismay! We had a pleasant afternoon and evening at the ranch, reviewing details of the deal and discussing our next moves. I left the ranch at 9 the following morning and was in Chicago at 1 p.m., meeting with our Midwest Division licensees and management.

Harvey returned to Miami and met with Paul Gerot, Dave, and me on November 29. It was an all-day conference in our new offices. We had moved into a new two-story office building which we had recently constructed at 7100 North Kendall Drive, having outgrown the office complex located in the rear of our Coral Way store 7 which had served us so well since 1957.

Gerot encountered problems with his Pillsbury board over the terms of the Burger King acquisition he had proposed. The merger proposal was troublesome to a number of the Pillsbury directors because they believed the price being paid for Burger King was too high. The Pillsbury Company was originally one of the largest flour millers in the country. Only in recent years had they gone into the business of producing and marketing consumer food products. This was due in large part to Gerot's initiatives and leadership in moving Pillsbury out of the basic commodity business (grain and flour) and into a potentially more profitable business. By the 1960s Pillsbury had become an important distributor of branded food products in the nation's grocery stores. The company's profit history, although growing at the time, was not very impressive.

Pillsbury's net profit in 1966 was barely at the level of $11 million. With 4,399,678 shares of Pillsbury common stock outstanding and selling on the New York Stock Exchange at $35 per share, the market capitalization of The Pillsbury Company was only $150 million.

To meet our asking price of $20 million, Pillsbury proposed issuing 400,000 shares of common stock and a convertible preferred issue worth approximately $5 million. We agreed to this formula, the effect of which would result in the Burger King stockholders' owning approximately 10 percent of The Pillsbury Company. This presented some difficulty for some of the Pillsbury directors, few of whom knew much, if anything, about the restaurant business other than the fact that it was a risky business with a reputation of having a high failure rate. Another difficulty lay in the numbers and the fact that The Pillsbury Company would be getting into a business which they knew nothing about.

There was a feeling that by departing from their basic business they could end up with a disaster on their hands. What if Burger King didn't produce? Gerot had his hands full. His proposal to issue almost $20 million of Pillsbury stock to acquire Burger King Corporation, a company with a tangible net worth of only $1.7 million and earnings of only $758,000 in fiscal 1966 seemed to a number of directors a very high price to pay.

As Paul Gerot explained to me later, he was seriously challenged by his board. "You are paying far too much for management," they argued. To which he replied, "Without this management I wouldn't want this acquisition at any price." Finally the board agreed to the proposed merger, asking for certain minor changes which were acceptable to us.

Afterwards Gerot flew to Miami to propose a definitive agreement. Harvey, Dave, and I worked with him in preparing a final understanding and turned the matter over to our attorneys, the New York firm of Shearman and Sterling, with instructions to prepare and approve the appropriate documents. On January 19, 1967, Gerot and I made a joint announcement stating our intentions to merge the two companies, and I notified everyone in the Burger King family about our decision.

From the time of the announcement of our intent to join The Pillsbury Company until June 21, 1967, when the merger was scheduled to take place, we were kept busy with lawyers and accountants hammering out details based on the agreement we had reached with Pillsbury management. This involved a considerable amount of traveling between Miami,

New York, and Minneapolis. The contract with Ben Stein to transfer the Burger King name and trademarks to Pillsbury was completed and finally our own contract relating to the merger was drawn, agreed to, and signed. The closing took place as scheduled on June 21.

I met Nancy and our four children at the Minneapolis airport on the day after the merger took place. I wanted them to feel that the family was a part of that special occasion. The children had grown up knowing Burger King was "Uncle Dave's and Daddy's company."

We took a cab from the airport into town so that I could introduce the family to members of the Pillsbury management group and show them some of their office facilities. This experience was an adventure for me and for the family. It was understood that I would be elected to the Pillsbury board of directors at their annual meeting of stockholders, which would take place in September. I would join the Pillsbury management team immediately and stay on as Burger King Corporation's president and chief executive officer.

Another reason for bringing the family to Minneapolis was a planned family vacation. After leaving the Pillsbury offices we went back to the airport and flew to Winnipeg, Canada, where we boarded a Canadian National train bound for Jasper in the Canadian Rockies. The train trip was another special event for the six of us. We had berths in a Pullman sleeping car and enjoyed a pleasant evening meal together as the train sped westward through the wheat fields and towns of Manitoba and Saskatchewan. Breakfast and lunch the next day in the dining car was also fun. Looking out the window of the train at the passing scenery conjured up thoughts of the exciting vacation trip we were going to enjoy together. The children had only been on an overnight train once before, on our first western vacation trip taken the year before.

On arrival in Jasper the next afternoon, we rented a station wagon which had been reserved. During the next five days we toured the magnificent mountain areas of the Canadian Rockies with their roaring streams, waterfalls, beautiful lakes, snow fields, and glaciers. Staying at elegant resort hotels such

The Remarkable Story Of

"INSTA-BURGER-KING"

Self-Serve Drive-Ins
WITH THE

MIRACLE **MACHINES**

A NATIONAL FRANCHISE CHAIN

Manufacturers and National Licensors
THE INSTA CO.

6777 HOLLYWOOD BOULEVARD, HOLLYWOOD 28, CALIFORNIA

FACTS ABOUT THE "INSTA" MACHINES

Insta-Burger Stove

1. It is not a stove — It is an automatic, multi-purpose machine.

2. It automatically unloads the cooked meat and the toasted buns.

3. It can cook at the rate of 400 burgers per hour — or only one at a time if preferred — and can be operated by inexperienced persons.

4. It cooks by radiant heat, and produces uniform burgers that are juicy and do not shrink.

5. It sears the meat on both sides simultaneously to retain the juices.

6. It needs only one electrical connection — a 115-230 volt, single phase, 40 amp. line. It is about 3½ ft. long, 2 ft. high, and only 15 inches deep, and weighs 225 lbs. The heating elements are General Electric Calrods, made to operate for 10,000 hours, and replaceable in 5 minutes.

Insta-Shake Machine

1. It is not a "mixer" — It is a manufacturer of milk shakes — and makes them straight from liquid dairy mix to fresh-whipped finished shake in one operation — in 4 flavors.

2. The machine is complete within itself — No extra flavor pumps are needed — There is no additional whipping with an outside mixer — The fresh-whipped, flavored, finished Shakes are delivered direct from the machine.

3. All Shakes come out at the same exact desired temperature — whether served at full speed or only one Shake at long intervals.

4. The machine capacity is so large that only one machine is needed whether only a few, or thousands, of Shakes are served daily. Refrigerated Reservoirs hold 14 gallons.

5. The Insta-Shake Machine is the only machine in the world that has an open-at-both-ends empty freezing cylinder and high-speed Beater — patented exclusive method of freeze.

6. Size, with cabinet and compressor, is about 4 ft. wide, 2½ ft. deep, and 6½ ft. high. It needs only one electrical connection — a 230 volt, single phase, 15 amp. line. It weighs about 1100 lbs. Aside from the refrigeration machinery and the beater motor there is only one moving part in the machine — the high-speed Beater.

Both Machines

Both machines have been thoroughly perfected — are of foolproof design — can be easily operated even by a moron — and have been operating successfully for years.

Service

1. No special service is needed. - The Insta-Burger Stove cannot stop operating except by the unlikely failure of its triple-sized General Electric motor, or its Speed Reducer which is under no strain, or its General Electric Calrods which are made to operate for 10,000 hours. — The Insta-Shake Machine cannot stop except by the unlikely failure of its double-size motor, or its oversize Copeland Refrigeration Unit.

2. In case of any failures, service is available by the neighborhood representatives of these large National companies — and there are no other parts in either machine that require service.

INSTA-BURGER-KING — THE GREATEST ADVANCE IN 50 YEARS IN FOOD SERVING!

An early ad promoting Insta Burger King (the precursor to Burger King) and the Insta machines originally used to make the hamburgers and milk shakes sold at the restaurants. The temperamental Insta broiler was replaced early on by a more efficient machine designed by Burger King cofounder Dave Edgerton, which is to this day a model for restaurant equipment of this type.

The Burger King restaurants, the first of which opened in Miami, Florida, in 1954, were a novel concept in food service. Distinguishing themselves from the carhop operations prevalent at the time, these restaurants were self-service drive-ins.

A true Miami invention—outdoor seating only. The early Burger King restaurants had uncovered patio areas for customers, but most patrons preferred to eat in their cars.

A new design for the Burger King restaurants. The slogan "Home of the Whopper" was added in 1957 to show that this new product was now a specialty of the house. The Whopper was a stunning success from the moment it was introduced.

Wherever you travel—Nationwide...

An ad appealing to the vacationing family, promoting Burger King nationwide. In 1961 McLamore and his partner Dave Edgerton began developing the Burger King franchise outside of Florida.

The opening of the 500th Burger King nationwide in Omaha, Nebraska, June 1969. McLamore (right) celebrates with the franchisees.

Jim McLamore (left) and Dave Edgerton, cofounders of Burger King, next to an airplane owned by Harvey Freuhauf, a valued business associate and a friend of Jim McLamore.

McLamore alongside one of the trucks in Burger King's Distron commissary subsidiary, which became a model for modern-day distribution systems to chain restaurants.

McLamore in Japan, 1969. Despite repeated tries, he was unable to interest Pillsbury in establishing Burger King franchises in Japan. McDonald's jumped in shortly after, and Japan is now its largest international market.

Don Shula (left), coach of the Miami Dolphins, next to Jim McLamore; Joe Robbie (right), manager of the Dolphins. McLamore was a part owner of the Miami Dolphins, which was a losing team in 1969 when he made his initial investment in an effort to keep the team in Miami.

Although he retired as CEO of Burger King in 1972, McLamore, who died in 1996, continued his involvement with the Burger King Corporation as chairman of its board of directors and as a director of The Pillsbury Company, which then owned Burger King. After Grand Metropolitan acquired Pillsbury in 1989, he continued to counsel and to promote the basic principles on which the success of Burger King was built: quality, cleanliness, and speed.

Almost a million Whoppers sold in one day! McLamore standing next to the display in September 1993.

An illustrious gathering of entrepreneurs in May 1979. (Left to right) Patrick O'Malley, chairman, Canteen Corp.; Barron Hilton, chairman, Hilton Hotels Corp.; J. Willard Marriott, founder, Marriott Corp.; Col. Harland Sanders, founder of Kentucky Fried Chicken; James W. McLamore, cofounder of Burger King Corporation; Kemmons Wilson, cofounder, Holiday Inns.

Jim and Nancy McLamore with Jerry Ruenheck (right), president of Burger King USA, his wife Karen, Lou Neeb (second from left), chairman and CEO of Burger King, and his wife Jean at the Vizcaya Ball, Miami, 1980.

McLamore and his wife Nancy in 1994. He recognized his wife as "an extraordinarily special woman," who maintained a cheerful household and raised their children while he worked 12-hour days, 7 days a week.

The McLamore clan in 1995.

as Banff Springs and Chateau Lake Louise added to our enjoyment, as did the golf outings at Banff and Jasper. Afterwards we drove to Canada's Waterton Lakes National Park, where we stayed at the Prince of Wales Hotel. Everywhere we looked we enjoyed spectacular vistas and scenery. We crossed the border into Montana's spectacular Glacier National Park, staying at the rustic MacDonald Lodge. Huge snowdrifts along the "Going to the Sun Highway" were something to marvel at in early July.

Driving to Great Falls, Montana, we dropped off the station wagon and flew to Casper, Wyoming, where we rented another vehicle for the drive to the Old Baldy Club in Saratoga. This was only our second visit to Old Baldy—an experience that was to become an annual occurrence for Nancy and me, a frequent occurrence for the children, and in more recent years, for the grandchildren as well. After a pleasant week at the club, we made the drive to Denver and the flight home.

I needed that vacation. For years I had been spending over a third of my time away from home on Burger King business looking for locations, working on leases and financing, and meeting with franchisees. The negotiations with Pillsbury and the more recent meetings with Pillsbury management added to the demands on my time. It was wonderful to have the opportunity to spend a few weeks with the family, and I returned rested and enthusiastic about beginning my association with Pillsbury. In particular I was excited about the support I expected to receive from Pillsbury. This, I believed, would be of significant help in the future development of Burger King.

I returned to Miami challenged about my new role as a member of the Pillsbury management team and as a director of the company. My personal situation after the merger took on a totally new dimension.

My salary was increased to $67,500 per year from the $32,500 salary I had been receiving prior to the merger. On top of that I was informed that I could expect to receive a bonus in the event Burger King met certain performance objectives. I had never received any income from dividends before because I never had any money to invest in the stock market. The Pillsbury stock I had received at our closing would pay me over $90,000 annually in dividends starting immediately, and there was the likelihood that dividends might be increased in the future. I anticipated that the value of my Pillsbury shares would increase over the years. This was based on my expectancy that Burger King would boost Pillsbury's earnings which, in turn, should have a positive effect on the price of their stock. All of this added personal income was of considerable help in relieving the financial strain I had been under. I had the additional comfort of knowing that I could find a ready market for my Pillsbury stock in the event a financial emergency arose.

Pam had gone off to Florida State University in 1966, and Lynne was preparing to enter Miami University in Oxford, Ohio, in 1968. As far as my own personal financial situation was concerned, I was pretty much relieved of any further financial worries, and I was ready to focus all my attention on running the business. It was very important to me that I do a good job as a member of the Pillsbury management team. I had a lot to prove to a lot of people, and most of all I wanted to prove to the Pillsbury board, Paul Gerot, and the Pillsbury officers that they had made a very good investment decision in acquiring Burger King. At 41 years of age I felt very good about myself and confident and excited about the future both from the standpoint of my personal situation and the prospects for the rapid growth and development of Burger King.

Looking back on our deal to merge with Pillsbury, I believe that Dave Edgerton and Harvey Fruehauf were absolutely correct in their assessment of the matter. Both of my partners believed that we should have remained an independent company. Although they agreed that we needed to fortify our financial position, they would have preferred that we do it on our own. I preferred to sell out for reasons that were perhaps a bit too self-centered. I don't believe I acted too intelligently in assessing our entire situation at the time. Perhaps we could have explored a number of financial alternatives which would have kept our many financial options open and improved our personal stake in the business. The reality was that Burger King was destined to become a major player in an industry that was ripe with opportunity. The three of us knew that, and we knew that it would take some inept management to throw the company off track. Our system and our formula for doing business was too good and too strong to have that happen. Harvey and Dave were right and I was wrong about responding to the first buyout offer that came around. Here again was a decision I made before carefully thinking it through. I was driven by the immediacy of my personal and professional financial goals and aspirations. I had not exercised enough good judgment in considering all the aspects of the matter. I had been in business for myself for 20 years, and I still hadn't learned to reflect and consider before jumping into situations like this. As we approach the year 2000, Burger King Corporation's value falls within a range of $1 to $2 billion. It is the second largest full-scale restaurant chain in existence. This is a tribute to a lot of people and organizations which helped to create this value over many years. One can only speculate about the results of a different strategy.

Pillsbury—
Coming Aboard

In negotiating with Pillsbury I made it a condition that Burger King was to be treated and operated as an autonomous subsidiary. On June 26, just five days after the merger took place, Bob Keith wrote a policy statement, which to some extent served to reinforce this understanding. In it he said, "We have concluded that Burger King will operate in an autonomous fashion, and the conduct of Pillsbury people must be such that there will be no evidence of invasion or no evidence of takeover." Keith went on to say he felt that within Pillsbury were capabilities which in time would be of value to the growth and development of Burger King, but that "*at least during the first year of operation*," it would be my prerogative to use these resources or not.

I viewed that as a reasonable statement, and to some extent reassuring, but I knew what it really meant was that the honeymoon was over. Things were going to be run a bit differently. I expected that Pillsbury would take a more active role in determining the strategic direction of the company and jump in on a number of operating and tactical decisions as well. Unfortunately, that is precisely the way things were going to work out. Burger King's entrepreneurial, hands-on, and seat-of-the-pants style of management was going to be challenged.

Pillsbury's Annual Meeting of Stockholders took place on September 12, 1967, and I was asked to present the Burger King story. I explained our strategy for expanding the business and speculated about our great growth potential. Paul Gerot retired from Pillsbury management as of that meeting and was recognized for the leadership he had provided during his 38 years of service with the company. I made remarks to the effect that it was Gerot who had been the key engineer of the Burger King acquisition. I acknowledged that it was our high regard for him and the representations he made which had convinced us to join the Pillsbury Company. I was genuinely sorry to see him step down.

I did not attend the September meeting of the Pillsbury board. I would be elected at the shareholders' meeting which was scheduled to follow. Robert J. Keith was elected chairman and chief executive officer. Terrance C. Hanold was elected president and chief financial officer. Keith had made Hanold's election as president a condition of his moving up to chairman. I was later to understand that this ultimatum did not sit well with the board. A number of directors felt that Hanold might not be the right person to serve as president. I didn't know anything about that at the time, but my problems with Hanold were to surface almost immediately.

My first meeting as a member of the Pillsbury board of directors was in November. Bob Keith asked me to make some comments about Burger King, and I used the occasion to give reassurance to the board that they had made a wise decision regarding the acquisition. I gave them a little history of the company and reviewed the progress we had made in recent years. It was hard to hide my enthusiasm about the great potential of the growing fast-food industry and Burger King Corporation's leadership and participation within it. Knowing that several members of the board had felt that Pillsbury might have paid too much for Burger King, I made a particular point of expressing the belief that within a relatively short period of time Burger King would become the main driving force and profit contributor to the company. Although I was sincere and quite serious about that, I felt that I might have been more professional and less exuberant in expressing myself. As it turned out, my comments proved to be very prophetic and a highly accurate prediction of things to come.

I asked the chairman to permit me to make a presentation to the January 1968 meeting of the Board. I wrote a letter on December 19 outlining the proposal I wanted to make. It contained the suggestion that we create a public offering of Burger King stock within the near future. I intended to base my remarks on the fact that McDonald's and Kentucky Fried Chicken had recently become public companies and were currently selling at extraordinarily high price-earnings multiples. McDonald's was currently selling at 40 times earnings and Kentucky Fried Chicken was at 54 times earnings. They were able to buy in franchisees by offering very high prices for these businesses. The "currency" they were using was their own highly valued stock. Common stock selling at such high multiples was often referred to in financial circles as being "Chinese money." It was an ideal way to raise the funds needed to expand the business. I told Bob Keith that I expected that Burger King's after-tax earnings in our next fiscal year would exceed $2.5 million and could grow easily to $5 million within a few more years. Burger King, as a public company, selling on the basis of 30 times earnings would have a minimum market capitalization of $75 million; at 40 times earnings it might be valued as high as $100 million. Assuming that our earnings were to grow up to $5 million, the company could easily be worth between $125 and $200 million, which would represent a substantial premium over the $20 million of stock they had just issued to acquire the company in June. My thought was that this would create a huge profit opportunity for Pillsbury while helping Burger King grow much more rapidly. I was driven to suggest this strategy because, after only six months as a subsidiary operation, I was already beginning to question Pillsbury's ability and its resolve to support the rapid expansion and real estate development strategy we wished to follow.

Burger King franchisees were well aware of the high prices investors were paying for restaurant stocks at the time. I believed that many of them would be interested in selling their business back to Burger King, particularly if it was a public corporation. Most franchisees wanted to stay in the system and continue to grow within it. For these franchisees it would be reassuring to know that there would always be a market for their businesses. The chairman seemed enthused with the idea and put me on the agenda for the January 3 meeting.

When I addressed the board that morning, I called attention to recent acquisitions of major restaurant chains by large corporations—most of which were consumer food-product companies like Pillsbury. The list was impressive, and it helped create an awareness about the growth potential in the food-service industry. Specifically, I called the directors' attention to the following consolidations, mergers, and acquisitions which had recently taken place:

United Fruit owned A & W Root Beer, with 2520 outlets

Marriott owned Big Boy Restaurants, which 557 outlets

Consolidated Foods owned Chicken Delight, with 1578 outlets

Beech Nut Foods owned Dobbs House, with 455 outlets

Greyhound Corporation owned Polly Davis Cafeterias and Hornes Roadside Shoppes

Servamation owned Red Barn Restaurants, with numerous outlets in a number of states, mostly in the East

Litton Industries owned Stouffers Restaurants with 104 full-service restaurants

R.J. Reynolds Tobacco owned Chun King Foods

Pillsbury owned Burger King Corporation, then with 315 restaurants

Ogden owned ABC Consolidated

General Foods owned Burger Chef, with 610 restaurants

Pet Foods owned Schrafft's Restaurants, with 180 outlets

Ralston Purina owned Jack-in-the-Box Restaurants, with 250 drive-in operations, mostly out West

Borden owned Burger Boy and had recently announced plans for adding a number of new units.

The entire away-from-home eating markets, which was less than $10 billion when I opened my first restaurant in 1949, was only $23 billion in 1966, and the fast-food portion of that market was barely $3.5 billion. By 1996 Burger King alone would boast of systemwide sales of over $8 billion, and the industry itself would have grown to over $225 billion! The real opportunity years for the restaurant industry were still in front of us in 1967, so it was understandably difficult for people to think in terms of this being the right time to jump in with both feet in an industry that had yet to prove its real potential.

I believed the concept of Burger King becoming a public company was a workable idea which offered a huge potential for Pillsbury. I also thought that it would be very good for Burger King, its employees, and its family of franchisees. Most important, I thought it would be an excellent way to expand the business. My six months as a member of the Pillsbury management team convinced me that Pillsbury was going to be timid and a bit reluctant to follow McDonald's aggressive lead in developing a growing portfolio of restaurant properties. I felt that if my proposal was adopted, Pillsbury would feel much more comfortable about Burger King's acting as a par- tially owned, but still independent company. They would hold a significant interest, but not obligation to pursue a highly leveraged approach to financing growth.

The board listened to my presentation with interest and asked some good questions. However, there was no further development of the idea by management, and the matter was ultimately dropped.

I learned an important lesson about corporate procedure: It wasn't advisable for an inside director to bring his own agenda directly to the board of directors. This was a job for management. It was their prerogative, it was their turf, and it was their responsibility. I had short-circuited the system by not knowing that this was prohibited procedure. Being unfa- miliar with this new world of corporate procedure and being the new kid on the block, I should have had more sense than to make such a grandstand play. One thing I did learn in making the presentation was that it was becoming apparent that the strategy involving Burger King's future growth had already been determined. Pillsbury would use conventional methods to finance Burger King's growth, and the pace of development would be much less aggressive than I had hoped it would be.

Pillsbury invested several millions of dollars in additional Burger King equity, and they approved our borrowings up to maximum levels. Regrettably these conventional financing arrangements placed limits and restrictions on our future borrowing ability. This, in turn, dictated that in the future we would need to conform to standard debt-equity ratios considered acceptable and appropriate by the rating agencies. By following conventional financing methods, we put a limit on the amount of debt which could later be available for real estate development.

McDonald's had no such restrictions because their growth strategy did not provide for the use of conventional financing methods. Their unique financing method enabled them to own and control all of their real estate because they financed each location on its own individual merits. Over the years this strategy paid off handsomely and vaulted them into the enviable position as the largest owner of retail real estate in the United States. This strategy and their overall approach to real estate ownership has been enormously beneficial and advantageous to their shareholders.

At my urging, Pillsbury management took a look at the McDonald's financing strategy, but they backed away from making a commitment to a similar program. In that decision, aside from the loss of the tangible financial rewards that might have been gained, Pillsbury lost a certain influence over the conduct of the franchisee community. This would become an increasingly important factor in future years. As landlords, McDonald's could be more effective in insisting that franchisees comply with their required standards of restaurant operation. Poor operators could be eliminated when leases were canceled. It was a bit more difficult for Burger King to act in this fashion when our only leverage rested in our ability and right to enforce provisions contained in our franchise agreements. The real trump card was the lease itself. In McDonald's case, any failure to meet the company's standards of operation could result in the franchisee losing both the lease and the business. I doubt that many McDonald's franchisees were willing to seriously challenge the parent in situations of this kind.

A sad moment for all of us occurred on October 14, 1968, when Harvey Fruehauf passed away. He had always been a good and valued friend, counselor, and mentor. I felt his loss deeply. I flew to Detroit to attend his funeral and spend some time with his wife, Angela, who had always taken a keen interest in the strong personal relationship which Harvey and I had enjoyed during the past 12 years. I read a memorial resolution I had written which was adopted by our board of directors. It speaks of the high esteem that all of us felt toward this remarkable man.

> WHEREAS, Harvey C. Fruehauf, Chairman of the Board of Directors of Burger King Corporation, became deceased on October 14, 1968, after 12 years of loyal and dedicated service to our Company, and

> WHEREAS, Mr. Fruehauf, in addition to his complete dedication to the welfare of the Company, served as a great inspiration and mature counselor to the corporate officers during this time, and

> WHEREAS, Mr. Fruehauf, by his contributions of wisdom, kindness and good judgment imparted a philosophy of high ethics and sound business sense to the Company's founders, David R. Edgerton and James W. McLamore, all of which has made a significant impact on the fortunes of the Company, and

> WHEREAS, Mr. Fruehauf will be sorely missed as a friend, colleague and advisor by all of our employees, associates, officers and Directors, all of whom knew him and held him in such high regard,

> NOW, THEREFORE, be it resolved that the Board of Directors hereby express the sorrow so keenly felt by the passing of Harvey C. Fruehauf, and

> BE IT FURTHER RESOLVED that this testimonial be spread upon the permanent records of the corporation and a certified copy hereof be transmitted to Angela Fruehauf, his beloved wife.

Earlier, on June 18, 1968, H. Glenn Jones our senior vice president of finance passed away after a long illness. Glenn was a good friend and a loyal and dedicated employee who joined Burger King in 1962. We were fortunate however to attract Leslie Paszat who joined the company soon after Glenn's passing. Les would play a key role in the company well into the 1970s.

Terry Hanold and Paul Gerot joined the Burger King board on March 10, 1967, a few months before the merger took place. Dave Edgerton resigned as an officer and director of Burger King on August 21, 1969. He could see the shift in both operating style and corporate culture, and he didn't care for either one. Dave's contributions to the Burger King organization ever since the beginning were legendary. His leaving was the end of an important era in the company's history. His departure served to remind me that things would never again by quite the same.

In 1971 Bob Keith and Gus Donhowe, the Pillsbury treasurer, joined the board. At the same time Paul Gerot resigned, which was a disappointment to me because I had such great respect for his calm, thoughtful, and intelligent style. I felt that of all the Pillsbury people Paul understood the Burger King organization as well or better than any of them. Bud Fruehauf resigned from our board on November 21, 1973, and Tom Wakefield resigned a few years later. With these major changes in the makeup of Burger King's board of directors, the company became, for all practical purposes, an operating division of the Pillsbury Company. The management of Burger King fell into a fixed pattern and adopted much of Pillsbury's corporate style and methodology. By the end of 1969 Burger King had ceased to be operated as an autonomous subsidiary and began to act in rigid conformity to the rules imposed by the parent.

As early as 1968 I was extremely frustrated with certain aspects of our new relationship. Many of the comments and suggestions I made regarding issues seemed to be constantly at variance with those of Pillsbury management. This raised serious questions about whether I would ever succeed as a professional corporate manager. I had been my own boss throughout my 20-year business career. During this time I was able to act quickly and independently in response to any given situation, problem, challenge, or opportunity. In the new scheme of things it was necessary to consult, review, debate, and clear major actions with others. This wasn't a familiar or comfortable style of managing for me. I thought it was inefficient and difficult to become accustomed to.

In spite of this, I made a concerted and diligent effort to learn and adapt to this unfamiliar management style. I didn't want to lose sight of the fact that Burger King was an exciting business opportunity with extraordinary profit-making potential. I reminded myself that as the CEO, I had the responsibility to deliver these profits. I wanted to be highly effective in achieving my goals, and I was determined to do the very best I could in this regard.

Fitting into the Corporate Mold

In 1968 Pillsbury's top brass sent an industrial psychologist to Miami with instructions to report on the way Burger King was managing its business. He was directed to interview each one of our top executives including me and report back with his assessment of our management style, strengths, and weaknesses. I was not familiar with this kind of a process, but we cooperated fully with this fellow. I thought he made a lot of quick conclusions, one of which was that I was much too involved with the details of running the business.

After he reported these conclusions to Minneapolis, I came under increasing pressure to delegate more responsibility to other members of my management team. The idea was for me to step away from running the company in the direct and hands-on manner which had always characterized my style of leadership. It was explained that it would be in the long-term best interest of the company for me to back away from the nuts-and-bolts side of the business and concentrate on the "big picture." It was their view that I should become more of a strategist and leave the day-to-day details of running the business to others.

I tried to understand the reasons that prompted this suggestion, but I could never quite get comfortable about it. I could understand that Pillsbury managers might have been trained to do this and that large corporations probably had to function this way, but I couldn't agree that this was a positive step for us to take at this particular time. I suppose that as a new member of the management team, I was expected to do things the way they did them in Minneapolis. Developing a different management style would be difficult for me, and I was very disappointed and upset to be asked to change the way I had been running the company so early in our relationship. I always felt the need to stay close to our top managers and very close to the decision-making activity. Over the years I had developed a deep sense of commitment toward our franchisees, and I didn't want to weaken or tarnish that important relationship. To maintain my sensitivity to the business, I needed to keep informed about such things as real estate acquisitions, the granting of franchises, opening of new territories, financing the business, and the many other matters which contributed so much to our success during the early years. The idea of my backing away from such a direct and total involvement was unthinkable as far as I was concerned. It didn't make sense to create such a major disruption in the style of management which had worked so well during these critical years.

Dave and I considered that it was important and necessary for both of us to keep deeply involved with Burger King's day-to-day business activity. We learned this during the early days when our business survival demanded it. It was working pretty well when the "expert" told us we had been all wrong. Warning bells began to ring in my ears. I began to think our entrepreneurially driven business was going to have a difficult time surviving in this strange new corporate relationship. Up to this point our management style had produced superior results and a corporate morale that was at an all-time high. We were averaging an annual return in excess of 75 percent on equity. We were one of the leading companies in our field. We were doing great, and our future prospects were very bright. It wasn't the right time to destabilize our leadership initiative. However, the message was clear, and we would have to begin to "do it their way." This was the opening salvo of the operational takeover of the Burger King business. Perhaps we should have expected that. I was just surprised that this sort of thing was happening to us so soon.

There are many examples of entrepreneurially driven companies succeeding famously by adhering to a hands-on style of management. Wal-Mart's fabulous retailing success certainly drives home an interesting point. Sam Walton spent most of his time in his stores, talking with and inspiring his employees and picking up ideas on how to improve his business. This was one of the most important keys to their extraordinary success. Well into the 1990s, and even after Walton's death, that practice continued to be an important factor in the way they ran their business. It seems traditional and ongoing that succeeding CEOs of Wal-Mart, as well as all of their top operations managers, spend a major portion of their time in their stores, working close to the people who serve their customers. This kind of direct and active involvement by top management plays an important role in generating employee enthusiasm and building an esprit de corps throughout their entire organization. The hands-on management approach has elevated the Wal-Mart Company to the very pinnacle of success. They are ranked as one of the top retailing enterprises in the United States. The Pillsbury suggestion in 1968 that I back away from managing Burger King in this same fashion and focus more exclusively on corporate planning and strategic issues struck me as being totally inappropriate, particularly during that critical stage in our growth and development.

Respecting Pillsbury's suggestion, I elevated Art Rosewall to the position of group vice president, and ultimately put him in charge of restaurant and franchising operations. Art was an experienced administrator, and he set about building an organizational structure to take over these responsibilities. Pillsbury management was pleased to see me make this organizational change, but it seemed to me that some of the spark went out of the organization when this change was made. Some of it started with me. Stepping away from the daily business activity resulted in my losing some of the intense enthusiasm that I had always felt in the past.

I attributed much of our past success to the role I had always played as a motivator of people. In addition to my principal duties, I felt I was responsible for creating dreams, building aspirations, and promising victories. Twenty-five years later, when I was serving as president of Fairchild Tropical Garden, I suggested to the managing director that our news publication publish a column headed "Dreams and Aspirations." We had never had a fund-raising campaign before, but within a few years we had raised over $10 million. Everyone got excited. People like to be on a winning team. They plead for and respond to challenge and an opportunity to become involved with something. A leader sitting behind a desk shuffling papers is in a pretty difficult position to motivate people and get them to feel that they are playing a role in building the business. There is an old adage that says, "The pack runs as fast as the lead dog." In my situation I felt that I needed to stay directly involved with the business, but this was going to change.

A decentralization move was under way, designed to replace what originally had been a highly centralized business structure. Such a change would make it easier for Pillsbury to absorb the Burger King organization into their own administrative structure. This was probably part of their original intention. As it turned out, Burger King management became less and less involved in the real decision-making process. One of its many downsides was the inefficiency it would create.

In July of 1969 Pillsbury's CEO flew to Saratoga, Wyoming, where I was spending a two-week vacation with the family. He wanted to discuss succession planning at Pillsbury. He arrived in the company's Sabreliner jet, and after checking into his room at the club, he got right down to business. He said that he had come to discuss corporate leadership and to ask me if I would be interested in becoming the next chief executive officer of The Pillsbury Company. The question took me by surprise, but I didn't need much time to think about it. I told him that I didn't view myself as the right candidate for the position, and I suggested that we leave it that way. It was a very short conversation. Earlier I had given some thought to the possibility of moving up the Pillsbury corporate ladder, but after experiencing corporate life during the past two years following the merger and living through my current frustrations, I concluded that I was not the logical candidate for the job.

The thought of moving to Minneapolis didn't appeal to me inasmuch as I was so deeply committed to living in Miami. I felt that I would not enjoy or be good at managing a large diversified company. I had no training or experience in that regard. The CEO had sent me a handwritten note months earlier saying that he thought I was one of the finest executives he had ever met, and I believe that he was sincere when he wrote that. I believed strongly I had been the right person at the right time as far as Burger King was concerned, but I had no other illusions.

In November of 1969 at the urging of the United States Department of Commerce, I joined a five-man trade mission to Japan. It struck me that taking this trip was consistent with backing away from Burger King's day-to-day operations. I looked at this as a "big picture" event, the purpose of which was to determine the feasibility of establishing the Burger King concept in Japan.

I spent two weeks in Japan. There were no American fast-food restaurants in operation there at the time, but there was a Kentucky Fried Chicken restaurant under construction at the site of the Osaka World's Fair. This unit was scheduled to open during the spring of 1970. The market looked like an explosive opportunity to me. I met with trade officials and government representatives of all of the major Japanese trading companies and several dozen business organizations. I looked into the way Japanese business ventures were organized and operated. I visited Osaka, Yokahama, and Kyoto and spent considerable time in Tokyo making contact and special arrangements with representatives of the various organizations which were interested in coming to the United States to discuss their interest in establishing a joint venture with us. When I returned to the United States, I shared my enthusiasm with Pillsbury management and expressed the belief that establishing a Japanese joint venture was an astonishing opportunity which would be quite easy to handle. The companies I talked to in Japan had both management and locations available. I didn't need much more than that, and I was ready to take our best shot. The top brass in Minneapolis felt that their International Division should be in charge of this project. I thought this notion was simply absurd. They didn't know the first thing about the restaurant business. I presented the concept to the head of international operations who also thought it was a crazy idea. Both of us thought that this was a matter for the Burger King organization to handle, but top management didn't see it that way. I kept the matter alive by sending Japanese delegations to Minneapolis after they visited with us in Miami, but nothing ever happened and the matter was finally dropped.

McDonald's viewed the opportunity quite differently. They jumped in feet first by opening their first restaurant on Tokoyo's Ginza on July 20, 1971, 19 months after my trip to Japan. The 50-50 joint venture they established grew to over 1100 restaurants by 1996. They reported that this was by far their largest and most profitable international restaurant division. Ever since the opening of the first unit, the restaurants have been a huge success.

The failure to capitalize on the Japanese opportunity was frustrating enough, but I continued to be disillusioned with Pillsbury's unwillingness to pursue the huge domestic potential that existed in the United States. This was an extraordinary opportunity simply begging to be exploited. The lack of support for the Japanese venture was consistent with the overall lack of enthusiasm for the Burger King business in general. During 1970 and 1971 Pillsbury management developed an increasingly negative attitude toward franchising and real estate development. This was the basic business that had built Burger King, and it was difficult for me to understand how they felt we could grow the business without placing a focus on franchising. They were preparing to downsize franchising. Many times at our Burger King board meetings, with our top management team in attendance, I was challenged to support the position that franchising and real estate development were in the company's future long-term best interest. Pillsbury management simply didn't agree that they were. The mounting tension which this caused became a problem tending to widen the gulf that already existed between the Miami and

Minneapolis organizations. Our differences on this major policy issue heightened a growing negative attitude, which the
Miami management team came to regard as a "we versus
them" working relationship.

This was turning into a real corporate problem. I felt that
if we couldn't resolve this basic strategic issue, we would find
ourselves missing out on the biggest corporate opportunity we
had in front of us. It was only natural that this subject would
be hotly debated in the Burger King boardroom. On one such
meeting with our entire top management group in attendance,
I presented plans for revitalizing our franchising program.
Minneapolis management, not only attacked the plans, but
openly criticized the policy more strenuously than they had
done in the past. The discussion could only be interpreted as
nothing short of *ordering* a change in our corporate direction.
In a state of utter frustration, as the meeting was about to
break up, I suggested the Pillsbury people take a hand
grenade, pull the pin out, and lob it on top of the table before
getting on the elevator. The "hand-grenade comment" really
struck a nerve and was often referred to in trying to resolve
our differences. When the big blowup came, it marked the
beginning of my exit as the chairman and CEO of Burger King
Corporation.

From the standpoint of our long-term strategic objectives,
the early 1970s were critical decision years. During the years
1967 and 1968 McDonald's and Burger King were opening
about the same number of restaurants. We were restricted by
our limited capital and borrowing capacity, and we were
stretched pretty thin as far as our management was concerned. We were still able to keep up the pace because
McDonald's was cutting back on their own growth plans. They
appeared to be concerned that the United States might be
entering a difficult economic period that could adversely
affect their business. We were of the opposite view. As far as
Burger King Corporation was concerned, we were ready, anxious, and able to generate all of the growth we possibly could.
This is where we hoped that the Pillsbury parent would come
charging in to give us a boost, but the financial support we

expected never came. Our management team began asking the question "Where is the cavalry?"

McDonald's founder, Ray Kroc, appeared to be disenchanted with talk about a cutback and so was his newly appointed CEO. This may have contributed to the resignation of Harry Sonneborn as McDonald's president in 1967. Following Sonneborn's departure, the new CEO gave the signal for rapid expansion. McDonald's growth expanded beyond anything they had previously considered in the past or anything we could ever have possibly imagined.

During the 1970s when Pillsbury was orchestrating a cutback in Burger King's growth, McDonald's was surging ahead at an extraordinarily rapid pace. From their opening of just 105 stores in 1967, and 109 stores in 1968, McDonald's opened 211 stores in 1969, 294 in 1970, 312 in 1971, 368 in 1972, 445 in 1973, and 515 in 1974. The cavalry had charged all right, but the guys on the horses were wearing the golden arches! By the end of 1974 we were eating trail dirt. At that very critical time back in 1970, we opened 167 stores (most of which were in the pipeline when we merged with Pillsbury). I was terribly disappointed when we were forced to cut back to 107 stores in 1971 and to just 91 stores in 1972. We had fought the good fight, but by this time it was clear to our management team that we had lost the war. McDonald's had won the battle. They were number 1 and, unless they stumbled and fell from their dominant position, would probably never be successfully challenged. It still bothers me to think what Burger King might have accomplished if we had demonstrated the courage to stay the course.

The emphasis and commitment to franchising was responsible for Burger King's becoming one of the world's giant foodservice organizations. Our cooperative relationships with franchisees coupled with their valuable contributions of time, energy, and resources were the keys to our success. We have been at variance with certain franchisees over a number of issues from time to time, and occasionally we have had to address our grievances in court, but that was an inherent risk in the franchising business. We expected to have certain uncooperative and difficult franchisees who turned out to be poor operators and some were like that, but by far the vast majority of them were dedicated and hard-working people who fully supported the system. They were the real backbone of our business. To argue that they were not was incomprehensible. It demonstrated a total lack of understanding about the real dynamics of the Burger King business. My business relationship with Pillsbury was not going particularly well because of our differences concerning many policy issues, with this one being one of the most important. I had no illusions about my own personal status. Differing with my superiors so frequently placed me in a difficult, if not an impossible, situation.

This was a terribly frustrating period. I had failed in various attempts to convince Pillsbury management that their positions on certain strategic issues were wrong. Witnessing the steady cutback in our rate of expansion was difficult for me to accept. The fact was that it was driving me to distraction.

The strategic philosophy concerning Burger King expansion came to light in a memorandum I received from top management on October 7, 1971. It was entitled "Financing and Planning Principles and Constraints." The memo outlined the way Pillsbury planned to direct Burger King's growth into the future. There were four key points:

> "Earnings alone will dictate how much growth we can finance."
>
> "Whatever real estate we develop will first be used to build company stores."
>
> "Only as a last resort will we consider developing stores for franchisees."
>
> "Only to the degree that *we must* will we *permit* franchisees to develop their own stores."

This statement of policy and strategic direction affirmed my greatest fears. Pillsbury would be pressuring us to open and operate company stores while cutting back on franchising and abandoning real estate development. I had been at variance with Pillsbury management on a number of important issues leading up to this definitive policy position, but the realization that this was actually happening was devastating. I put in a call to Minneapolis after reading the memorandum and asked, "What the hell did you fellows buy this company for?" It was a short and very unpleasant conversation.

After this bitter encounter I knew that I wouldn't be staying long as a member of the Pillsbury management team. I couldn't be the team player I was expected to be if the price was sacrificing the huge global opportunity that Burger King represented. I was looked upon as some kind of maverick, unwilling to buy into the Pillsbury philosophy and method of doing things. I understood that if I disagreed with management on matters involving corporate strategy, it wasn't smart to be too vocal about it. I had no one who would listen to me. In desperation I took my concern into the Pillsbury boardroom, but that didn't have much of an effect and put me in an even more difficult position. This was going over the head of management, and that in itself wasn't a very smart move. I was learning a valuable lesson about the role of corporate directors. The lesson was that directors don't interfere with management's introduction of new ideas and strategic directions because it takes time to prove whether these ideas are good or not. Directors usually wait an agonizingly long period of time to reach a conclusion about things like that. In Burger King's case they hadn't reached that point. With management fully in support of what I felt was a terrible strategic mistake, this was the way it was going to be, and I had better get used to that. Unfortunately, there was more to come. Pillsbury management wasn't quite finished in tearing the heart out of Burger King's strategy for the future.

After receiving the October 1971 memorandum which gave a strong indication of a shift in corporate direction, I received a nine-page, hand-written memorandum from Minneapolis. It was dated January 22, 1972, and marked *confidential*. This one upset me as much as the October 7 bombshell. This one presented a rationale supporting the policy statements in the October memorandum. The assumption and conclusions were extraordinary in their lack of perception about the worth of the Burger King franchising program. On January 28, 1972, I responded with my own paraphrasing of the comments contained in this confidential memorandum and invited dialogue and discussion on the subject. If these positions prevailed, they would undermine the entire Burger King opportunity as I saw it. I began to think in terms of the value of my investment in Pillsbury stock. Anyone with common sense and good judgment could see that Burger King was Pillsbury's major growth and profit opportunity, but here was an affirmation of management's intent to downsize and restrict our growth and momentum.

The memo of January 22, 1972, set forth Pillsbury's perception of franchisee attitudes, which they considered detrimental to our business. It was hard to believe that Minneapolis really believed this fantasy of disillusion and misperception. In their own words, it was Pillsbury's conclusion that a Burger King franchisee was a person who:

1. Is ingenious at shifting his losses over to Burger King rather than absorbing them.

2. Automatically threatens company with antitrust suits as a bargaining tool.

3. Resists performance of contract duties and demands concessions from Burger King under threat of litigation.

4. Only in the beginning is deeply and daily involved in operations of store.

5. After obtaining five stores is divorced from function of store manager. He is then nothing more than a district manager. At ten stores, he is simply a regional manager.

6. After three or four stores are obtained, licensee's function as an operator phases out and his interest as an investor becomes paramount. Such licensees are only mediocre development prospects.

7. Upon receiving additional stores the licensee's declining personal commitment to operations and growth is guaranteed.

8. Fits a pattern, or a "franchisee life cycle"—going initially from intense personal involvement in stores to general manager. Gets fed up with day-to-day detail.

9. At certain stage of growth resists ideas of renovating, enlarging or upgrading his Burger King store. More interested in cash flow than improving sales by reinvestment.

10. By concentrating new licenses in hands of existing multiunit licensee's, we accelerate the pace toward the end of licensee's life cycle. Repurchase of the license is a normal consequence of its issuance.

The memorandum was a blow to the Burger King management team, which was acutely aware of the benefits franchisees were contributing to the system. We had respect for franchisees. Pillsbury people had very little. Feelings about the memo ran from disbelief to disappointment to anger. This was clear evidence reflecting Pillsbury's growing negative attitude toward franchisees, and it added to our concern that they were determined to establish a strategic direction which would put the Burger King business on the back burner. Our Miami group had grown up with the business and had been witnessing and relishing the explosive growth we were enjoying ever since the 1950s. Now with a near total disregard for our current momentum, we were about to throw away a golden opportunity. It was hard for us to either accept or understand this kind of thinking. We had yet to experience a single failure after opening over 800 restaurants since 1954, and yet in 1972 we were looking at plans to abandon the aggressive growth strategy that had built the company and brought us so far.

The Minneapolis announcements were really in support of a sharply reduced growth strategy that Pillsbury must have decided upon a few years earlier. We had reached the high point in new-store growth in the fiscal year which ended in May of 1970, with the opening of 167 units. This was a 34 percent increase over the preceding 12-month period and indicated our momentum and how active we were in building the company. By the middle of 1970 we had a total of 656 units in operation. Our rapid expansion was the direct result of momentum we had brought to Pillsbury when we came aboard a few years earlier. These were planned openings which were already in the system before we joined Pillsbury. As 1970 rolled around, on a near-riskless basis, we were opening an average of three new restaurants a week. As the new policy took effect, our rate of expansion declined sharply, with new-store openings falling far behind our competition as noted in the following table.

	Units opened	
Year	McDonald's	Burger King
1967	100	70
1968	109	108
1969	211	108
1970	294	167
1971	312	107
1972	368	91

The real test in measuring the success of a business strategy is to look at results. Our performance was dismal. We had stopped nearly dead in the water while our competition was opening restaurants at an accelerated pace with every intention to nail down the top spot for good. If grown men were allowed to cry, we would be in need of bath towels.

McDonald's stepped up the pace by 1974, opening an average of 10 new restaurants every week during the year. Most of these were operated by franchisees, but the real estate was either owned or controlled by McDonald's. This was their golden egg. McDonald's view of the value of franchising and real estate development was exactly the opposite of Pillsbury's. Their growth strategy was a preemptive strike establishing them as the market leader, a position I doubted they would ever knowingly or willingly give up. I told our management team in Miami that we had lost the race for the top. Our best hope was that we could hold onto the number 2 position.

When negotiating the Burger King acquisition in 1966, the Chairman and CEO, Paul Gerot, made it clear to his Pillsbury board that he had no interest in acquiring Burger King Corporation unless I agreed to stay on and run the company. I was 40 years old at the time and relatively inexperienced in dealing with the complex financial and contractual matters that attend mergers of the kind we were discussing. Burger King had played a very important role in my life during the past 22 years, and I was anxious to continue my role as president and CEO of the company. I had no intention of retiring. I wanted to stay on and assist in the realization of our dreams and aspirations. I believed that I was the most qualified person to do that. In my discussions with Mr. Gerot I agreed to remain at the helm for the next five years. With that commitment from me, he was prepared to recommend the merger to his board.

I made no commitments to stay active in the business once the five years were up. Future participation would depend on the level of support Burger King would receive from Pillsbury, and even more it would depend upon my effectiveness as a CEO and a member of the Pillsbury management team. I hoped to be very effective in these roles, and I was particularly anxious to prove to the Pillsbury people that the Burger King acquisition had been a smart and financially rewarding business decision for them.

My five year-contract was up in 1972. At this point I had been in the restaurant business for over 25 years. It occurred to me that there might be a little more to life than just growing the business a little bigger and getting a little richer in the process.

Pillsbury management might have decided before 1972 that I wasn't fitting into their plans. I had no way of knowing that, but over the years, I seemed to be constantly at variance with them on a number of important issues.

In 1967, when I became a Pillsbury director, I might have been the largest individual stockholder on the board. This had no effect on influencing corporate policy, and it shouldn't have. However, I did feel that at least to a certain extent, I was representing the nearly 10 percent of Pillsbury shares then held by the former stockholders of Burger King Corporation. Furthermore, I felt that I had a special responsibility to express my views about Pillsbury's strategic direction, particularly as it related to the Burger King subsidiary, which certainly was something I knew quite a bit about.

I believe that my presence on the Pillsbury board might have been an irritant to some, because I felt that it was my obligation and responsibility to study and comment on operating plans and corporate strategic issues. When I agreed or disagreed with management, I considered that it was my duty as an "inside" director to make these feelings known. Criticizing top management put me in a difficult situation. In challenging top management's thinking in the boardroom, I was risking the loss of friends in important places.

At the same time that Pillsbury management began backing off in its support of the Burger King business, they began to recommend that Pillsbury get into a number of totally unrelated businesses. This struck me as a very ill-conceived strategy. It was clear that we knew very little about any of these proposed acquisition targets, yet management convinced the board to invest in quite a few of them. We acquired *Bon Appetit* and *Bon Voyage* magazines. We got into a computer time-sharing business, Call-A-Computer, as a joint venture partner with a North Carolina–based life insurance company. I was an old friend of the president of this company, who told me later that his investment in this venture had resulted in a serious financial hardship. We acquired a Minnesota-based home building company, PEMTOM. We got into the gardening business with the acquisition of a nursery and flower and plant marketing business, Bachman's European Flower Markets. Still later we bought a winery in California, Souverain Cellars. At the time an annual report noted, "It is the company's intention to make the Souverain Winery one of Pillsbury's important businesses." Two years later another annual report noted, "Our involvement in this business [Souverain] and its disposition were both costly." We expanded into the poultry business by acquiring J-M Poultry Packing

Co., which had a chicken business in Arkansas and Louisiana. These acquisitions brought one disappointment after another. Not only were these acquisitions extraordinary in their diversity, but they were made with a complete lack of familiarity with any of these different businesses and hence were doomed to dismal failure.

It was difficult to understand how management could develop such enthusiasm for new, unrelated, and unfamiliar businesses while they neglected the one major business which we already owned and knew a great deal about. It was my view that we should have stood steadfastly and solidly behind Burger King. Why we distracted our corporate attention and burdened our financial situation with these investments was a mystery to me. It came as no surprise that we suffered serious losses when they were finally divested.

The Pillsbury Company acquired the Green Giant Company in 1979. In 1968, during my first year as a director of the company, management had presented a proposal urging that we acquire this company. Green Giant was an established but cyclical Minnesota-based company engaged in the marketing of canned and frozen vegetables. Management believed that Green Giant would make a good strategic fit and urged us to approve it. After examining the proposal I concluded that it was a terrible idea. Based on the proposition put before the Pillsbury directors, the Green Giant stockholders would wind up with approximately 40 percent of our total shares. Green Giant was in a commodity type of business with limited long-term growth potential. It was my judgment that this situation could hardly be viewed as anything worthy of our interest. I was particularly opposed to the idea of diluting Pillsbury's interest in Burger King. The proposal didn't make any sense, and I told the chairman that I couldn't support it. When the recommendation was brought to the board, I spoke out strongly in opposition to it and I was pleased when it was turned down, although I knew that my opposition had offended management. I had failed to act as a team player, and this was a clear violation of unwritten corporate rules. I may not have been an experienced corporate director at the time, but I couldn't help but know that I had placed myself in a delicate position with management.

After Pillsbury made a number of diverse acquisitions and created a dislocation of corporate resources, a lot of other things started to go wrong, the most important of which was dropping the Burger King ball when we should have been running with it. It was disappointing to lose ground to our main competitor when we should have been thinking of ways to stay pretty much on their heels.

At the same time these things were going on, the stock market was trying to determine what Pillsbury was all about, what we intended to be, and where we were headed. The crazy acquisitions we had made blurred our corporate image as far as the financial community was concerned, and the price of our stock began to decline as a result. This contributed to a drop in employees' morale in Miami, and I doubted that it could have been much different in Minneapolis. In 1967 I traded my Burger King stock for Pillsbury stock on the basis of its market price of $45. After six years it had dropped to a low of $17.25 a share, a loss of more than 60 percent in value. I attributed much of that to bad management and the clumsy way we had dealt with important strategic issues, particularly with regard to Burger King. I wasn't a bit happy about the price of our stock, which aside from being a personal financial disappointment, was a terrible report card on our corporate performance. The investing public had sent Pillsbury a pretty significant message, showing its lack of confidence in our management and our strategic direction. In this very confused environment, investors and stockholders alike were raising serious questions about the future potential of The Pillsbury Company.

Burger King was too big, too profitable, and too promising for Pillsbury management not to wrap their arms around it. Within a few years of the merger, Burger King was run more and more by the Pillsbury people in Minneapolis. Their initial commitment of autonomy was a thing of the past. This was somewhat understandable inasmuch as management had a definite oversight obligation to see that Burger King realized its maximum advantage. The 1700 miles separating Minneapolis from Miami were a barrier to accomplishing that, and it seemed inevitable that management wanted to remove any restrictions. What followed was that more and more Pillsbury people were assigned to oversee the Burger King situation. Initially, many of our managers, most of whom were at the staff level, were directed to work closely with their counterparts in Minneapolis. This created a large bureaucracy which gradually broke down the integrity of the management organization in Miami. Helping plan the strategic direction of Burger King was a responsibility for Pillsbury, and we expected them to become involved in that process. Unfortunately, we became nothing more than an operating division. Some of the spark began to leave the company at that point. Pillsbury had a certain amount of difficulty trying to understand the Burger King business. Their overlay of corporate management and the growth of a heavy bureaucracy developed into the kind of problem that often occurs when a big company takes over a smaller, leaner, and more entrepreneurially oriented business. Pillsbury imposed a different management style and corporate culture on a company that didn't quite understand what was happening.

This often happened in acquisitions, usually with disappointing and unsatisfactory results. I expected that Pillsbury would gradually absorb Burger King and force it into their corporate mold, but I hoped that the process would be orderly. It was in everyone's interest for Burger King to fit comfortably into the Pillsbury organization, even though management styles and corporate cultures were quite different. I didn't anticipate that in accomplishing such a transition the strategic direction of Burger King would get so seriously rearranged. This made the entire process much more difficult. Tensions continued to mount.

My departure as CEO of Burger King took place in May of 1972 at the end of my five-year commitment. When exiting this role, I was disappointed that I had failed to keep Burger King on track. Although this may have been due to the ill-advised strategies imposed from above, the fact was that by

1972 we were becoming a second-rate player in a burgeoning food-service marketplace. This is what really bothered me. Burger King's earnings were steadily on the increase. This wasn't the problem. The most important thing on my mind was the hope that Burger King would continue to prosper and grow and somehow return to its roots, which had always been based on franchising and real estate development. It still carried the potential of becoming one of the great restaurant chains in the country, if not in the world. That was my vision, and I believed in it strongly. Much would depend upon Burger King's future leadership and the corporate direction it would take in the years to come. In 1972 we were not headed in the right direction, but I hoped that would change. I would no longer be involved in that process except for the fact that I would remain a director of The Pillsbury Company and continue my involvement with Burger King Corporation as chairman of its board of directors. The chairmanship title would be purely honorary.

My departure coincided with the selection of a new management team at Pillsbury. There was never any talk of hiring an outsider. Bill Spoor was named chairman and CEO and assumed the additional title and responsibilities of president a few years later.

Fortunately, the new management team recognized almost immediately that Burger King should be designated as Pillsbury's growth vehicle for the foreseeable future. It began to receive strong support and resumed a more active franchising and real estate development posture. The 1973 Pillsbury report announced that Burger King planned to open 200 restaurants in fiscal year 1973, and the 1974 report disclosed that the opening of an additional 223 restaurants would increase our total number to 1199 units. This was an impressive rebound from the mandated cutbacks of previous years. McDonald's opened 960 new restaurants in that same two-year period, which was over twice as many, but at least we were returning to our original mission, which was to maintain our position as a major player in the restaurant business. Our main competitor was pulling out in front of us with such speed and determination that it appeared unlikely that we could ever catch up, but I was pleased to see that we were finally getting back into the fray.

I was disappointed about Pillsbury's lackluster support for Burger King during the years following our merger, but I tried to take these setbacks in stride. I felt I could learn from this experience by not getting too worked up about things over which I had no control. Besides, I felt that the basic concept of the Burger King system was so right and so strong that it would take a pretty inept management group not to recognize and capitalize on its huge potential. I was pleased to see a new leader come in and take charge of a situation which really needed to be jolted back to reality. The return to the business of franchising and real estate development was to Bill Spoor's credit. He did something else which helped put The Pillsbury Company back on track when he orchestrated the divestiture of the many ill-conceived non-food-related acquisitions that Pillsbury had made between 1967 and 1972. As far as I was concerned, with a sharper corporate focus, the future outlook for Pillsbury and Burger King began to look much brighter.

Stepping Down

In May of 1972 when I retired as the CEO of Burger King Corporation, I wasn't sure what to expect so far as my future was concerned and I was very apprehensive. Not only was I leaving the familiar and stimulating world of Burger King, but I needed to find something equally challenging to take its place. This wasn't going to be easy. I knew that I was at the end of an active career in the restaurant business that had begun 25 years earlier. The big question was how I was going to adjust to a vastly different way of life.

I was 46 years old, which was an awfully young age to think about taking it easy. I was in very good health. I certainly had no intention of retiring in the sense of having nothing to do, but I had only a vague idea as to what I would do. I had decided earlier that I would not go back into the restaurant business. This was because I intended to maintain my affiliation with Burger King. My financial investment was there and so was my loyalty. There were too many wonderful friends, franchisees, colleagues, and memories associated with Burger King to just walk away and head out in a business that could be considered competitive or disruptive. I was taking the consulting agreement I had made upon retiring seriously, in the sense that I felt obligated to stay involved at least to the extent that my services might be needed.

My major preoccupation focused on finding the right kind of stimulating challenges. Nancy kept trying to reassure me that I would come across plenty of opportunities of that sort, but I needed to be convinced. The very thought of being inactive and unchallenged was very unsettling. I wasn't exactly sure which direction I would take, but I certainly knew where I had to start.

The first order of business was to move out of the Burger King headquarters building. The last thing our management team needed was to have the cofounder and former CEO of the company sharing office space with them and in a sense "looking over their shoulders." I rented space in the original Burger King office building which was located across from the Dadeland Shopping Center just a few blocks away. It was quite close to home, and because of its convenient location, I wouldn't need to face a difficult traffic situation going to or from my home. This building had been sold to the Southeast Banking Corporation in 1969, when we moved into the new seven-story office building just up the street.

I leased a fairly sizable area on the second floor, which a few years earlier had served as part of the Burger King law department. It was a pleasant corner office with windows extending from floor to ceiling. I occupied this office from 1972 to 1988, when I moved into the newly completed Burger King World Headquarters building on Old Cutler Road at SW 184th Street.

When I stepped down as CEO, Pillsbury asked me to stay on as chairman of the Burger King board of directors, and inasmuch as I intended to remain a director of The Pillsbury Company, I was in a position to maintain my contact with Burger King. I was fortunate to have Janet Wheeler, my secretary of long standing, join me in time to establish my new office in 1972. Janet had been with Burger King for 12 years, having joined the company as a secretary and bookkeeper in 1960. By 1988 when I moved into the World Headquarters building, Janet had completed 28 years of service to the company. It was understandable that she finally decided to call it quits. All of us would miss her. She was very familiar with most of my friends, business associates, and many of our franchisees. Everyone, including Nancy and the children, regarded Janet very highly. She was almost like a member of the family, and we hated to see her leave.

I was proud of the fact that in 1972 when I left the company, Burger King was recognized as being one of the largest and most successful restaurant chains in the country. I felt confident that we would continue to grow and keep our leadership position in the dynamic food-service industry. The management team was now under Art Rosewall's direction, and I anticipated that this team, with Pillsbury's support, would maintain its forward momentum. There was a lot riding on that, notably my investment in The Pillsbury Company as well as my pride. I had seen too many big, successful restaurant companies fail not to believe that Burger King itself could be vulnerable to the fickle winds of change in our swift-moving marketplace.

Dave Edgerton and I enjoyed a wonderful relationship during the years we worked together. We both developed a deep sense of personal fulfillment in witnessing Burger King's extraordinary progress and achievements. Burger King had reached levels of growth, stature, and importance that we hardly thought was possible when we first started out. Our intense concentration and focus on running the business had been an intoxicating experience. We were fascinated and challenged by our work. Our constant focus centered on building a successful business. During the past 18 years Burger King had demanded my full time and attention. I enjoyed the stimulation of being a part of such a dynamic situation, but this was about to change. In stepping down as the Burger King CEO I had every hope of finding something equally important and challenging, but I knew this wouldn't be easy.

I decided to become more involved in activities I was already familiar with. These included community service, philanthropy, investments, education, real estate, golf, gardening, reading, the family, traveling, public speaking, trade association work, and corporate directorships. I wanted to remain actively involved with the business community, particularly in the Miami area, which was my home and favorite place in the world. One thing that required a lot of attention was my personal investments. I had been able to increase my net worth substantially during the past five years in spite of the poor performance of my Pillsbury shares, and I was confident that I could do better than that whenever I put my mind to it. I had not given much thought to making many outside business investments in recent years simply because I was so busily engaged in managing Burger King. Now I had the time to look into that and do a lot of other things.

I had made a few outside investments before leaving Burger King. One of them was an investment in the Miami Dolphins, which I made in 1969. This was a struggling, losing team in the old American Football League. The AFL was an upstart organization trying to compete with the NFL. Professional football was just coming into its own, and Miami was proud to have a team representing the city. In 1966 Joe Robbie was granted a franchise to field an expansion team. The franchise agreement designated Robbie to be the managing general partner. Joe didn't have any money to invest in the franchise, and by 1969 he was in a delicate financial condition as a minority investor in a partnership which he had put together. He was having some difficulty with a few of his limited partners who owned 60 percent of the team. Being heavily in debt himself and unable to come up with any more capital of his own made this situation very tense. The Dolphins were not much of a draw at the gate, and with all his debts, the franchise was in a deep cash-liquidity crisis. Sunday games rarely drew more than 40,000 fans to Orange Bowl stadium which could accommodate almost twice that number.

The Dolphin's share of AFL television revenue was only $500,000 a year, which was a mere drop in the bucket compared to the $40 million or more that each NFL team earned annually in the 1990s. Robbie, in his frustration, began threatening to move the team to another city as he sought solutions to a difficult financial and partnership situation.

In a meeting at my home, which was attended by Robbie, four friends and I agreed to invest in the Dolphins on the presumption that suitable financing could be arranged to enable us to buy out the current limited partners. At the time I was on the board of the First National Bank of Miami. In these days chain banks were not permitted, and First National was the largest bank in Florida. I told the group that I would take the idea to our president and determine if the bank had any interest in refinancing the proposed new investors. The bank liked the idea and came up with a financing package which we all found acceptable. As the new limited partners we guaranteed financing which, among other things, enabled Robbie to increase his share of ownership. With the five of us joining Robbie as part owners, the Dolphins stayed in Miami. This was a commitment Robbie made to us at the time we agreed to step in and help him stabilize his own investment position. Robbie made the commitment that the Dolphins would remain in Miami, if the financing could be arranged. We put a great deal of importance on this, sensing the beneficial impact it would have on our city, our community, and the State of Florida. I believe that Joe also felt this way.

Within months of making this investment, a series of significant events took place. The first was the merger of the AFL into the NFL. This was followed in rapid succession by Robbie hiring Don Shula to be head coach. Don had recently served as the head coach of the Baltimore Colts. What happened next electrified the world of professional football.

Robbie, as the managing general partner, was the Dolphins CEO, and he handled the team's business affairs. The investment of the new partners in the Miami Dolphins was completely passive. For me it involved nothing more than attending the home games and occasionally traveling on the team plane to games we played in other cities. This activity was limited to weekends during the fall months, but was made very interesting by Don Shula's extraordinary accomplishments in bringing the team to three consecutive Super Bowl contests in 1971, 1972, and 1973. It also provided our family with the opportunity of knowing many of the players, coaches, and in some cases, their wives and children. The Dolphins won their first Super Bowl following the remarkable 1972 season, when they won 17 consecutive games without suffering a loss. The 14-7 Super Bowl win against the Washington Redskins at the Los Angeles Coliseum brought out a feeling of great community pride unlike anything that had ever happened in Miami before. The Miami Dolphin investment was a "fun" investment and a profitable one as well. The limited partners including me sold our interest to Robbie a number of years later, but all of us savored the enjoyment of being an important part of building a remarkably successful sports franchise.

The National Restaurant Association began to take a considerable amount of my time. I joined the board of directors in 1966 and moved rather rapidly. At the time of my retirement as CEO of Burger King in 1972, I was on track to become the NRA president, a position I assumed in 1974. The story leading up to my presidency casts an important light on the character and dimension of the food-service industry at that time.

I was one of the first restaurant-chain executives to be elected to the board of directors of the NRA. This was probably due to the fact that I was known in industry circles, having served previously as president of the Florida Restaurant Association in 1964 and president of the Miami Restaurant Association and the Pan American Hotel and Restaurant Exposition a few years before that. I had gained recognition in the trade press for speeches and articles about industry issues and franchising.

In 1967 as an incoming new member of the board of directors, I was sensitive to the fact that many board members were unaware of the potential impact that chain-restaurant growth and development was going to have on the industry. It was my judgment that restaurant franchising, which was very new at the time, would trigger a rapid escalation and expansion of chain restaurants all over the country. It was also my sense that this kind of growth would come very rapidly, with the chains assuming a dominating presence on the national scene. It struck me that either the board didn't recognize this potential, or perhaps they just didn't *want* to recognize it. At the time the NRA board consisted almost entirely of single-unit restaurant operators. I didn't believe they were particularly well informed on this subject. The composition of the NRA board was a fair reflection on the makeup of the industry at the time. There were relatively few restaurant chains in the country, and the industry was still pretty much made up of the more familiar Mom-and-Pop operators. In 1966 there was not a single restaurant chain in the United States that could lay claim to being of national stature. Few could even come close to being thought of this way.

The NRA president asked me to make a presentation to the NRA board in early 1967. This particular board meeting was attended by a number of restaurateurs from many different countries. As invitees of the NRA they were in Chicago to attend the NRA's annual convention and trade show. My presentation pictured the current escalation and buildup of new restaurant chains. I predicted how differently the food-service business would be constituted in the future, emphasizing my belief that franchising would play a key role in bringing all this about. I suggested that the NRA should consider inviting leaders of the industry's chain-restaurant organizations to serve on the board, arguing that these modern-day food-service executives could bring a valuable national perspective to NRA discussions and deliberations.

In 1969 I accepted the chairmanship of the NRA's important Government Affairs Committee. This required me to spend quite a bit of time in Chicago and Washington attending to matters of interest and concern to the food-service industry, and it brought me in contact with many restaurateurs from all over the country. This certainly sharpened my perspective on changes that were taking place in our rapidly expanding industry.

Long before retiring as CEO, I maintained an active involvement with a number of community boards and other outside interests. When I stepped down in 1972 as Burger King's CEO, I was at least partially prepared for a change in daily routine.

My entire business career was filled with activity in local, state, and national organizations. I thought it was important to do this. During the 1950s it was Junior Achievement, Parent-Teacher Associations, Little League sports, the United Way, our church, and the Miami Restaurant Association, which I served as president in 1953. During the 1960s I became more involved in outside organizations. I served as a director and ultimately president of the Florida Restaurant Association. I helped organize the Royal Palm Tennis Club (serving as treasurer for many years and later as president). I joined the board of the First National Bank of Miami, served as trustee of the Northfield Mount Hermon School in Massachusetts, a director of the Doral-Eastern Golf Tournament, a trustee of Fairchild Tropical Garden, a director of the National Restaurant Association, and a member of the Society of University Founders at the University of Miami. I thought it was important to be involved with activities which were totally unrelated to my business. At least this previous experience gave me some idea of how to keep busy and active.

As I was coming to grips with rebuilding my life after retirement, I began to understand why so many people who lead hyperactive business careers often die within a few years of retirement. Many of them are simply unable to cope with facing a drastic change in their pattern of daily living. After ending extremely active professional careers, they don't know what to do. My business career was filled with decision making, heavy traveling schedules, meetings, tough choices, and pressure-related job activities, so I understood what that was all about. Having lived that kind of life myself, I was aware of its intoxicating effect. I knew that when my action-packed lifestyle was suddenly altered, I would have to fill the void with something else or face certain problems associated with withdrawal and a change of pace. I didn't realize at the time just how much my previous outside activities would contribute to a comfortable transitional experience.

In most major corporations retirement usually takes place somewhere between the ages of 55 and 65. Unless a person prepares carefully for that day and for that event, the shock of retirement can have a profound effect. Sudden withdrawal can lead to all sorts of psychological disorders. The trick is to prepare carefully in advance in order to avoid the trap, and this is not always an easy thing to do.

I spent a lot of time thinking about this long before I retired. I felt that a big part of the problem centers on the fact that during a long business or professional career, many people never take the time to develop outside interests. I learned that this is of paramount importance when it comes to adding balance to a person's life. I avoided that trap because during my own business career I had given freely of my time to many activities which were completely unrelated to my highly focused world of Burger King. I was never an unwilling casualty after retirement, because I knew how to keep myself busy and stimulated. I would become involved with new and diverse interests, and I already knew what it took to do that. I planned on doing this during the period leading up to May of 1972. I was already an active participant in a number of diverse activities that could keep me mentally and physically sharp. With this sense of determination, I felt reasonably certain that the transition from Burger King to a totally new life would go quite smoothly.

Getting Adjusted to "Retirement"

The 1967 merger agreement between The Pillsbury Company and Burger King specified that I would stay on as the CEO until May of 1972, a period of five years. By mutual agreement this could have been extended, but that was never considered by the parties. I wasn't comfortable in my capacity as the manager of an operating division (which Burger King had become), and Pillsbury felt that they could function more freely with more control and less constraining influence coming from me as a cofounder and longtime CEO of Burger King. I didn't fit their corporate mold, and I had yet to adjust from my hands-on management style. Being at constant variance with Pillsbury on key strategic issues made my presence on the management team a disruption and a troubling annoyance. I felt sure of that. There were plenty of reasons for us to separate.

Nevertheless, my retirement discussions with Pillsbury were cordial, open, and very professional. Everyone understood that I would leave in 1972, so my departure would come as no surprise to either organization. With these decisions made well in advance, I had ample time to consider what I would do after my very active 25-year career in the food-service industry came to an end.

I was not troubled by the realization that I would be relinquishing the CEO job at Burger King. I would miss that, of course, but this position had long ago ceased to be the job of a chief executive officer. That function had been taken over by the Pillsbury executive office. Burger King, as an operating division, was reporting to management in the same way their other operating divisions reported. I wasn't prepared to do that for an extended term.

What did trouble me was the task of rebuilding my life once my active business career came to an end. I had always been intensely interested and involved with my work. This was a totally absorbing part of my life during the previous 25 years of owning and operating restaurants. I was deeply concerned about the implications of making an abrupt change in my lifestyle. This was going to be one of my major challenges. I had never been faced with anything like this before. Bridging the gap was not going to be easy. I felt certain about that.

I shouldn't have been concerned about keeping busy and involved. When I settled into my new office, I received many calls asking me to take on various responsibilities. There were so many offers and invitations that I had to back away and think about how much time I could afford to give to these proposals. I decided to take my time about that. First I needed to sort out my priorities and decide which of these offers were the most important to me. I had to consider community service, investment opportunities, philanthropy, hobbies, family affairs, learning experiences, service on corporate boards, and a wide variety of other pursuits. I needed to evaluate all of these projects before jumping in.

Hobbies came quickly to mind. I loved gardening, and South Florida was a perfect place to enjoy a hobby like that. I recalled a time when I was still active in Burger King and preparing to leave the O'Hare Inn and take the bus to the airport for the trip home. It was snowing quite hard outside on that Friday afternoon. With my business finished and a few hours to spare before flight time, I was sitting in my room in front of the window, watching the snow drift down, reading a book on tropical gardening, a favorite subject of mine. I was thinking about the garden projects I wanted to take on during the next day in sunny Miami. Gardening was and is a consuming passion of mine. I feel very fortunate to have such an interesting hobby to help take my mind off other matters.

Many business people become so highly focused on their careers that they don't take time to interest themselves in something different. Failure to recognize this can extract a heavy price, and in certain cases it can be life threatening. Boredom and a person's lack of purpose can do a considerable amount of psychological and physical damage. I felt fortunate that I did not fall into this category. I had a multiplicity of interests to stimulate my mind.

Three months before stepping down I bought the property adjoining our home in Miami. The property consisted of a house and a lovely rolling piece of land with many oak trees, all situated on the same lake which fronted our own residence. This property added an additional 1.5 acres of land and gave us a total of 500 feet of lake frontage. The land itself had many promising features, which I felt could be turned into an interesting addition to my garden. Ever since building our own home in 1964, I had spent a considerable amount of time and effort creating a lovely garden. The thought of adding another 1.5 acres to this project filled me with stimulating thoughts and ideas.

One of the attractive features about Miami is its extraordinary climate. For a gardening enthusiast this presents an unusual opportunity to work with plants 12 months out of the year. South Florida's mild subtropical climate is a compelling reason to live there. The unique environment of South Florida had much to do with attracting me to Miami. I felt that the adjoining property would make a perfect addition to our home and garden, and it would provide me with a great opportunity to create a place of unusual beauty. I planned to start on this interesting project while I was attempting to sort out all of my priorities and options following retirement. By taking possession of the property in April, I was in position to tackle something which could absorb much of my time, energy, and attention. I saw this as offering a therapeutic release from any inner tensions which might build as a result of facing a radical shift in my professional career.

When my retirement date rolled around a month later, the CBS affiliate in Miami, WTVJ-TV, came to our home and did a special television report about my departure from Burger King. The producer selected the newly acquired property as the site for the interview, which featured me dressed in my gardening clothes. I recalled the fun and excitement I had experienced over the years and mentioned that I had yet to decide what I wanted to do. I said that I expected to remain close to South Florida and continue to stay involved with worthwhile projects, whether they were local or national in scope. I called particular attention to my gardening hobby and the enthusiasm I felt for the project which was immediately ahead.

Quite often, flying home after a long business trip, I would read books on tropical horticulture, garden design, or related subjects. Books of this kind provided me with a diversion from busy airports and monotonous flights in cramped seating. My Saturdays and Sundays at home were often spent in "the yard" creating projects, such as planter beds, waterfalls, sprinkler systems, and outdoor lighting, or tending to the plants themselves. I enjoyed doing this sort of thing so much that I had trouble forcing myself to get out and play golf, which was yet another passionate hobby. Having another acre and a half of land added to my private garden and plenty of time to work on it offered assurances that I could avoid boredom. There was a little wishful thinking in all this, but at least for the time being I had something that could help me keep mentally and physically occupied.

My concern about keeping involved and stimulated reminded me that I needed to take stock of my personal situation. I had kept most of my stock in The Pillsbury Company, but after five years it was worth less than when I received it. This investment, which represented a significant part of my net worth, had so far proved to be disappointing. I felt that my future investments would have to do much better than that.

I intended to stay actively involved as a director of the First National Bank of Miami, The Pillsbury Company, and Burger King Corporation. I also planned to join a few more corporate boards after I retired. I was traveling quite extensively in connection with my duties as the upcoming president of the National Restaurant Association. I was also deeply involved as a trustee of the Northfield Mount Hermon School and active in the Young Presidents Organization. The YPO meetings were very well structured and organized to include highly regarded experts in all fields of activity. They were interesting and educational, and they were usually held in unique and fascinating locations. This gave Nancy and me a chance to travel and visit new places, which was something we had not been able to do when I was so actively involved with Burger King.

My long-standing contact with the South Florida business community and many of its leaders had me on track to begin a term as the vice president of the Greater Miami Chamber of Commerce. I had looked forward to becoming more deeply involved with this very diverse organization.

Nancy and I had purchased a residential lot at the Old Baldy Club in Saratoga, Wyoming, with the intention to build a summer residence there. A few months after retirement we hired an architect to design the home, which would be based on a plan that Nancy had developed. Working with the architect and builder took a little bit of our time and provided an added stimulation to our lives. This was a fun project for Nancy. With trips to various meetings and the work I was doing to create an extension to my garden, I kept reasonably busy, but I remained on the lookout for additional activities that could be challenging and worthwhile.

Fortunately, they weren't long in coming. A few months after retirement I received a call asking if I would consider standing for election as a trustee of the University of Miami. This was a job that I was very pleased to accept. Because I felt the University was one of the truly outstanding institutions which deserved a lot of community support, I wanted to get involved in the process. On the heels of the call from the university, I was asked to become a director of the Community Television Foundation which operated WPBT–Channel 2, our public television station in Miami. I regarded this as another valuable community asset. This was followed by a call from Fairchild Tropical Garden asking me to become a trustee. I loved Fairchild Garden and had spent a lot of time there getting ideas about how to build and enhance my own private garden. Without hesitation I accepted all three assignments and willingly assumed all of the responsibilities that went along with them.

While on vacation in Utah, I received a call from the chairman of Southeast Banks, Hood Bassett, telling me that he was representing an organization of banking executives in the Southeast. This organization was asking me to offer my candidacy to serve as one of the seven governors of the Federal Reserve Board in Washington. Hood told me that his group was in position to suggest the nomination of a person from our part of the country. His question was "Would I be willing to serve if nominated and confirmed by the U.S. Senate?" I flew to Washington and had dinner with one of the present governors, who explained what my role would be. The thought of spending so much time in Washington influenced my decision to decline the nomination. I simply couldn't accept the idea of living anywhere outside of Miami.

A number of friends tried to interest me in running for the U.S. Senate, but I had no interest in politics and never gave that any serious consideration. I did become a member of the Orange Bowl Committee and agreed to serve as the chairman of the upcoming United Way Campaign in Greater Miami. With these various activities to attend to, including some foreign travel and the enjoyment of my investment in the Miami Dolphins, the world of retirement became extraordinarily busy, just like Nancy predicted it would. There was much more to come.

The University of Miami and the Community Television Foundation had certain problems, and soon after going on these boards, I became deeply involved in solving them. These two organizations took much more time than I thought they would when I first joined them, but the real time consumer was the National Restaurant Association. As the incoming vice president and still chairman of the Government Affairs Committee, I was spending much more time on the NRA than I had originally planned. I expected that my year as president in 1974–1975 would be quite busy, but I had anticipated that it would be another year before the pace of activity would quicken. It was at this point that Henry Bolling, my good friend and current president, asked me to take over many of his duties. He had recently gone through a difficult surgical procedure and simply couldn't meet the heavy travel commitments which the job required. I agreed to do this, which meant that during the next two years, I would be traveling extensively on NRA business.

I was pleased to accept the NRA responsibility because it put me in front of various audiences all over the country which were related to the food-service industry. These occasions afforded important new learning experiences and the chance to make new friends. Over many years I had addressed various industry groups and had come to know many restaurateurs and food-service executives from different parts of the country. This was a great learning experience and a perfect opportunity to keep informed about new developments taking place in a growing industry that had become such an important part of my life. My travel schedule during the next few years was heavy and a bit tiring, but it was just what I needed when I was sorting out my options and trying to figure out what I wanted to do.

After winning the College National Championship at the age of 64, Bobby Bowden, the coach of the Florida State University football team, was asked if he might be considering retirement. He answered that after retirement there was only one big event to look forward to and he wasn't quite ready for that. Active people, particularly those who have only a single interest, have reason to be concerned when they face retirement. Even though I had a business career that was quite balanced, I was constantly on the lookout for a lot of "big events" to keep me busy and stimulated. I didn't want to get trapped into a life of dull monotony and inactivity.

After my election to the board of trustees at the University of Miami in 1973, I accepted all the leadership positions I was asked to assume and moved rather quickly in assuming major committee responsibilities. After serving as the chairman of the finance committee and later the executive committee, I was elected chairman of the board of trustees in 1980, a position that I was to hold for the next 10 years, culminating in my election as chairman emeritus (for life). To say that this activity kept me busy would be quite an understatement. It became almost a full-time job.

A similar challenge was waiting for me in 1973 when I joined the board of the Community Television Foundation of South Florida. The first challenge was to resolve an impossible "share-channel agreement" we had with the Dade County School Board. The Federal Communications Commission issued a license to the Dade County School Board to broadcast on the UHF channel 2 frequency in 1955, during the heyday of "Educational TV." A citizens' group was formed to consider ways to develop public ownership of this facility, but because this group had only limited resources at the time, it needed the support of the school board to work this out. The share-channel arrangement was entered into in 1970. The school board retained programming control during weekdays until 3 p.m., using the call letters WTHS, and the foundation agreed to operate the station during late afternoon hours, evenings, and weekends, using the call letters WPBT. This created mass confusion. I took on the responsibility of resolving the matter and talked the school board into turning over their interest to the foundation at no cost. Gradually the confusion disappeared and channel 2 became recognized as a premier television broadcaster in the South Florida area.

While I was chairman of the board of directors of WPBT–Channel 2, I suggested that we offer a business news program. At the time we were unable to compete with the major networks' evening news programs. Our president, George Dooley, liked the idea and in 1979 we began presenting a 15-minute program, *The Nightly Business Report*. After the format was changed to 30 minutes, it became one of the most popular shows on public television. The program is now broadcast worldwide every weekday evening from our studios in Miami.

I believe I accomplished a great many things as chairman of the board of directors before stepping down in 1979. Conceiving the idea of the *Nightly Business Report* was one of them. The acquisition of additional properties adjoining our studios was another and perhaps even more important contribution.

During the 1970s, I went on the boards of the Storer Broadcasting Company, Ryder System, and Southeast Banking Corporation. These three highly respected Miami-based companies had already earned national distinction as leading companies in their respective fields. I joined the board of a small independent oil and gas company in Midland, Texas, and served as a director of Arvida Corporation for a very brief period of time, when this leading community real estate developer was undergoing extensive corporate repositioning. With my service on these seven corporate boards and the attention I was giving to the various investments I had made, I was able to keep in touch with the fascinating world of business, which was always something of great interest to me.

My investment decisions ran the full gamut from good to bad. The oil business did rather poorly, and I lost some money putting some beef cattle on feed in a Denver feed lot, but I learned important lessons about avoiding the kinds of investments I didn't fully understand. I also learned to examine the character, reputation, and experience of the people I was dealing with. What was particularly gratifying to me during these years immediately following retirement was the fact that I was no longer under the kind of pressure and stress I had experienced in the corporate world I had just left. My cup was beginning to fill up, and it would soon reach the point of running over.

CHAPTER
EIGHTEEN

Burger King Grows

1972 to 1988

During the early 1950s the first restaurants appeared which ultimately developed into what became known as "fast-food chains." Burger King, McDonald's, and Kentucky Fried Chicken all came from very humble origins, but they were able to establish a small foothold during this decade. With the dawn of the 1960s these three industry pioneers began to attract a modest amount of regional attention, but at that early date there was no indication that these small entrepreneurial ventures would ever trigger the international explosion of growth and development that took place in the years which followed.

As the country entered the 1960s the American lifestyle began to take on an entirely new character and focus. This produced a rapidly increasing demand to "eat out" more often, which was a phenomenon attributed to a number of economic factors and social changes. During the latter part of the 1940s, family income began to increase as more women and teenagers entered the work force. Servicemen returning from World War II and the Korean War married and began raising families, which led to the development of what became known as the "baby boom." This in turn triggered an exodus from urban centers and a rush into the growing areas of suburbia, which brought about large-scale construction of new homes, the development of shopping centers, and the construction of new highways. There was high consumer demand for all sorts of material goods, including automobiles. Television was still in its infancy, but it began to have a profound effect on American lifestyles. People developed new and different ideas about how they wanted to live and function in a rapidly changing world. The food-service industry responded to these changes with the certainty that people in the United States were going to be less inclined to eat at home. In the future they would demand service in restaurants, which would combine features of speed, convenience, and quality in tune with the times and the consumers' increased affluence, mobility, and sense of values.

The mom-and-pop restaurants which had succeeded and dominated the restaurant scene during the twenties, thirties, and forties were soon challenged by the emergence of chain restaurants conceived to cater to modern-day tastes and preferences. Conditions were ripe for the success of these chains, and this led to their ultimate preeminence in the marketplace.

During the 1950s restaurants such as Burger King found that they could attract customer interest and be operated very profitably. The first key to this success was the introduction of limited menus, which enabled these restaurants to consistently and quickly deliver quality food at rock-bottom prices. The second key was the basic simplicity of the restaurant operations, which enabled management to easily train franchisees to operate these businesses. The third key was that franchisees of multiunit restaurant chains could join together to advertise their business to create consumer awareness and demand. Dave and I jumped on the opportunity when we first sensed the importance of this situation. As early industry pioneers, we had an important head start as far as our size and experience was concerned, and we were determined to capitalize on this advantage.

During the late 1950s and early 1960s companies such as Burger King were opening less than a dozen restaurants a year, but they were still considered to be industry leaders and big in terms of their relative size. Of interest is the fact that those restaurants then considered "The Big Three," Burger

King, McDonald's, and Kentucky Fried Chicken, still enjoy the same nationally recognized status well into the 1990s. Perhaps as many as one hundred aspiring fast-food companies fell by the wayside since Burger King established itself as a leader, because competition was stiff. Although the systems we used were basically quite simple and easy to copy, it took good management and effective marketing strategies to succeed. The marketplace was a harsh teacher. To the struggling participants success didn't come easy. It had to be earned.

By the late 1960s Burger King had established itself as an advertiser big enough to use local, regional, and even network television. This was possible because our franchisees were required by contract to pay 4 percent of their sales to support our joint advertising and marketing programs. This factor contributed significantly to our ability to grow the business during the seventies, eighties, and into the nineties.

By the early 1970s, we had shown most of the television markets across the country what a Whopper looked like and how it was made. By that time the American public knew what Burger King was all about. With our restaurants proudly displaying the sign "Home of the Whopper," our two brand names became fixed in the minds of millions of people, who came to regard our restaurants as good places to eat. We conveyed the simple message that at Burger King our customers would receive good food, excellent value, and quick service. Our selling proposition was that the Whopper was the very best hamburger in the country, and we hammered that message home using the terrific impact we could only get by using television. Our idea of the great American meal was a Whopper, fries, and a Coke, and we sold that idea. We believed that this was the right message, offering the right combination at the right moment in time.

Our competition wasn't exactly standing idly by watching us do this. McDonald's was busy doing pretty much the same thing we were, but they had also targeted the children's market very early, nailing it down with effective marketing strategies, which included the innovative use of a clown they named Ronald McDonald. Other chains began to use television advertising as soon as they could afford it. Led by Burger King and other fast-growing chains, the food-service industry grew rapidly by targeting consumers eager to be served. As these modern-day restaurant chains grew and prospered, the restaurant industry became one of the country's largest television advertisers.

Restaurant chains were motivated to grow as rapidly as possible so that they could take advantage of the effectiveness of television advertising. In our case we were determined early in the 1960s to become national in stature so that we could then tap the added cost efficiency of using network television. This was the best buy in terms of our cost-per-viewer impression. During the seventies and eighties network television advertising not only served to build restaurant sales for the few companies who were large enough and able to afford it, but it helped to expand the entire food-service market by creating awareness and an accompanying consumer demand for restaurant services and eating out. Advertising also focused interest and attention on owning restaurant franchises. The result was that the food-service industry enjoyed a long period of extraordinary growth.

For years the restaurant industry was regarded as one of the most failure-prone businesses in the United States. Restaurant franchising changed all of that. In Burger King's case, by the early 1970s we had opened over 800 restaurants and had never experienced a failure. Specialized chains like ours, by having been tested in the marketplace and by offering training, backup, and support, helped to ensure the success of their franchisees. In time the restaurant business earned a reputation of being a relatively safe, reliable, and profitable way for people to get into a business of their own. The food-service market by the 1990s exceeded $275 billion, which was an extraordinary increase from the $10 billion it had been in 1949, when I opened my first restaurant in Wilmington, Delaware. Absent the introduction of franchising and the resulting growth of the multiunit chains, we would never have witnessed such a revolutionary change.

It was most unfortunate that during the extraordinarily explosive growth period leading up to the early 1970s, Burger

King lost the opportunity to challenge for the number 1 position in the fast-food industry. During the vibrant 1960s, all of us felt that we had a reasonable chance to reach that pinnacle of success. During the five-year period following the 1967 merger with Burger King, Pillsbury began to cut back on our restaurant expansion and franchising at a time when the industry leader, McDonald's, was intent on quadrupling their own. By 1972 we had to concede that it would be virtually impossible for us to challenge them for the lead. This wasn't a very happy thought for our management team, which had proved that we were pretty good at running our company and building a lot of successful restaurants.

As the 1970s began, the industry found itself in a unique position. Chain restaurants had been virtually unknown and unnoticed during most of the early 1960s and so was restaurant advertising. By the 1970s franchised-restaurant sales reached levels which had previously been considered as being out of reach. This growth and the accompanying increase in advertising expenditures began to build a strong consumer demand for restaurant services. With this kind of activity in the marketplace, a lot of smart people who had studied the industry's growth potential were poised to jump in and take over if the leaders demonstrated an inability or unwillingness to take the initiative themselves.

McDonald's effectiveness in dealing with this situation is attested by the fact that by the early 1990s they were able to report earnings before tax in excess of $1.5 billion and boasted of having 12,418 restaurants in operation at year-end 1992. At the same time Burger King reported operating profits of approximately $250 million with 6648 restaurants in operation. We had been able to stay in the number 2 position, but we paled in comparison to the industry leader. The years 1972 to 1988 were an important expansion period for Burger King, but for McDonald's they were nothing short of spectacular.

Arthur Rosewall directed Burger King during the five years immediately following my departure, but declining health forced him to withdraw from active management in 1977. In February of that year Don Smith was brought in to serve as president and CEO of Burger King. A former McDonald's senior officer, Smith remained at the helm until May of 1980 when conflicts with Minneapolis headquarters resulted in his withdrawal. During his three-year service with the company, Smith introduced and insisted upon much higher standards of restaurant operations than had previously been in effect, while giving support to a number of excellent marketing programs, which were produced under the direction of the chief marketing officer at the time, Chris Schoenleb.

Following Don Smith's departure, Lou Neeb took over as chairman and CEO, having previously served as president of Steak and Ale, a company which Pillsbury acquired in 1976. The founder of Steak and Ale, Norman Brinker, was then serving as a director of Pillsbury and was acting as a Pillsbury vice president and CEO of Steak and Ale. When Neeb left Burger King in 1982, Brinker took over as chairman and CEO of both Steak and Ale and Burger King. He elevated Jeff Campbell to the position of chairman and CEO of Burger King, a position held by Jeff into calendar year 1988. Over many years Brinker demonstrated extraordinary skills in recognizing trends and building highly successful restaurant concepts. He stepped into a leadership vacuum after Don Smith's departure and stabilized a very difficult situation.

Jeff Campbell had previously worked for Chris Schoenleb in the marketing area during the early 1970s. As an energetic and highly creative member of this department, Jeff was involved with implementing the highly successful "Have it your way" campaign. He rose rapidly in the ranks, playing an important role building sales, which by 1975 were running at an average annual rate of $420,000 per restaurant per year.

While serving as a member of the marketing department, Campbell asked for duty as a line officer and served as the Northeast region's vice president where he proved to be quite successful. With operating experience under his belt, he returned to Miami in 1981 to take the top job in the Burger King marketing department. By that time our average restaurant sales had grown to $728,000. Within four years they rose to over $1 million. It was at this point in 1983 that Brinker elevated Jeff to the position of chairman of the board and CEO of Burger King Corporation, a position he held for the next five years.

One of his first initiatives as chairman was to introduce "operation shape up," a program designed to build on Don Smith's determination to improve restaurant operations. Business responded well as a result of this initiative. Also during the early part of the 1980s, working with the J. Walter Thompson Advertising Agency, Burger King marketing programs reached the pinnacle of success by producing good, solid, and well-executed advertising messages which packed a big wallop. The 1983 Pillsbury annual report proudly announced that: "Burger King commercials became the talk of the country for their candid creativity."

It is important to note the significance of our various marketing strategies over the years. Advertising campaigns are designed to deliver specific messages to the public. In Burger King's case our need was to tell a story about who and what we were and describe the benefits our customers would enjoy as a result of eating in our restaurants. Depending on the quality and execution of the message, our advertising could be highly effective in building sales or produce very little impact. Creativity was the key to this strategy, and our challenge was to get our message across with as much impact as possible.

One of the initial campaigns launched in the early 1970s was the "Have it your way" campaign, which was not only very effective advertising but put Burger King on a new course. The promise contained in this advertising was that we would give our customers a special, new, and unique service which they could not get at other fast-food restaurants. We made the point that we would dress our sandwiches exactly according to our customers' wishes. This was a direct strike at McDonald's, whom we believed to be vulnerable because their production and service methods did not enable them to provide this kind of special treatment and handling for their customers. This very successful campaign was followed by "Make it special, make it Burger King," which emphasized the personal treatment and made-to-order good food our customers could expect in our restaurants.

The marketing savvy and leadership of Campbell and Kyle Craig (marketing) during the early 1980s resulted in the creation of one successful advertising campaign after another. The campaigns were highly focused on the quality of our hamburgers, and they positioned Burger King in the public's mind as the preferred place to go for hamburgers. The very successful "Aren't you hungry" campaign was a blockbuster success built on showing our open-flame broiling, with hamburgers dressed with a mouth-watering array of goodies and condiments. The "Battle of the burgers" campaign attacked our competition head-on by referring to consumer surveys which showed a definite preference for Burger King's Whopper.

These creative and well-executed campaigns were responsible for helping to more than double our average store sales during the period of 1981 to 1987. This extraordinary success was driven by Burger King's insistence and emphasis on excellence in restaurant operation. We focused on delivering the promise our advertising was making. The restaurants had to be well-run or the advertising would count for little. This important fundamental is occasionally overlooked by marketing people who are often more concerned about producing creative selling messages than insisting upon excellence in restaurant operations.

The four very effective marketing strategies introduced prior to 1985 were built on the success generated by one of our earliest campaigns, "It takes two hands" (to handle a Whopper). This was created by BBDO during my years as CEO. This campaign sent out a strong message about value, quality, and the uniqueness that people could find only at Burger King. When this was followed by the highly successful "Have it your way" campaign, we began to build a strong foundation which helped to establish Burger King as one of the top providers of restaurant services in the United States. Unfortunately, the marketing strategies which followed, beginning in 1985, fell far short of delivering the same kind of results which were produced by these earlier campaigns. This was also the moment when the world of Burger King started to unravel.

Throughout the early 1980s Burger King continued to make significant progress in terms of the number of restaurants it opened and the profits it earned. These were good times in an expanding economy with the food-service market continuing to grow at an impressive rate. As expected, the demand for Burger King franchises picked up along with that. Contributions made to the cooperative advertising fund continued to pour in, and by 1985 we had over $175 million per year available for marketing activities. By 1985 the number of Burger King restaurants in the United States had climbed to 4225. This gave us an important physical presence which, when coupled with our powerful advertising campaigns, provided us with a significant marketing advantage.

Following his string of successes in Miami, Campbell was asked to move to Minneapolis to head up Pillsbury's restaurant division. In doing so he kept the mantle of chairman and CEO of Burger King. Unfortunately, things started to become a bit mixed up after he left Miami. Jerry Ruenheck, who had served as Burger King president and chief operating officer ever since Don Smith's departure in 1980, stepped down in 1985 to become a franchisee. Kyle Craig, who had been extremely effective as the chief marketing officer following Campbell's move to the chairmanship, left to head up other Pillsbury restaurant operations and was ultimately put in as the CEO of Steak and Ale. Later he left Pillsbury and went on to serve as president of Kentucky Fried Chicken—USA. Kyle's loss was keenly felt within the Burger King organization.

After departures by Ruenheck and Craig followed by Campbell's move to Minneapolis, there was a period of management instability, resulting in a high turnover in the executive suite. During 1986 three different executives served in the capacity of chief marketing officer, and as incredible as it may seem, for one lengthy period of time, no one served in that important capacity. The work of the department was turned over to various members of the marketing staff, who dealt with our challenges in a rather disorganized manner on a completely ad hoc basis.

With the departure of key members of top management a lot of things began to go downhill. The changes and disruptions in the executive offices and marketing department led to the launching of one disastrous advertising campaign after another. The first of these was the infamous "Herb the Nerd" campaign which was followed by a succession of subsequent failures. The "Herb" fiasco was mentioned in *Advertising Age* as being the worst advertising campaign of the year. What followed in rapid succession didn't represent much of an improvement. Even Burger King's own marketing research people referred to the period of 1985–1987 as the "blurred image era."

As desperation set in and one ill-conceived campaign followed another, we lost our focus. The public was left to wonder what Burger King was all about. They were totally confused about our message. To complicate matters, menu prices were steadily increased, and this proved to be a very unwise and flawed strategy, which gradually brought about a steady erosion in customer traffic. Unfortunately, this situation was never adequately addressed. The loss of focus in our advertising and the steady upward ratcheting of menu prices marked a critical juncture in Burger King history. The public was confused about the selling proposition, and they began to have second thoughts about Burger King's being a good place to go for value. This was an unfortunate shift in public perception which, if left unchecked, could seriously damage the company's prospects for the future.

We had built the business by projecting a clear image of who and what we were, and the central message was always centered on the subject of value. Value is more than a matter of price alone. It involves aspects of service and ambiance as well, and we were failing on all counts. Unfortunately, it would be years before management would fully understand the significance of all this. In the meantime, customer traffic continued its steady decline. Management appeared willing to accept this as long as high profit margins were maintained, and they continued to raise menu prices. Things were beginning to fall apart, and as far as I was concerned, the prospects for the future looked to be anything but bright.

1985 was not a good year for either Pillsbury or Burger King. One disappointing loss was Win Wallin's decision to leave as vice chairman of The Pillsbury Company. For a number of years Win had been responsible for overseeing Pillsbury's restaurant operations which included Burger King. He had been a highly regarded Pillsbury executive, respected by both Burger King management and its franchisees. His stature, intelligence, and mature leadership acted as a stabilizing factor in nurturing many important relationships.

In May of 1985, Pillsbury acquired Diversifoods for $390 million in cash. This company consisted of a conglomeration of restaurant operations including the ailing Godfather's Pizza chain, the Chart House restaurants, and 377 Burger King restaurants located in the greater Chicago area, Louisiana, and the neighboring Gulf coast as well as parts of Virginia.

Chart House, our largest franchisee, acquired Godfather's Pizza during the time when Don Smith was CEO of Burger King. It proved to be a very costly mistake. Following this acquisition, the corporate name of Chart House was changed to "Diversifoods." The sales and operational problems which existed in the Godfather's organization were responsible for driving down the price of Diversifoods stock to a fraction of its former level. Employees' morale suffered as a result of the serious marketing, sales, and image problems that were associated with the company. Restaurant operations and the physical appearance of the restaurants suffered as the result. Diversifoods was not in the best of shape when Smith left the CEO position to take on another assignment.

Pillsbury was rather obligated at that point to acquire Diversifoods in order to preserve the integrity of the Burger King name. The 377 Burger King restaurants had been so poorly run in recent years that our reputation was badly damaged in a number of important markets. It would be enough of a problem to clean up the Burger King situation, but the bigger challenge was making some sense out of a sick pizza business, which we knew nothing about. There was also the problem of managing the Chart House chain of full-service specialty restaurants, which were spread out from coast to coast. I began to regret even more Pillsbury's failure to acquire Chart House on terms which Art Rosewall and I had recommended in the early 1970s. Now they were forced to pay a king's ransom for a sick business which earlier would have cost but a fraction of the price.

Adding to our difficulties was the fact that in 1985 Bill Spoor, having reached retirement age, stepped down as CEO of Pillsbury. The departures of so many corporate leaders created serious leadership voids. With key positions in many of his divisions to fill, the new Pillsbury CEO, Jack Stafford, faced significant challenges in building an organization which could manage an extremely diverse and complex number of businesses under rather difficult circumstances. Unfortunately, these problems came at a time when a variety of operational storm clouds were gathering. Jack had lots to be concerned with and to think about.

Pillsbury's fiscal 1986 report covering 1985 results acknowledged almost apologetically: "After three years of spectacular growth, year-to-year sales per restaurant increased only slightly." In Burger King's case, comparable restaurant sales adjusted for menu price increases had actually dropped below those of the prior year. Left unsaid was that our customer counts were in a free fall.

During the years 1985 to 1988 the revolving door in the executive suite at Burger King seemed to turn faster and faster. These changes in management created a certain amount of disorientation. Long-term strategic planning gave way to dealing with shorter-term tactical issues, operational problems, quick fixes, and just putting out fires. At this critical juncture Burger King management made a number of unfortunate decisions, all of which were destined to have a negative impact on our business.

The first decision involved the introduction of untested new products to an already overcrowded menu. This was the first of several ways management hoped to stem the tide of declining sales and customer traffic. The second decision was to continue raising menu prices as a means of increasing profit margins. Management saw this as an opportunity to increase restaurant profitability. Both strategies were grossly flawed from a strategic point of view, and they wound up producing the exact opposite effect of what was intended. Unfortunately, the problems created weren't recognized for an agonizingly long period of time.

New products were introduced in a never-ending stream without management sensing the damage which might be caused. Burger King was founded on the simple premise that a limited menu was our key to success. Our expanded menu confused the public. It also confused the employees who were filling our customers' orders. This created in-store production problems which reduced our speed of service and lowered the overall quality of our product line. The added confusion made it difficult for employees to fill our customers' orders accurately. This became our number 1 customer complaint. Menu price increases brought on a steady erosion of the customer base. It became glaringly apparent that we were pricing ourselves out of the market. The tragedy of the situation was that we steadily lost customer traffic for years because top management consistently overlooked or failed to recognize the significance of these unwise decisions and the damage they were doing to our business.

Throughout 1986 and into the 1990s sales and traffic counts continued to deteriorate, and a series of ill-conceived marketing plans and advertising strategies were not able to stop the bleeding. Advertising expenditures in the 1985–1986 year exceeded $190 million and grew to $227 million by 1988. None of this heavy spending was able to stop the steady decline in sales and customer traffic. By the fall of 1988, with franchisees deeply disturbed and in near revolt, Grand Metropolitan entered the scene. The ensuing battle for control of Pillsbury and Burger King only aggravated the situation. Change was in the wind all right, but the question remained as to what effect this change would have on Burger King, its franchisees, and the future.

Years later Burger King was forced to admit that during a period of eight years from 1986 to 1993, we lost an average of 34 percent of our previous customer traffic per restaurant. The two questions demanding answers were: How did we get into this mess? and How were we going to get out of it?

I could see what was wrong and, interestingly, so could our marketing research people, but management was not seeking any advice on the subject. During the battle with Grand Met, when I was a director of The Pillsbury Company, it was easy to see that the interests of Burger King were not a matter of major concern. The fact was that during this battle Burger King and its family of franchisees were thought of as pawns in Pillsbury's battle to remain independent. Meanwhile, sales and profitability continued to decline. These were dismal and disappointing years. Unless changes took place, Burger King would be faced with big trouble.

Hostilities from London

Ryder Systems' board of directors, of which I was member, held a three-day meeting in Williamsburg, Virginia, beginning on Monday, October 3, 1988. Being a light sleeper, I woke up early Tuesday morning and walked down the hall at the Williamsburg Inn to a breakfast room especially set up for members of the Ryder board. A few of the directors had arrived and were seated at one of the tables. As I entered the room I received some startling news. Herman Schmidt, a retired vice president and general counsel of Mobil Oil Corporation, shot the question, "Jim, did you see the CNN story on Pillsbury this morning?" He went on to say that the morning edition of *The New York Times* had run a full-page advertisement announcing a cash tender offer by Grand Metropolitan Plc of Great Britain to buy all Pillsbury shares at $60 per share. To say I was shocked was putting it mildly. I thought that Pillsbury might be vulnerable to a takeover threat, but this was startling news. Our stock closed on the New York Stock Exchange the night before at $38 per share, so we were looking at an offer to buy the company for a 60 percent premium over the last trade.

This unsolicited, hostile takeover bid was as preemptive as it was extraordinary. Grand Met was obviously quite serious about acquiring Pillsbury and had laid a top-dollar offer on the table. The offer appeared to be high enough to discourage other would-be suitors or white knights from entering a bidding war, and it looked as though it was calculated to counter any defensive tactics that Pillsbury might put up in an effort to remain independent. Grand Met had obviously planned a vigorous offensive campaign, and they seemed to be prepared to deal with any defensive tactics that might result from their actions. Pillsbury needed to respond right away, so I expected to receive a call very soon from our Minneapolis headquarters. The call wasn't long in coming.

There was good reason to think that Pillsbury might be a target for a takeover. To begin with, the company had been the subject of a lot of negative press during the preceding two or three years. Much of it involved management turnover and changes that had taken place in the executive offices of the company. Bill Spoor had served as Chairman and CEO for 13 years, from 1973 until 1986. He was strongly supportive of John Stafford, and he had recommended to the board that he succeed him as CEO.

Stafford came to Pillsbury with an excellent reputation and background having served as the chief marketing officer of the Green Giant organization. After Green Giant was acquired by Pillsbury in February of 1979, Jack had made many significant contributions to the company in key leadership roles. He rose rapidly in the organization. The board elected him president of The Pillsbury Company in 1984, and he and Spoor worked together in harmony. In 1986 Spoor reached retirement age and on his recommendation, the Pillsbury board elected Stafford to the post of chairman, president, and CEO. Unfortunately Stafford soon encountered a number of operational disappointments in the exercise of his managerial responsibilities.

In the first place he inherited a business that had a number of problems. The Steak and Ale restaurant subsidiary headquartered in Dallas had overexpanded, and it was operating outside of their management's span of control. Sales and profits had declined from former levels, and the company was faced with closing a number of their restaurants.

The profitable Bennigan's Tavern concept was also showing some of the same trouble. Controls were weak. Management was stretched pretty thin and had become increasingly less effective. These problems began to show up on the bottom line about the same time as the Burger King situation started to unravel.

Leading up to 1986, Burger King management was under increased pressure to increase profitability. During the period of 1980–1984 menu prices had held very steady and profitability had increased noticeably. With highly successful marketing programs like "Have it your way," "Aren't you hungry," "Make it special," and the "Battle of the burgers," sales and customer counts increased steadily during this four-year period. Unfortunately, costs were also rising with the result that margins were being squeezed. In the recent past, restaurant profitability had increased dramatically, but management seemed to be preoccupied with the possibility that future profitability might come under pressure. Their solution to the problem would be a simple one, and the word went out to raise prices.

Beginning in 1986 Burger King's comparable store sales began to decline, and customer traffic fell off at the same time. Raising menu prices was exactly the wrong course of action, taken at the wrong time. By 1988 customer counts were in a free fall. Alarm bells were ringing, but nobody seemed to be listening. Marketing strategies were so poorly conceived and awkward that Burger King became the subject of negative reporting and ridicule in the food-service and advertising trade press. Even the national media was giving Burger King a bad time, citing in particular the infamous "Herb the Nerd" advertising campaign that had been such a colossal bust. Predictions were that this campaign would go down in history as one of the least effective and most costly marketing fiascoes of all time. Unfortunately, there were other advertising campaigns to follow that were almost as bad.

Stafford had the misfortune to preside over Burger King's change of agency from J. Walter Thompson to N.W. Ayer. Hot on the heels of the "Herb" disaster, Ayer brought out another questionable and ineffective campaign called, "We do it like you'd do it." Spending on the various campaigns and the costs related to them ran into the hundreds of millions of dollars, and still Burger King was facing a steady decline in traffic and sales. Mixed in with these high-profile disappointments were minicampaigns like "Burger King Town," "Good food for fast times," "Bigger and better," and "Torch" (Broiling is better). Not only were these campaigns not working, but we were projecting new and different images. Our own marketing research pointed out to management that our customers were very confused about what Burger King was trying to say. Management did not have a grip on the problem, and with the declining traffic counts and negative sales performance, our franchisees were becoming increasingly hostile and impatient. It was a bad situation, which had been developing for several years, and it was going to get much worse.

At the time I was not particularly well informed about all that was going on inside the Pillsbury operating divisions, but there was plenty of evidence of trouble there. The declining share of market in both our consumer-product sales and restaurant divisions was evidence that Pillsbury was having trouble on a number of different fronts. Stafford was in trouble because of these disappointing results. The Pillsbury board didn't like the numbers they were looking at. To make matters worse, Bill Spoor's interest in trying to help solve the problem was interpreted by the press and others to mean that he intended to return to the CEO job to lead Pillsbury out of the dilemma. This was not a fair interpretation of the situation, but the perception of it fueled speculation that there was dissension in the managerial ranks. It also focused attention on Pillsbury's sales, marketing, and profit woes and on problems with Burger King and its franchisees.

The Pillsbury directors faced the management issue at a board meeting in Naples, Florida, in March of 1988. Stafford, with considerable grace and dignity, tendered his resignation, and the board elected Bill Spoor to succeed him. Bill was asked to serve as the interim CEO until a replacement could be found. The press gave considerable coverage to this event, and Pillsbury took a pretty sound drubbing in the financial press. *Fortune* magazine wrote a story about "the management caldron at Pillsbury." All the articles which focused on the notion that Pillsbury was in trouble and that in order to deal with the problem the company had reinstated a tough-minded CEO, who would take vigorous and unpopular actions as a means of restoring the company to the level of profitability and market position it had enjoyed in the past. Press relations reached a low ebb and almost ensured that there would be caustic reviews to document the company's plight. All of this was on my mind when the news of Grand Metropolitan's $60-a-share tender offer was announced on October 4, 1988.

Prior to that time there had been rumors circulating about the possibility of Pillsbury becoming a takeover target. What attracted Grand Metropolitan? Certainly the company's visibly weakened market position in key business areas, coupled with its own management problems, made the idea of a corporate raid or takeover at least seem possible.

At this particular time in history, corporate takeovers were the most talked about subject in the business world and in the financial press. The country was awash in cash thanks to junk-bond financing, which was used to create gigantic pools of cash. Cash was readily available to corporate raiders or other parties who were actively engaged in funding corporate takeovers. Michael Milken and his associates in the investment banking firm of Drexel, Burnham, Lambert dominated the field of junk-bond financing and were deeply involved in this controversial activity. Corporate raiders suddenly had access to huge pools of capital, and for that reason the threat of corporate takeovers became the subject of tense and focused discussion in boardrooms all over the country. Junk-bond financing brought about some of the largest corporate takeovers in the history of the country. It was the use of such huge amounts of debt financing that was largely responsible for the collapse of many financial institutions, most notably in the insurance, commercial banking, and the savings and loan industries. Many financial institutions were scalded by engaging in this kind of practice.

Beginning in 1986 Burger King began to show negative comparable store sales and sharply declining customer counts after a series of marketing disasters. Franchisees were upset and vocal in their criticisms of Burger King and Pillsbury. These concerns, which were expressed with a level of hostility and resentment, soon gained attention in newspaper articles and magazines. Management could only watch and wince as confrontational stories continued to be aired. Pillsbury's corporate weaknesses and vulnerability became increasingly more visible and evident to the public and the financial community at large.

In February 1988 I received a call from Donald Smith, who had been Burger King's president and CEO from January 1977 to May 1980. Don presided over several of the most prosperous years in sales and profit improvement in Burger King history. He was highly regarded by franchisees who found him to be an operationally oriented, effective executive. Smith had done much to improve their business during the years he had been in charge. Don had had a long career with McDonald's and was serving as one of their top executives when he was recruited by Pillsbury to become Burger King's president and CEO. The franchisees developed a healthy respect for Smith because they shared a common interest rooted in the importance of maintaining the highest standards of restaurant operations. Smith reinforced the rules, and franchisees understood that he wouldn't tolerate any departure from prescribed operating procedures. They towed the line. They liked Smith's decisiveness, and they appreciated the fact that he was a team builder who had exceptional leadership skills. There was never a question about who was in charge when Smith was sitting in the president's chair.

The problem was that Smith, being as strong as he was, was dealing with equally strong and tough-minded leadership in Minneapolis. It wasn't long before confrontational differences of opinion arose regarding strategic issues and differences in management styles.

Smith wanted more freedom in running Burger King. He also wanted to be more involved in determining the strategic direction of the company, but he found himself in the position of having to take too many matters before the Pillsbury management group and the board for approval. As frustration set in and more conflicts arose, personalities began to clash. This heightened more of the we-versus-them attitude that had prevailed since the merger took place in 1967. Miami executives seemed to feel that they were in the position of coming to Minneapolis in beggar's clothes with outstretched hands asking for favors. They felt left out of the strategic planning process. It was their view that tactical approaches to problem solving and most operational issues were decided upon long before they got to town.

Problems like these are not particularly unusual in parent-subsidiary relationships. Pillsbury and Burger King were two very different companies, each having unique corporate styles and philosophies. These differences often lead to personal conflicts, which can make it difficult to maintain smooth working relationships. By the time Grand Met entered the picture, this situation had existed throughout most of the 21-year history between the two companies. Smith's frustration ultimately led to his departure. In 1980 Pepsico asked him to take over their Taco Bell and Pizza Hut subsidiaries. Smith seemed pleased to get out, and there was reason to believe that the management in Minneapolis was equally pleased to see him go. Burger King franchisees saw it differently. They felt that Smith's departure was an unfortunate loss of leadership.

After a short tenure at Pepsico, Smith left to take over food-service operations at Hershey Foods, which owned the Friendly Ice Cream Corporation, a restaurant company with over 600 operations in 16 states, mostly in the Northeast. Later on he went on the Holiday Inn board which had acquired Perkins Family Restaurants, a restaurant chain located principally in the Midwest. Perkins had been a lackluster performer in recent years, and this presented Holiday Inn with a problem they didn't need at the time. They had plenty of other problems of their own. The directors decided to restructure Holiday Inn and unload Perkins. This resulted in a leveraged buyout wherein Smith gained a significant interest in the Perkins chain based on his agreement to take over its management and restore the company to acceptable levels of profitability.

The Bass Brothers and key manager, Richard Rainwater, of Fort Worth were the principal architects of the deal and became the principal partners in the leveraged buyout, or LBO. Within a few years Smith turned Perkins around and produced a success for the company and its investors. In the process he created a personal fortune for himself and obviously impressed the Bass Brothers' organization. Smith called me from Boca Raton in February of 1988 and asked if he might come by the house and bring along a friend he wanted me to meet. The meeting took place the next day with the three of us seated around our pool. I had no idea what he wanted to talk about. His friend was a financial deal maker and a former associate of the Bass Brothers. The purpose of their visit became evident after Don explained his deal with Holiday and Perkins. They wanted to discuss the possibility of acquiring Burger King Corporation from The Pillsbury Company.

As a director of The Pillsbury Company I wanted to avoid any discussion on the subject, and I told them at the outset that I was unwilling to go over it with them. I told them that this was something the two of them should talk to Bill Spoor directly about, and I suggested that this was their only logical course of action in pursuing the matter. I didn't want to put myself in the middle of this situation. Don may have thought that I was frustrated by the gradually worsening conditions at Burger King and might be willing to act as an intermediary in approaching Pillsbury, but I wanted no part of that.

It was clear that Smith had talked to quite a few of our franchisees. This was reported in the press at the time in articles about our franchisees' growing dissatisfaction with Pillsbury's stewardship of Burger King. Smith tested the idea of his taking over Burger King in talks with key franchisees. I wanted to stay out of any discussion on the subject because of conflicts that could easily have arisen as a result of that. I offered to arrange contact with Pillsbury if they wanted to review the matter with management, and I left it on that basis.

The following morning I advised Pillsbury's general counsel about Smith's visit and offered to review what had taken place during our discussion if management wanted any more information about our meeting, but no one called back to ask any questions. This seemed odd to me in light of the increasing speculation that Pillsbury might be a takeover target in the future. The Bass brothers were known to be a major player in the takeover business and had probably taken a hard look at Pillsbury in the process of considering a buyout of Burger King. I began to wonder how many others had been looking us over. All of this added to my surprise that no one at Pillsbury called me back to discuss the previous day's encounter.

At the time Don Smith was attempting to open discussions concerning the possibility of acquiring Burger King, Pillsbury received word that Bill Farley, an investor and takeover specialist in Chicago was accumulating Pillsbury stock. By the middle of 1988, Farley had bought close to three million shares of Pillsbury at an average cost of $38 a share. Farley had earned the reputation of being a corporate raider during the past few years because of his aggressive acquisition of shares in a number of companies. By acting in this fashion he was holding out a threat that he might try to take over a company. This tactic often resulted in the company's buying back the large block of shares he had bought. This was usually done at a price above market value, giving Farley a considerable profit. The practice was called greenmail.

At one point during the summer months of 1988, with Pillsbury stock dropping $3 or $4 a share, Farley was "underwater" by as much as $10 million. In addition, he was obligated to pay a very high rate of interest on the money he had borrowed to finance his purchase of stock. Formerly an investment banker and analyst, Farley had an eye for vulnerable corporate situations which might become a future takeover target. It seemed obvious to me at the time that The Pillsbury Company was one of his next targets. I wondered how many others had the same idea in mind.

With Farley showing a $10 million paper loss, it seemed as though he might have made a serious mistake in taking such a major position in Pillsbury stock. He was willing to borrow huge sums of money to finance his purchases of shares in various companies, but this one looked like he was on shallow ground. Farley had made a fortune doing this sort of thing in the past, and it was becoming increasingly clear that this time he had his eye on Pillsbury. There is an interesting sidelight to Farley's venture: Months after the Grand Met takeover of Pillsbury was completed, I was lecturing at a Young Presidents Organization seminar in Buenos Aires and ran into Bill Farley, who was in attendance. I asked him how he finally made out on the Pillsbury stock he had accumulated. He told me that he had made a profit of $77 million. I had to respect his instincts.

Our directors probably knew that Pillsbury was being looked at, but aside from knowing about Farley, they had no idea who was doing the looking. The question was where the first strike might come from and what form it would take. This was not a subject the board was willing to discuss. Grand Metropolitan supplied the startling answer on October 4.

The surprising announcement of Grand Metropolitan's offer on October 4 resulted in the calling of a special meeting of the Pillsbury board a few days later. It was imperative that the board respond to the offer and consider all matters relating to it. For Pillsbury stockholders the offer was very significant. Shares of Pillsbury stock had increased 60 percent in market value in the anticipation that a takeover was imminent. The arbitrageurs had jumped in with both feet. They believed a bidding war might drive up the value of the stock even further. Stockholders would be very attentive to any response the directors of the company would make.

The first reaction of many stockholders in such a situation is to urge the directors to accept the offer. There are two reasons for this. The first reason is that the price being offered is at such a premium to the market that it is "too good to refuse." The second reason is based on the possibility or threat that the offer could be withdrawn. To stockholders it is often a case of a bird in the hand being worth two in the bush. Grand Met had offered a 60 percent premium over the previous day's market close, which was a huge increase in the value of the shares. Stockholders have no authority to act in response to offers to acquire their company. That authority rests solely and entirely with a board of directors who have the authority and obligation to act on behalf of the shareholders.

In December of 1987 the Pillsbury board of directors adopted a so-called shareholders rights plan, the short name for which is a poison pill. Essentially this plan enables the board, in the event a takeover of the company is threatened, to issue rights to its shareholders to buy any acquiring company's stock at a price substantially below the market. The effect of this is to make any acquisition prohibitively expensive to a would-be acquirer. As a practical matter, so long as these rights are in place, the hostile bidder is forced to deal directly with the board of directors and attempt to negotiate a settlement. Without a shareholder rights plan in place, stockholders might tender their shares at the bid price, which could enable the hostile bidder to acquire a majority or all of the shares on their own stated terms. With a majority of shares in hand, any hostile bidder could effect the desired acquisition in any number of ways. This is an oversimplification, of course, but in the Pillsbury–Grand Met case a shareholder rights plan was in effect. It forced the two companies to negotiate in the event no other options were available.

The directors of Pillsbury were required to examine the tender offer by Grand Met carefully and consider all of its implications. One of the board's first responsibilities would be to determine whether the $60 offer by Grand Met represented the full value of Pillsbury shares. If they concluded that it did not, the board had an obligation to consider a better offer from another party or to restructure the company in such a fashion that would enhance the shareholders' value over and beyond the tender-offer price.

Our attorneys were Skadden, Arps, Slate, Meagher and Flom, one of the better-known firms specializing in corporate takeover matters. They were on retainer and in position to advise Pillsbury on the legal issues involved and to suggest a strategy the directors should follow in discharging their fiduciary responsibilities to shareholders.

In addition, the directors needed to retain financial consultants to counsel them on matters dealing with valuations, financial restructuring, and a host of other issues relating to the response they must make. Four major U.S. investment banking firms were retained: Drexel, Burnham, Lambert; Wasserstein, Perella & Co.; First Boston; and Shearson, Lehman, Hutton. Kleinwort-Benson, a British investment banking firm, was also retained. The retainers paid to these investment bankers were sizable. My recollection is that the fees exceeded $40 million.

The first action of the Pillsbury board at a meeting held in October was to issue rights to Pillsbury stockholders as prescribed in the shareholder rights plan. The rights gave stockholders the option to buy stock of any hostile acquirer's company at half of the market price in the event the proposed acquisition ever took place. This poison pill played a key role in determining the direction of the battle that would soon take place.

Based on studies provided by the investment bankers, the Pillsbury board determined that the $60 per share price was "inadequate" and advised shareholders not to tender their shares. In the bankers' judgment, the value of Pillsbury stock was in the range of $68 to $73 per share, and they presented their reasons in support of this opinion.

Efforts to locate a white knight proved futile, so management attempted to find ways to restructure the company in the hope that they could demonstrate to shareholders that the "pieces" resulting from such a restructuring would add up to an amount over and above that which Grand Met was willing to pay. In that case The Pillsbury Company might be able to remain independent.

The key piece under consideration was Burger King. The restructure involved a plan to dispose of Burger King Corporation via a spin off of the company to Pillsbury stockholders. Part of this plan was to have Burger King, *before being spun off,* borrow a sizable sum of money—perhaps in excess of $1 billion. After this was done, it was planned that Burger King would pay a huge cash dividend of a like amount to The Pillsbury Company. Pillsbury would in turn pay out the entire sum in cash dividends to Pillsbury stockholders. This dividend would play an important part of determining the valuation of the pieces of The Pillsbury Company to shareholders. It was planned that after the spin-off and the payment of the huge dividend, the remaining value of what was left in The Pillsbury Company would add up to a figure in excess of the Grand Met offer. Determining the value of the sum total of these pieces would be the responsibility of the directors. They would arrive at this determination based on the advice and representations made by our four U.S. investment bankers.

The key pawn in building this defensive strategy was Burger King Corporation, and there were two reasons for that. First of all, a spin-off would present a serious tax liability in the event any company subsequently acquired Pillsbury. It would probably be so onerous that it would force Grand Met to withdraw its tender offer. The IRS would view any normal spin-off of Burger King to Pillsbury stockholders as a tax-free transaction, but if Pillsbury were later to be acquired, the IRS would view the Burger King spin-off as a sale. The accounting treatment would be forced to acknowledge that an enormous capital gain had taken place. The resulting capital-gains tax would be huge.

To obtain the cash needed to pay such a large dividend to The Pillsbury Company, Burger King would make arrangements to borrow over $1 billion. If this could be arranged, and the investment bankers thought it could be, Pillsbury would be able to declare a $15 a share dividend to their stockholders.

A borrowing and subsequent payout of an amount of this magnitude would not only place Burger King Corporation in a precariously delicate financial condition, but render it practically incapable of providing for its future expansion needs and seriously undermine the company's ability to adequately service its franchisees. Such an action would render Burger King insolvent for all practical purposes.

The final indignity in the investment bankers' plan would result from a subsequent spin-off of the common stock of a mortally weakened Burger King Corporation to Pillsbury stockholders. It was the bankers' opinion that the remaining Burger King "stub" (its shares trading in the open market) would be valued in the range of $11 to $12 a share. It was felt that these two actions plus the "tax pill" created by the spin-off would surely keep a hostile suitor at bay. The $15 per Pillsbury share paid out in the form of a cash dividend and the stub of 88 million shares of Burger King stock selling at $12 would mean that the Burger King disposition would add up to a value of $27 per Pillsbury share. This would be a significant factor in helping convince the Delaware court that the whole of Pillsbury was worth more than the $60 a share being offered by Grand Met. Our investment bankers planned that the spin-off would consist of 88 million shares of Burger King stock, and they expressed the belief that these shares would trade on the open market at $12 per share. Assuming this happened, the market value of a nearly insolvent Burger King Corporation would be in excess of $1 billion. I found this difficult to believe.

Reaction of the Burger King franchisee community to news of such a plan was varied. On one hand there was an almost universal opinion among the franchisees, and many members of Burger King management, that an independent Burger King company with its common stock trading in the open market would be far more desirable from an operating standpoint than remaining a division of The Pillsbury Company. Franchisees were frustrated with Pillsbury's handling of Burger King affairs in recent years, and a sizable majority of them favored a separation.

It was the general feeling that an independent Burger King management would be better than what currently existed. Franchisees felt that way for a variety of reasons. They didn't approve of Pillsbury's regular practice of selling Burger King company stores and valuable real estate in order to meet profit goals. To franchisees this evidenced Pillsbury's lack of a long-term commitment to the business. There was also a general feeling among franchisees that the Burger King management crisis could be stabilized. The high turnover in the executive offices at Burger King was a matter of great concern to them. They consistently pointed to the fact that in the past 17 years Burger King had been managed by 9 chairmen, 10 presidents, and 8 chief marketing officers. To the franchisee community at large, an independently operated Burger King Corporation would be looked upon as a desirable alternative to the way things were.

On the other hand, Pillsbury's price for granting independence to Burger King would be ruinous to the financial health of Burger King. Adding $1 billion in debt to Burger King Corporation and turning this huge sum over to The Pillsbury Company so they could pay this out to their stockholders in the form of a huge cash dividend would seriously undermine Burger King's ability to remain a viable competitor in the marketplace. Franchisees rebelled when they realized what might happen to them. The implications of such a move were downright scary. Since the 1967 merger, there was never a time when more bitterness and resentment attended the relationship between the franchisee community and The Pillsbury Company.

During the desperate weeks that followed Grand Met's tender offer, Pillsbury management became immersed in an attempt to devise a restructuring plan which the board could support. It was important to be able to show that the pieces of Pillsbury added up to a value greater than the $60 per share that Grand Met was offering. Burger King, being the key to all this, was thought to be capable of delivering a value of $27 per share or almost half of the $60 Grand Met tender offer. This assumed that the spin-off would actually take place and the market would respond the way the bankers had predicted.

The important question was determining the realistic value of Burger King stock once it had been spun off to Pillsbury stockholders. What value would the investing public put on the shares of Burger King as a grossly overleveraged company? The investment bankers decided to make a judgment about this by projecting Burger King's profitability and financial condition based on management's future operating assumptions as to sales, expenses, and profits.

When the initial projections by Burger King management were delivered to Pillsbury, they were sent back with instructions to present a set of projections which would show a more optimistic outlook and a higher earnings potential. The bankers could not make their case with the first set of numbers they received. At this juncture Charles Olcott, who was under extreme pressure as Burger King's president and chief executive officer, resigned rather than sign off on figures he could not support. He thought that his initial presentation had plenty of "stretch" in it, and he was unwilling, as he said, "to pump any more air into the numbers."

This was a sad moment in Burger King history. Olcott's meeting with the newly elected Pillsbury CEO was uncompromising in its demand. Olcott told me later that he was instructed to sign off on higher profit projections for a stripped-down Burger King Corporation or he would be asked to resign. As Olcott explained to me later, it was either a choice of being a team player and going against his sense of ethics or getting fired. Olcott, a highly principled person, told me later, "Jim, I just couldn't do it. The initial figures were already full of air. I couldn't blow them up any further. I just said to hell with it and got out."

In the critical meeting of the Pillsbury board in Minneapolis on Sunday, November 6, the discussion centered on the Burger King spin-off idea. Pillsbury management presented Burger King's profit projections based on the latest set of operating assumptions they had put together. The figures were high enough to justify the spin-off concept, and they formed the basis upon which the investment bankers arrived at their opinion that the spun-off shares would sell in the market for around $12 per share. The board was hard pressed to challenge that opinion. After all, these highly paid bankers were the experts.

In my capacity as a director of Pillsbury I could not discuss any of these forecasts and assumptions with Burger King management, but instinctively I didn't like them. It was pretty clear to me that there was too much "blue sky" involved. I wished that I could have pinned down some of our management on the specifics in private, but this wasn't an appropriate thing for me to do. I didn't like the data I was looking at, and at the same time I was being pressured to accept the findings and recommendations of the bankers. All I could do was direct some pointed questions to the bankers about management's forecasts and conclusions. Did Burger King feel comfortable that given current market trends they could deliver these numbers? They said "yes" to that and also to a number of other challenges I threw out to them, but I felt they were hedging and under pressure to make the numbers fit. I wanted to know if the investment bankers had met with our management and were able to convince themselves that these projections about sales growth, profitability, and costs were reasonable.

I was quite well aware that we were into our third straight year of declining restaurant sales and customer counts. I also didn't have any confidence that the company's management had figured out how they were going to reverse that trend. It turned out that I was right about that. Comparable store sales and customer counts continued to decline for the next five years. Although the bankers assured me on the points I had raised, I harbored serious reservations about the whole thing. I felt that they were supporting the figures in order to justify the value they wanted to put on the Burger King shares once the company had been spun off. I told the directors about my reservations and stated my reasons for feeling the way I did, but the board had the assurance of Pillsbury management and the bankers that the figures were supportable. The directors, including myself, were not in a position to seriously challenge the numbers and the representations, so in the final analysis we could do little more than rely on the opinions of our advisers.

The critical moment for the Pillsbury directors came when the Burger King spin-off plan came to a vote. My position was right where the franchisees would line up when the news broke. I liked the idea of Burger King becoming an independent company, but the idea of leaving the company grossly undercapitalized and nearly insolvent was repugnant to me. I didn't like the plan, but when the matter was presented, I voted for it. It was already clearly evident that all the other directors were going to vote for the idea, and I felt that my negative vote would do more harm than good.

At this juncture there seemed to me to be every reason for the entire board to appear to be united. Aside from that, my principal obligation was to consider what would be in the best interest of the Pillsbury stockholders. This plan, *if it worked,* might be very good for Pillsbury stockholders. I was frustrated in my lack of confidence in the figures that management and the bankers were throwing our way inasmuch as I couldn't see how a financially weakened Burger King could survive. I seriously questioned that a spun-off Burger King's common stock would be able to command $11 to $12 in the marketplace. Still, if I was wrong about that and the bankers were right, this plan might prove to be a good deal for Pillsbury stockholders. It was my duty and obligation as a director of The Pillsbury Company to address the concerns of these stockholders. I could sympathize with Burger King, but I couldn't act in their behalf.

I thought about other fiduciary responsibilities. Certainly I had an obligation to consider the best interests of our employees in this matter. Our franchisees would be negatively impacted, if such a spin-off occurred. There was no question about that. I had an obligation to look after their interests, too. Our franchising relationship clearly assumed that franchisees had a right to expect that the company's financial integrity would remain intact. Our suppliers, creditors, and employees had some rights, too. It was a very complex and frustrating situation.

My principal mission as a director of The Pillsbury Company was to find the best deal for our stockholders. Now, privately at least, I was beginning to hope that Grand Met might provide the best answer in that regard. There was concern on the part of Pillsbury management and the bankers that it might be difficult to market Burger King shares after a spin-off unless our franchisees were in support of the idea. Accordingly, on November 14, Jerry Levin was sent to Miami to meet with employees and franchisees in order to convince them that the numbers were valid and that Burger King, after the spin-off, would remain a viable, dynamic company.

Levin had recently been named chairman and CEO of Burger King following Charlie Olcott's resignation, so it was to be expected that his appointment would be greeted with concern. Franchisee support for the spin-off concept was, at this point, critical to the plan's success, and it would be Levin's responsibility to sell them on the idea. Before taking on that assignment, he needed to convince Burger King management that the deal was a good one. Much later, after Grand Met acquired The Pillsbury Company, I asked a member of middle management to write a note telling me how our employees felt during the heat of battle about these new and shocking developments. I received the following memorandum:

REFLECTIONS ON THE GRAND MET ACQUISITION

A few weeks ago the expected happened—550 people were laid off at Pillsbury and another 550 at Burger King. This was less than two months after the acquisition by Grand Metropolitan, the fourth largest British conglomerate.

It was a down and out dirty fight. No doubt about it. The Pillsbury top brass felt that they were fighting the good fight. This was a battle for independence, for the sanctity of the Pillsbury name, its traditions, and the people who fought long and hard to build the hundreds of brand names that comprised the company's portfolio. But, unlike that momentous occasion of July 4, 1776, the Americans lost. What Pillsbury did not count on was that not only its shareholders but its employees would say "enough is enough." The shareholders were unlikely to see $60 a share in their lifetime. Vague promises of restructuring and the Burger King spin-off were not as good as cold, hard cash. To hell with tradition. The Pillsbury Board and Senior Management team had their chance many times over and continued to blow it. As for the employees, they were groping for any leadership at all. Years of chronic instability and mismanagement had taken their toll. The cheerful announcement by Jerry Levin of a Burger King spin-off, in which each share of Pillsbury stock would yield an additional share of the new publicly held Burger King, produced shock waves. Employees were expected to feel a sense of pride and cohesion. But what they saw was their hard-earned retirement income converted into stock that would decline in value at a geometric rate the date

> after issue. With almost obscene bravado, Jerry let the mass of employees know that he would be leading the new independent Burger King...and, by the way, only one-third of the staff would probably remain.
>
> The employees knew, far better than the shareholders and industry analysts, the true state of the company. The employees would take their chances with an outsider, and decided to trust their luck with an unknown company, Grand Metropolitan.
>
> The employees seemed to understand that nothing good could possibly come of this. No matter who won the battle, a corporate blood bath would surely follow.

I believe the memorandum fairly reflected the view of most employees and most franchisees. The Burger King family was extremely upset about Pillsbury's stated intention to defrock the company.

It was about this time, during the heat of the battle and largely as a result of the publicity about a potentially damaging franchisee revolt and retaliation, that Pillsbury decided to abandon plans to effect the spin-off of Burger King Corporation. This idea was proving to be much too difficult to sell to the many constituents who might be affected by this action, and there seemed to be little doubt that from a legal point of view we might be stepping into a litigation mine field.

In November, at a hearing in Delaware's Chancery Court, Judge Allen made some significant comments. He told Grand Met's attorneys that he had looked at Pillsbury's confidential financial information and saw more value than the $60 per share bid. In effect he said that if circumstances remained as they were, the pill could stay in place, and he went on to suggest that Grand Met "must demonstrate some movement" if he were to change his mind. He scheduled a hearing for December 12 to consider the spin-off issue and to hear other arguments as to why the pill should or should not remain in place. What Judge Allen was saying to Grand Met was in effect: "I see more value than $60 and if you want to stay in the arena and move this along, you had better get your best offer on the table."

To Pillsbury the judge was saying, "Show me how and why you can place a higher value than $60 on your shares. What values do you see and what is your basis for drawing these conclusions?" He said in effect, "You can't just say 'No' to Grand Met unless you come up with a better value for your shareholders." This served notice to the Pillsbury directors that they were required to come up with a better plan than the one contained in Grand Met's proposal. In the absence of an acceptable plan, Pillsbury ran the risk that the judge might enjoin the spin-off and pull the pill, thus enabling the shareholders to decide for themselves whether or not to accept Grand Met's $60 a share offer.

By early December, Grand Met increased their tender offer to $63. Pillsbury was given a matter of days to accept it under threat of its being withdrawn. With the hearing before Judge Allen set for December 12, the pressure on Pillsbury was intense. Discussions between opposing lawyers indicated a higher figure was available if the matter could be settled soon between the parties.

The Pillsbury board met by telephone on Sunday, December 11, and learned that discussions between investment bankers representing both sides indicated that a $66 offer might be arranged. There was even a hint of $67. The directors were made aware that the Grand Met CEO, Sir Allen Sheppard, had left a formal $65 offer on the table with the understanding that it would expire at midnight. This put even more pressure on the Pillsbury directors, requiring us to look at all of our available options. With Judge William Duffy about to hear the arguments the following day in Delaware's Chancery Court, Pillsbury's options were very few in number.

It all seemed to boil down to this: We could accept the $65, or reject it and try to negotiate a higher price, perhaps $66 or $67. Our final option would be to litigate in arguing support for keeping the pill in place and only agreeing to remove the pill if we could settle the matter at $68, but not lower than that. Litigation would take up to three months and chances of winning were not very promising. Our attorneys reminded us that we would "be in the swamps a long time," if we wanted to go that route. Meanwhile, the business would suffer immensely. The uncertainty surrounding this ongoing battle had the effect of numbing corporate activity and employee morale.

Stockholders and arbitrageurs were clambering for settlement, and the parties were not that far apart. The Pillsbury board met again by telephone Monday morning, December 12. Judge Duffy scheduled a court hearing for 2 p.m. Grand Met's $65 offer expired the night before at midnight. All we had to look at now was the $63 tender offer. In our telephonic meeting the board passed a resolution officially rejecting the offer as being inadequate. Our attorneys gave assurances that, in their view, we could negotiate a $66 settlement. I argued in favor of making this settlement rather than running the risk of an adverse court ruling. This point seemed to have the support of most of the directors, but no official action was required at that point. The matter would go before the Delaware Court that afternoon, and the ruling that would come out of that hearing would surely dictate our next course of action.

Judge Duffy heard arguments later in the day (December 12) and ruled on December 16. The long-anticipated ruling enjoined Pillsbury from spinning off Burger King and struck down the pill as the key antitakeover defense. That sealed the fate of Pillsbury. All there was to do now was to consider litigating the issue or negotiate the best deal we could with Grand Met.

The final meeting of the Pillsbury board took place in Minneapolis on Sunday, December 18. Lawyers for both sides had met in New York a few days earlier, following Judge Duffy's ruling, and agreed that Grand Met would submit a $66 offer for the Pillsbury board's consideration. After hearing from our attorneys and bankers, all of whom were in attendance, the board acted on their collective advice, passing a resolution acknowledging that $66 a share was a fair price and that the offer should be accepted by Pillsbury stockholders. The resolution passed with Bill Spoor casting the only negative vote. A merger agreement was signed the same day providing that all Pillsbury stock tendered by January 3, 1989, would be purchased for $66 per share and that all remaining shares would be acquired and paid for in a so-called back-end merger at a later date.

A few days after Pillsbury capitulated, Ian A. Martin, chief executive of Grand Metropolitan's U.S. operations, said that management changes at Burger King should be expected. "We most certainly will bring in someone from the U.K. with extensive food retailing experience," Martin said. "That's almost certain." The *Miami Herald* reported that Martin expected to meet with Burger King franchisees, citing the fact that franchisee relations with Pillsbury had deteriorated as the result of the proposed Burger King spin-off plan. A *Miami Herald* article noted that many franchisees supported Grand Met during the lengthy takeover battle and applauded the London firm's victory. Bill Pothitos, a franchisee and chairman of the National Business Planning Council was quoted as saying, "I'm very pleased the way things worked out." I believe he spoke for a sizable majority of Burger King franchisees who felt that they had been beaten up pretty badly over the past several years. These people were ready for a change—any change—and few of them appeared to be disappointed about the Grand Met takeover.

I left Minneapolis on Monday morning, December 19 and headed home to Miami. In the airport I picked up a *USA Today*, *The New York Times*, *The Wall Street Journal*, and copies of the local papers. All of them had extensive coverage about the Grand Met victory. The local press speculated on the changes this British firm would force on Pillsbury, its thousands of employees, and the community itself. The local press speculated that there would be disruptions in the lives of men and women in the Twin Cities and that many people would be faced with losing their jobs and means of livelihood.

Where did all this put Grand Met? They would pay $5.7 billion to the stockholders of The Pillsbury Company and take over the company. Current Pillsbury earnings seemed to indicate that the company was fully priced at $5.7 billion, but Grand Met claimed that they knew how to build and market brands and expressed their intention to substantially reinforce the Pillsbury presence in the marketplace. The Pillsbury Company owned some of the best-known brands and trademarks in the world including Burger King, Whopper, Häagen

Dazs, Green Giant, Totinos Pizza, Van de Kamp, Pillsbury's Best, and the Pillsbury Doughboy. It was the hope of everyone that Grand Met would be very successful and would ultimately be able to justify their having made such a sizable investment. As I left Minneapolis on that Monday morning, I wondered how they would approach the management challenge that was waiting for them in Miami at the offices of Burger King Corporation.

Ian Martin took over as chairman of both The Pillsbury Company and Burger King Corporation following the formal acquisition of The Pillsbury Company on January 9, 1989. He sent a young 43-year-old named Barry Gibbons to Miami and gave him the title of chief executive officer.

Shortly after Barry arrived in Miami I called him from my office on the fifth floor of the Burger King World Headquarters building. I introduced myself as the cofounder of Burger King and a recent director of The Pillsbury Company, adding a note of welcome and expressing the hope that I would have an opportunity to meet him "in the near future."

He responded by asking if he could come right down, saying he was anxious to meet me. Within a few minutes he was in my office and after a very pleasant introduction, I got right to the point I wanted to make. I felt that he might consider it appropriate, and perhaps expect, that I would vacate my office after our recent hostile encounter, and I offered to do this saying, "After all, we have been through a bitter fight and I have been on the opposite side. I don't want to send out a signal that I disapprove of Grand Met or yourself, because I do not feel that way. My interest is completely singular. I am anxious to see you and Grand Met make a notable success of the Burger King business and to the extent I can be of any assistance, I am willing to help." He looked at me intently saying, "Mr. McLamore, your reputation precedes you. I knew quite a bit about you before I arrived here. As a founder of this company, you have the respect of the many people who are associated with Burger King, and you would do all of us a great service and honor if you would keep your office here and continue to remain involved." I was deeply touched and complimented by this remark, and I told him so.

I remained in my offices at the Burger King World Headquarters until August 24, 1992, when Hurricane Andrew dealt the building a cruel blow, causing over $30 million in damage and requiring that the building be vacated. What was far more significant was the extraordinary damage and devastation done to the homes and lives of our many employees who lived in the direct path of this killer hurricane. Grand Met, in response to Barry Gibbons' leadership, made a particular point of looking after the interests of Burger King employees and families in the aftermath of this natural disaster. However, these employees had no way of knowing how their future lives would be affected by another storm that would come in on the winds of reorganization and reengineering, as Burger King attempted to reposition itself for the future.

Stumbling Blocks for Grand Met

In paying $5.7 billion in cash for The Pillsbury Company, it was generally conceded that the value of the Burger King piece might have been close to $1.5 billion, although this figure is pure conjecture. What was certain, however, was that Grand Met inherited some problems as far as Burger King was concerned.

During 1985 Burger King started to experience a steady loss of business. Unfortunately, this downward trend continued for the next seven years before reversing itself in 1993. Average store sales declined during this period, even though menu prices continued to increase. The most noticeable decline was reflected in the loss of customer traffic. Our average check increased, but this only indicated that our customers were paying more for their food than they had in the past. The decline in customer traffic was a dangerous and ominous sign, but if management felt troubled by it, there was very little indication of any real concern. Our own marketing research people called attention to the loss of customer traffic and suggested that a possible reason for the decline might be related to menu price increases. Management must have had hearing problems because nothing of significance was done to deal with the situation. Business was in a free fall as menu prices were increased in an apparent attempt to recapture lost operating profits. The quality of restaurant operations suffered as profits declined.

This was becoming a serious matter when Grand Met took over The Pillsbury Company. Burger King's average restaurant sales and customer traffic counts were then in the third year of decline. The problems this created began to show up in rather ominous forms.

Franchisee failures were more frequent and a sense of desperation developed in certain markets. Under pressure to increase profitability, the newly appointed Grand Met management went along with a strategy of increasing menu prices even further, which struck me as the wrong way to deal with the problem. This unfortunate development soon brought trouble to both Burger King and its franchisees.

From the mid-1960s to 1993 the selling price of our signature product, the Whopper, was increased from 39 cents to a range of between $1.79 and $2.89. During the same period the original regular 12-ounce soft drink increased from 10 cents to about 79 cents in most markets, although the size of the soft drink had increased to 16 ounces. French fries had risen from a single regular-sized portion selling for 10 cents to three sizes ranging from 79 cents to $1.29. Rising costs of ingredients and packaging accounted for some of the increases, but certainly not all of them.

Whereas food and packaging costs previously represented 43 percent of the customers' dollar, costs were currently running less than 30 percent, which meant that the public was receiving far less food for their money than they had received in the past. The business had been built on the simple proposition of offering our customers outstanding value. We had lost that initiative, and there was no attempt to restore it until calendar year 1993 rolled around. It was a long wait.

During that long wait, many different marketing and advertising strategies were launched in an attempt to reverse the trend. Burger King spent hundreds of millions of dollars on expensive advertising and marketing programs, all of which failed to produce tangible results. At a distance, it was obvious that this was not the fault of our marketing and advertising campaigns. It struck me that our company was failing to deliver value to our customers, who were screaming in our ears and trying to tell us what was wrong. Unfortunately, management didn't get the message.

Jerry Ruenheck left the office of president in 1985 in order to become a franchisee. I hired Jerry in 1969 and witnessed his rise in the managerial ranks. I was aware of the contributions he made during his 16 years of service. His departure as president ushered in a period of high management turnover in the executive office. The new Burger King president introduced a marketing campaign built around a character called "Herb the Nerd." This costly and grossly ineffective campaign was the first of many subsequent campaigns, none of which was able to stem the erosion of restaurant sales and profits.

I agreed with the critics about the "Herb" fiasco. The absurd idea behind the campaign was that it would encourage viewers to be on the lookout for Herb, who might drop in unannounced at various Burger King restaurants nationwide. In the event Herb was spotted, customers who witnessed the event would receive a reward of some kind. This enticement was supposed to flood our restaurants with new business. The campaign was a classic bomb which wasted tens of millions of our advertising dollars. Unfortunately, it was the first of a number of equally ineffective campaigns which followed one on top of another.

Certainly, ineffective advertising is a serious business liability, but there was something even more threatening going on at the same time. Unfortunately, this went largely unnoticed. The problem involved the "value message" we were sending out. Not only were we badly misdirected in pricing our products, but we were delivering poor service to our customers. You can't be wrong on two counts like that and still survive in the restaurant business. We had other problems brought about by offering a proliferation of poorly conceived and badly presented menu items. Having made this mistake, management discovered that we were unable to fill customers' orders as accurately as we had in the past when the menu was much simpler. This led to a reduction in product quality and much slower service to our customers. Even good advertising couldn't overcome problems of this kind.

It was difficult to understand why the company no longer focused on the basic fundamentals on which the business had been built. Our restaurants needed fixing, and our operating strategy was woefully deficient. In such a situation it is useful to remember that advertising is like a two-edged sword. It is risky and unwise to invite people into a restaurant when the products and services aren't right or the business is poorly managed and not meeting customers' expectations. Good advertising might bring in new customers at first, but damage occurs when they are shown how ineffectively their needs are being met. Disappointments like this are a ticket to disaster. At the time many of our restaurants were in bad physical condition, and then were poorly run. This was the result of the squeeze on profits and the cost cutting which followed. The obvious challenge was to correct that deficiency, but there were no plans in place to lead the way.

From 1985 to 1993 many different advertising campaigns hit the airwaves. Each one had a theme and a particular message to go along with it. They came as a result of frequent changes in top management. Beginning in 1985 Burger King brought in one chief marketing executive after another. Each of them wanted to create a successful marketing strategy to lift the company out of the doldrums. This was the quick fix they were looking for. The public perception of the campaigns told a sad and different story. None of them rang any bells. Our consistency of focus went right out the window with all the changes that were introduced. We seemed to lack any real ability to create and reinforce a strong and consistent image.

During this difficult time I received a call from the editor of a leading trade publication. He asked me about the "fuzzy" image and the distorted messages which Burger King was sending. He simply couldn't understand what kind of message the company was trying to communicate. I believe most of the American people felt pretty much the same way.

The campaigns that followed "Herb the Nerd" were "Burger King Town," which was an attempt to position Burger King as the resident experts who know how to make the best hamburgers in "home towns" all across the country, and "Best food for fast times," a campaign designed to position Burger King as the best place for quality products in a fast-moving world. We were jumping all over the place and confusing people with messages which were frequently changing. I wasn't really concerned about the different advertising campaigns we were running at the time. There was a more urgent problem. Before launching advertising or promotional campaigns, we needed to upgrade the quality of our food and service and fix what was wrong inside the restaurants. That was the first order of business. The advertising situation could go on the back burner until we got our house in order.

We created one of our major problems when we introduced so many new menu items. This brought on even more confusion. Our customers already had a problem trying to understand where we were trying to position ourselves. We took the focus off hamburgers and put it on chicken, fish, desserts, and specialty sandwiches of all kinds. Even though the Whopper was clearly recognized as the most preferred sandwich in the United States, management took the focus away from hamburgers and our unique flame-broiled cooking process to promote other products. Before long we were no longer "America's Burger King." This was the hard-earned and lofty position we had fought for throughout the years. Some of the advertising was about in-store merchandising programs which never generated much public interest. With the waste of millions of dollars in advertising and product promotions, the free fall in sales and traffic counts continued unabated during the years leading up to the Grand Met takeover.

Another classic advertising failure was a campaign called "We do it like you'd do it." This multimillion dollar effort was intended to convey the message that Burger King prepared its food just like the public would do it if they had the opportunity to prepare the products themselves. The July 16, 1993, edition of *The Wall Street Journal* contained the observation that "the gutters of Madison Avenue are clogged with discarded slogans that once, in someone's conference room, probably seemed nothing less than brilliant—like Burger King's short-lived 1988 tongue twister, 'We do it like you'd do it, when we do it like we do it at Burger King.'" The article went on to say, "Sometimes a brand is haunted by a catchy old slogan that just won't die. Burger King has gone through ten mostly forgettable lines since, 'Have it your way' bowed out." "Have it your way" was a winner which was tossed out.

After downplaying hamburgers and later recognizing the mistake, the "We do it" campaign attempted to capitalize on our unique broiling method of cooking hamburgers. This is what distinguished us from our competitors. The message was that because our food was prepared like people would prepare it at home, our food must be very good. The television advertising presented scenes of fun on the beach and backyard cooking, but not too many shots of the products which were available in our restaurants. As this expensive campaign wound down, the sales needle never moved and traffic counts continued their free fall. Whether this was primarily because the campaign was ineffective or whether we were reeling from menu confusion and price escalations remained a matter of conjecture for some but not for me. I was convinced that the problem was centered on the fact that Burger King no longer offered value to its customers. I felt that we were simply pricing ourselves out of the marketplace. We should have been addressing that issue and using advertising to tell the American people that we were doing something to put value back in the equation.

In 1989, following the Grand Met acquisition, Burger King launched another costly campaign called "Sometimes you gotta break the rules." The idea behind this controversial campaign, at least in the minds of our marketing executives, was that Burger King was willing to go to extremes if that is what it took to bring our customers the very best in food and service. We weren't in a position to deliver on that promise, and the real issue was value, which was something we weren't advertising at all. So far as stimulating sales was concerned, the needle never budged and with good reason. It was a poorly conceived campaign. Sales and traffic counts continued their steady, exasperating decline, but nothing was done to correct the operational deficiencies in the restaurants.

Part of the problem with the "rules" advertising campaign

was that the public never understood the intended message. The only signal that came through to them was that it was okay to "break the rules." For a family-oriented business like ours, this put Burger King in a very bad light with the public. Irate parents flooded the company with mail and telephone calls complaining about Burger King's encouraging their children to "break the rules." Rather than helping our business, this advertising might have done more harm than good.

In the middle of these ill-conceived marketing campaigns, I received a call from Dave Thomas, the founder of the Wendy's restaurant chain. I met Dave in 1975 when I was serving as president of the National Restaurant Association. I was in Chicago at the time, attending the NRA Trade Show and Exposition. Dave had come to Chicago to attend the opening of Wendy's store 40, which was his first restaurant in the state of Illinois. Although we did not know each other at the time, he asked me to come to his restaurant opening and make a few remarks. My encounter with this interesting man developed into a long, lasting friendship. Years later, after Dave moved to Fort Lauderdale, we saw each other at various community functions and other gatherings, all of which contributed to our growing friendship and mutual respect. Dave and I were both concerned with the plight of abused and abandoned children. We both supported charitable activities in these areas in South Florida. The McLamore Children's Center, operated by the Children's Home Society, was a prominent Miami facility engaged in this work.

Dave called me to suggest that we should discuss some problems connected with the children's care. I suggested that we meet at my office, which was located in the Burger King World Headquarters. Inasmuch as he had never seen the building, I invited him to drop by for lunch. As we were walking to the dining area, he turned to me and said with a sort of twinkle in his eye, "Jim, about your advertising programs, don't change a thing. These campaigns are just fantastic." Looking at the mischievous grin on his face, I got the message that even our competition couldn't quite understand how we were trying to position Burger King in the minds of the public.

Our sales and traffic counts had been in a steady decline for years. Our competition was fully aware of that because all of the major chains participated in cooperative and regularly conducted industry surveys. Dave knew about our situation and was just "working me over" in a very friendly and inoffensive manner. I must have had a frustrated look on my face following his well-aimed remark because he asked me what I would do if I were still running the company. I answered by saying, "I'd do what Lee Iacocca does for Chrysler and be the spokesman for the company. I would tell the public that I created the Whopper over 30 years ago, and I would show this hamburger on television with the comment that the public considered the Whopper to be the best and most preferred hamburger in the country." A few months later I saw Dave in his first television commercial as the spokesman for Wendy's. I don't know whether he got this idea from me or whether it was something he had already decided upon, but Wendy's decision to use Dave as their spokesman proved to be one of the most highly successful marketing strategies in the food-service industry. This personal touch to the Wendy's marketing program helped to increase store sales significantly over the years which followed.

Dave used his homespun manner to successfully introduce a value menu and a number of new specialty products. Wendy's was one of the first restaurant chains to address the value issue head-on and was one of the first chains to capitalize on an enthusiastic consumer response. With Thomas as the chief spokesman conveying the value message, Wendy's store sales increased significantly, while Burger King continued to show flat to negative average store sales and traffic counts. Entering 1993 Burger King's average real-store sales were declining for the seventh consecutive year, and the average restaurant's customer counts had fallen off by over 25 percent since the end of calendar year 1984. The situation was critical and with sales reaching such low levels, many franchisees found themselves in a tenuous financial position. The tension between Grand Met and the franchisee community was already quite strained, and this only caused it to get much worse.

The problems of declining sales and traffic counts began in 1985 during the Pillsbury years, and it continued after the Grand Met acquisition in 1989, up to 1993. The record kept by the Marketing Department of Burger King Corporation tells a very sad story, as shown in the accompanying table. The table measures "share of traffic," which is the percentage of Burger King customers in the overall quick-service restaurant (QSR) "sandwich" category. These are fast-food customers who eat sandwiches, which include hamburgers. "Average restaurant sales" reflects the actual dollar sales, unadjusted for menu price increases. The "average customer count" gives the number of customers served in the average Burger King restaurant.

Year	Share of Traffic	Average Restaurant Sales	Average Customer Count
1985	17.0	1,014,000	943
1986	16.6	1,020,000	893
1987	16.5	1,012,000	872
1988	16.6	983,000	842
1989*	16.2	952,000	792
1990	15.7	955,000	735
1991	15.0	946,000	697
1992	14.6	961,000	687

*Grand Met takes over January 1989.

The loss in average restaurant customer counts went from 943 in 1985 to 687 in 1992, a loss of over 25 percent of our average customer base in eight years. If that trend continued, the impact on the company and its franchisees would be staggering. Jim Adamson was made CEO in mid-1993 at a time of disappointing sales, declining profits, frustrated franchisees, and real concerns about the future. Everyone was hoping that Adamson could reverse the trend and get the company back on track.

Getting Involved Again

Since stepping down as Burger King's chief executive officer, I had maintained a certain level of contact with company officials and a few franchisees but never again acted in any official managerial capacity. My involvement was limited to those infrequent occasions when I was asked to address a national convention of Burger King franchisees and speak informally on a range of subjects of my own choosing. I was no longer a presenter of or commentator on the company's plans for the future, and I never used these occasions to express approval or disapproval of company strategies or practices. These conventions were management's opportunity to present operational and marketing plans while reinforcing their relationships with the franchisee community. I would maintain a respectable distance from such involvement, but because I had been so deeply involved in establishing so many of these franchisees in business, I was always welcomed with open arms. I always felt deeply moved by the warmth of the reception I usually received.

My basic and simple message on these occasions was to remind everyone that the original Burger King operational system was the best in the business and that it was important to adhere to these standards. I felt it was very important for me to reinforce the notion of compliance with the basic and fundamental principles on which the business had been built: the quality of our food, the cleanliness of our restaurants, the speed of our service, and the courtesy of our employees. This has always been the basic formula for the success of the

Burger King business, and I tried to drive the point home at every opportunity that was given to me. This message sounds so simple that many people can't see the magic in it, but I know that the principles work and that these very basic and fundamental ideas have been responsible for building and maintaining our success over many, many years. It is only when we vary from them that we run into trouble. Unfortunately, the system was developing a great deal of trouble as we entered the 1990s.

Dave Edgerton and I envisioned that Burger King's success would be built around strict adherence to the simple principles of quality, cleanliness, and speed, but we also knew that we needed to put a heavy emphasis on getting to size quickly in every market we entered. We believed that the ultimate reward could only come as a result of our building a strong market presence. Notwithstanding our aggressive expansion goals, our franchisees were urged to concentrate on planning for intelligent growth and expansion while trying to stay away from the kind of rapid growth that might expose them to financial instability. We reminded franchisees about the importance of our becoming one of the nation's major advertisers because of the great strategic significance of heightening our competitive position. I have always had a deep appreciation for the important contributions our franchisees have made in helping to build the business. I cared about them, and they seemed to understand and appreciate that fact. The success of the Burger King system always depended on the success of our franchisees, so this was a matter of the utmost importance. When these people signed on as franchisees, I felt that they were placing their trust and confidence in us, and I always made a point of trying to justify that faith.

I believe that our franchisees respect the fact that I thoroughly understand the business, and most of them seem to respect my judgment on matters involving corporate strategy and restaurant operations. There is an element of mutual respect in this regard, which has been responsible for building many strong personal relationships. It is always most gratifying to receive a warm reception on those special occasions when I am privileged to address franchisee meetings. Burger King management had always known about the special relationship that existed between the company's franchisees and me, but until 1993 there had been very little reason to take advantage of this unique chemistry.

By 1993 many people in the franchisee community were up against hard times. Business was off significantly, and there was a general mood of despair and the feeling that, unless something dramatic took place, things were not going to get any better. A few of them seemed to have lost hope. Many franchisees were disillusioned about the stewardship of the company during recent years, and they were beginning to challenge the quality of leadership that was going to take them into the future.

In January of 1993 I received a call from Jerry Ruenheck, who was then serving as the president of the National Franchisee Association (NFA). He asked me if I would be willing to attend a gathering of franchisees at one of their upcoming meetings to speak about the problems that Burger King was currently facing and offer some suggestions on how best to deal with them. Before I agreed to accept Jerry's invitation to speak to this gathering, I met with Barry Gibbons, the Burger King CEO at the time, to discuss the matter. I said that I was inclined to do this, but only on the basis that my presence and remarks would make a constructive contribution to the situation. I told Barry that I felt strongly that many of the problems confronting Burger King at the time were of the company's own doing and that if I addressed the meeting, I would have to be candid in expressing these views. I saw no way to extricate ourselves from the current dilemma other than by identifying and commenting on the policies, strategies, and tactical decisions which I believed were to blame for the problems we were currently facing. I would have to be frank about all of this, and I offered to decline the invitation if he felt that my remarks would disrupt any plans he had to put the company on a positive new course. To Barry's credit he said that he understood that I would need to be honest and forthright in addressing these issues and went on to say that my comments might be a good first step in coming to grips with the current dilemma. Accordingly, he urged me to accept the franchisees' invitation to address their meeting.

This put me in an interesting position. It was the first time in the past 21 years that I had been asked by Burger King management to address franchisees on corporate policy issues and operational matters. I welcomed the opportunity to get involved in this process. I called Jerry to accept his invitation to address the NFA meeting, which was scheduled to be held in Tampa on February 25.

I felt that I knew exactly what was wrong with the way our business was being run and that I had some definite suggestions on how the problems should be dealt with. I was very pleased to have the opportunity to express my views on the subject. I had been sitting on the sidelines for a long time, but my considerable interest in the fortunes of the company and its franchisees made it important for me to keep well informed and up to date on not only how our business was being run, but about all the events which were taking place in the rapidly changing food-service industry. In the past, I never discussed my concerns about Burger King's strategic direction either publicly or privately, even though I often had serious misgivings about the way things were being handled. I felt that by doing so I would be disrupting the system, which would only disturb rather than assist management in the discharge of their duties. I felt that unless I could address the issues openly and constructively within the system and with the endorsement, approval, and support of management, any comment I made might only make matters worse. I had no appetite to add confusion, acrimony, or debate to an already tense and explosive situation. Now, for the first time in 21 years, I was being asked to tell both management and franchisees just exactly what was wrong and what I thought was in need of attention.

The NFA meeting took place on February 25. I knew I was among friends when my introduction was followed by a long, standing ovation. This troubled gathering seemed to understand that I knew what their problems were, and it seemed quite clear that they were hoping I might offer some suggestions and answers to help lead us out of the difficult position we were in. Burger King had been experiencing declining store sales and customer traffic for eight years at this point, and things were still on a downhill track. The situation was grim, and the mood in Tampa was somber.

Sitting on the sidelines during these years enabled me to see what was happening. What was wrong seemed so obvious and apparent to me that I was surprised that management wasn't doing something about it. The problem in a nutshell centered around this: Until the mid-1980s, Burger King had been running very effective advertising campaigns and at the same time maintaining a reasonable and competitive menu-pricing policy. During the period from 1980 to 1985, price increases were put into effect only to offset increased costs. Our gross profit margins remained stable and consistent. By 1985 our marketing research staff was able to report that the public ranked Burger King very high in terms of being a good place to go for value. Then something unfortunate happened. Acting on the advice of management, menu prices began to ratchet upwards to levels our customers were reluctant to accept. There was no doubt in my mind that this was a major contribution to the steady erosion of sales and traffic that developed.

At about the same time, something went seriously wrong in the marketing area. Major organizational changes had recently been made in top management at both Burger King and The Pillsbury Company. In one two-year period beginning in 1985, Burger King had three different chief marketing officers heading that very important department. Each one of these executives had different ideas on how to position the company, so marketing strategies began to shift all over the place. During the next seven years menu prices were steadily increased while a thoughtless array of new product introductions brought about confusion to customers and employees alike. This tragic period, which lasted eight years, brought about a 34 percent decline in our average restaurant customer traffic. *At the same time, we were spending over $1 billion in advertising, merchandising, and sales promotions* in the expectation of building sales! It wasn't hard to see what the problem was. Our own market research was warning us that our high menu prices were partly to blame for driving off our customers, but nobody at headquarters seemed to be paying too much attention to this research. The message never quite got through.

The first point I made in my Tampa address was that we were pricing ourselves out of the market and that we were no longer perceived as the place to go for value. This was the basic problem, and as far as solutions were concerned, I said that the only way to recover what we had lost was to begin offering the public substantially more value than we had been doing in the past. A few years earlier Taco Bell had fired the food-service industry's opening volley by dropping their prices dramatically on a number of their leading menu items. Wendy's and McDonald's followed a short time later by bringing out their own value menu as a lure to building traffic and sales. We had done nothing in response to these initiatives, while the industry had begun a war of discounting.

I then told the following story: Shortly after our competition put their pricing moves in place, I ran into our chief marketing officer in the hallway of our headquarters building and asked him how he planned to respond to these initiatives. I presumed that he must have had a plan in mind. I expressed my concern that if we failed to meet this competition head-on we would find ourselves in an even more seriously disadvantaged position. I was surprised when he expressed his complete disagreement with me and went on to say that our competitor's price discounting would ultimately backfire. I didn't understand what he was trying to get across and asked him to explain why he felt that way. His position was that our competitor's price discounting would convey a message to the public that their products were not worth what they had been charging in the past. This was the basis for his predicting that customers would become so disillusioned with the pricing integrity of these businesses that they would quit coming in. He concluded by saying that Burger King was going to hold the line on prices and stay the course so far as maintaining high profit margins was concerned. I couldn't believe what I was hearing. I told him that I felt we had to address the value issue right away and if we failed to do so, our business would suffer even more. Menu presentation and pricing are important strategic issues, and I knew for certain that in taking this "hold the line" pricing position, Burger King would soon be looking right in the face of an upcoming disaster. We were totally out of sync with the world around us.

By the time of the NFA meeting in Tampa there was no doubt that the system was really hurting. Many franchisees were deeply concerned about their future. A lot of factors other than high menu prices had contributed to the problem, but that was one of the main issues. The nation's economy had been flat for some time, and many people were out of work. Consumer confidence was very low at the time, and the public was looking for value and aggressively shopping for price. I reminded franchisees that the 1990s had already become known as the "value decade," and I suggested that the first order of business was to address the value issue head-on and quickly. I told the audience that if the company failed to lead the way with an effective value-engineering program, we were in for even bigger trouble in the near future.

The second point I made was that the Whopper was being underutilized as an important marketing tool. I reminded everyone that whenever Burger King ran a 99-cent-Whopper promotion our sales went right through the roof. This was solid evidence that whenever we offered our signature product to the public at a favorable price, our customers came back to our restaurants in droves. I suggested that many markets could introduce a 99-cent Whopper on a regular basis and that others should use it in combination with french fries and a soft drink, also at a favorable price. Building customer traffic would stimulate sales in the whole product line, and although margins might suffer slightly, our restaurants would be rewarded with a significant increase in gross-profit dollars. If we did this on a consistent basis with the Whopper and other high-demand menu items, our customer response would result in the growth strategy we so desperately needed. I urged management to use the Whopper as the main attraction in luring business back into our restaurants, predicting a resurgence of sales to the high levels we had enjoyed in the past. This strategy had proved successful in a number of key markets where innovative franchisees who had adopted this strategy were reporting sales and traffic increases of up to 40 percent or more since introducing the Whopper at the regular price of 99 cents. Prior to this, the Whopper had been priced in the range of $1.79 to $2.09 in most markets. The theory behind this discounting of the Whopper to 99 cents was that it would build traffic by taking a much-reduced, nominal profit on the sale of each Whopper in exchange for selling ancillary products at regular margins to a vastly increased customer base.

The Whopper had bailed us out before. The first time was in 1957 when we first introduced it. The important decision to create the Whopper saved the company from going under. Since that time this extraordinarily successful product had earned the recognition of being the most preferred large hamburger in the country. By 1993 we were selling over two million Whoppers every day, and surveys showed that the American people favored the Whopper by as much as 2 to 1 over any other hamburger. I expressed the view that this sandwich could be a very powerful and effective marketing tool, if it was used properly. Previously we had not used this product exclusively as a method of building sales.

I criticized a number of the company's marketing strategies, but even as I spoke, we were then spending tens of millions of dollars promoting "dinner baskets" which featured a steak sandwich, fried (frozen and breaded) shrimp, or a breaded thin chicken cutlet, all of which were of very marginal quality.

The dinner-basket idea was introduced to build evening sales by offering a full-meal kind of service. Service personnel would deliver the customers' orders directly to their table. An added feature of this service entitled our customers to receive free popcorn while they waited. This was a real departure from our proven system of service, and it turned out to be a major operational problem. The most popular dinner basket turned out to be a Whopper with french fries, which shouldn't have surprised anyone because these two items were long established as the most popular items on our regular menu. There was nothing new about this. Our customers were trying to tell us that they wanted Whoppers and fries and were not particularly interested in marginal-quality dinner items that we were ill-equipped to properly prepare and serve anyway. The dinner-basket concept was never thoroughly market-tested, but I am certain that our franchisees would have killed the idea if they had been given a voice in the matter. Even in the face of evidence that our restaurants were selling less than 20 dinner baskets a day, we kept the program alive for almost a year and a half. It was reported that we spent over $40 million trying to promote this idea. When it was finally discontinued, management was forced to admit that it had been a tragic failure. This was yet another example of how customers were sending important messages, but nobody seemed to be listening.

I spoke about recent thoughtless menu proliferations which created confusion and slower service, and which aggravated customers and employees alike. I had recently spent time studying our own market research which was advising management that fast-food restaurant customers across America now perceived Burger King to be the worst provider of value among all of the top chains. This research also revealed that the major complaint was our inability to fill our customer's orders accurately. This, I explained, was the direct result of adding a senseless variety of new items to an already overcrowded menu, which only served to confuse our entire production process. Our employees just couldn't handle it right. Another major criticism was that the company had yet to do something constructive to counter the difficult service problems that resulted from this expanded menu. Our marketing research staff deserved a lot of credit. They seemed to know exactly what the problems were, but management wasn't responding or doing anything to deal with the situation. Nobody at headquarters seemed to be listening, but if they were, it was painfully evident that solutions to the problem were nowhere in sight. I leveled heavy criticism at the way management had cut back on services to the franchisee community. Regional and district offices had been closed all over the country, leaving franchisees to service themselves. I complained that this very short-sighted policy was wrong and that it was bound to lower the standard of restaurant operations around the country.

The headquarters of Grand Metropolitan in London, England, is a long way from Burger King's headquarters in Miami. Moreover, Grand Met was noted for expertise in the areas of finance and marketing, for which the company had earned an international reputation. They were not as highly respected nor had they earned such high marks as a company having exceptional operations skills. If they had contributed to the decision to have Burger Kings cut back on services to the restaurants, they should be held responsible for the fallout that would surely occur as the result of this decision. Cost cutting is one thing, but cutting necessary servicing is something that will surely lead to irreparable damage.

I drew attention to past ineffective advertising campaigns and suggested that the current television spokesman did not convey an appropriate image for the company. The spokesman was an MTV character named Don Cortese, who appealed mostly to 18- to 25-year-olds. The recurrent theme of this advertising was "I love this place." Within a 10-month period after I had criticized this campaign to our franchisees in Tampa, the trade press, *USA Today,* and *The Wall Street Journal* had all singled out our "BK Tee Vee" campaign as one of the worst advertising campaigns of 1993. I thought it was important to get away from the kind of advertising we were doing and talk more to a broader, more diverse consumer market about our products while focusing on the value issue. I emphasized that we needed to establish the fact that we were the industry leader in selling quality hamburgers and other high-value menu items. The message I continually tried to hammer home was that our signature product, the Whopper, was the proper vehicle for getting these important points across.

At the time of the Tampa meeting the current policy gave our franchisees the authority to decide which advertising and marketing strategies would be used in their own areas. I expressed the view that this cumbersome arrangement had to be discarded in the interests of the entire Burger King system. For better or for worse, for good or for bad, the organization had to put its confidence in a single authority when it came to determining overall corporate advertising and marketing strategy, and that authority had to rest solely in the hands of the chief executive officer of Burger King. I took that position even though I was aware that the franchisee community currently lacked confidence in our company officials. Franchisees had lived through one marketing fiasco after another, and they had witnessed the waste of huge sums of their advertising dollars. The media planning and media buying functions had been in disarray for quite a while, and the creative executions of our still-unfocused advertising strategy were justifiably receiving stinging criticism from the press, outside observers, and of course the franchisees themselves. I could understand why the franchisees wanted to jump in and take charge of it all, but in my judgment, that simply wasn't going to work. I was convinced that the final authority in such matters had to be in the hands of management.

It was becoming increasingly evident that network television advertising would have to give way to more regional and local advertising inasmuch as each individual market had its own character, opportunity, presence, and marketing plans. We were looking for advertising strategies with a potential for returning the system to prosperity, but the problem really centered on the fact that the company had not dealt with the nightmare of operational shortcomings, menu proliferations, the pricing issue, or service in the restaurants. These issues had to be addressed before the system could be restored to competitive status. Advertising alone wasn't going to solve that problem. The job was to fix the business itself, and at this particular time our restaurants needed a lot of fixing.

A major responsibility of any marketing department is to identify problem areas and find solutions, but this had not been done. Reports from our research people that had pointed problems out had, unfortunately, been disregarded. In making my remarks, I had to call a spade a spade. Management's oversights and their inability to recognize and deal with operating deficiencies and other serious shortcomings had to be addressed before Burger King took another step. I said it was pointless to focus exclusively on advertising aimed at luring new customers into our restaurants when we were not operating them properly.

Another deeply troubling issue involved our competition. I told the franchisees that I couldn't understand why we hadn't gone after the double-drive-thru operations that were springing up all around us. At the time these new businesses represented a significant competitive threat. Their specialty was a hamburger made exactly like a Whopper. It was just a little bit smaller, but it was priced at 99 cents, about half as much as we were charging for the Whopper. The rest of their menu consisted mostly of french fries and soft drinks at prices which were also slightly below ours. There was no inside seating. Customers were served through two drive-up windows, which was exactly the way 60 percent of all fast-food customers preferred to be served, so they had an important competitive advantage in this regard as well. Their simple menu was about the same as ours was 30 years earlier. Their food was presentable, their service was fast, and their prices were low. They were throwing up some stiff competition which, up to that point, had produced no response on our part. I made the point that I had to believe American Airlines, United, or Delta would never let some start-up airline challenge them on their major routes without meeting them squarely on price and service. I couldn't understand why we were standing idly by and letting this aggressive new competition come in and run off with our customers. I reminded our franchisees of a comment attributed to Ray Kroc. Someone asked him what he would do if he saw his chief competitor drowning a little offshore. He is reported to have said that he would stick a running hose in his mouth. This was a time to get tough, and I expressed the belief that we should have gone on the attack a long time ago. By our inaction we were inviting our competition to enter the marketplace with some assurance that they would never be challenged.

In my concluding remarks I expressed my confidence in the future and made some specific comments on why I felt such a sense of optimism. One of our great strengths was in the fact that we still had a firm grip on the number 2 position in the marketplace, at least with regard to the number of restaurants we had in operation. We had advertising and marketing revenues of over $275 million a year to work with, which was a matter of considerable significance, but without question, our greatest strength was the fact that we had the nation's favorite sandwich, the Whopper. I reminded our franchisees that these two assets should be used to our maximum advantage. By restoring our competitive status in restaurant operations and marketing, we could position Burger King in the public's mind as the favorite place to eat, and this would soon begin to generate increased sales and profitability.

I could tell by the franchisees' reaction that they agreed with my assessment of the key problem areas. I had spelled it out in clear and unmistakable terms and delivered a message to management that they should get busy and start dealing with the issues. It would be interesting to see how they would respond to the challenge.

The franchisees at the Tampa meeting seemed pleased to see me taking a more active interest in the affairs of the company. Barry Gibbons and Jim Adamson, who was then the chief operating officer, continued to encourage me to become more involved in spite of the challenges and criticisms I continued to make about the way the business was being managed. A few months earlier at the company's request I traveled to Portugal to address a gathering of franchisees from Europe, the Middle East, and Africa. Previously I made some brief comments to several thousand franchisees gathered at a Burger King convention at Disney World in Orlando. Now, with management's encouragement, I would be traveling to different parts of the United States to speak to franchisee groups and our own regional, district, and restaurant managers. The promise I was receiving from top management was that suggestions I was making would be given proper attention. That was enough to get me to roll up my sleeves again.

On August 24, 1992, Hurricane Andrew inflicted severe damage on the Burger King World Headquarters building. A 17-foot storm surge and wind gusts which probably exceeded 200 miles per hour nearly destroyed the building and did destroy or seriously damage thousands of homes, including many owned by our employees. The terrible destruction caused $30 million of damage to Burger King headquarters building and took the building completely out of service for over a year, requiring that I find a new location for my office. Immediately after the storm I converted our guest house into a temporary office. During the following months this proved to be such a convenient facility that I decided to stay there permanently. At the time, I was serving as president of Fairchild Tropical Garden, which is located only a few blocks from our residence, and inasmuch as I was spending a great deal of time at the garden, the new office location was very convenient. Another compelling reason for this relocation was that I would be situated on the site of my own three-acre garden and could enjoy looking over the work that is constantly taking place there. I liked to comment that I was "15 minutes closer to the golf course," even though I was so busy during these times that I rarely seemed able to get out to play.

Barry Gibbons expressed his regret at my decision not to return to the World Headquarters building and his feeling that my presence at the home office had always been regarded very positively by the company and the employees who worked there. This very nice compliment reassured me that I was still viewed as a resource to the company, and this expression by Barry pleased me very much.

Immediately following the Tampa meeting I met with Jim Adamson to discuss the message I had delivered to the franchisees. I stated my concern about current policies, advertising, customer service, marketing plans, operations, and product improvement issues that I felt needed to be addressed. Along with my comments I offered certain thoughts and suggestions for addressing these issues. There was a healthy exchange of ideas, and I had confidence that Jim would give these matters the serious consideration they deserved.

Jim urged me to go to Toronto in late May to address another gathering of members of the National Franchisee Association. I told him that I would be pleased to do that, but cautioned him again that I would continue to speak out in criticism of the company's way of handling certain matters. He said that he understood that and expected that this would be a condition of my going there. I'm sure that he felt confident that any remarks I made would be constructive in nature and designed to identify the problem areas, offer suggestions for correcting them, and challenge the franchisees to get behind the company's plans to find solutions and solve the problems. I had previously explained that before arriving at solutions and corrective actions, it would be necessary to discuss the reasons the problems had arisen in the first place. This is what I intended to do in every meeting I planned to attend.

I received another warm reception in Toronto. My message was essentially the same as I had delivered in Tampa three months earlier. It was apparent to the management personnel who attended this meeting that the franchisees and I were on the same wave length. They knew that my comments had touched the core of the problem. The issues were value, menu proliferation, flawed marketing strategies, the quality of our products, and breakdowns in the way we were delivering service. I spoke about these matters in specific terms and offered suggestions for dealing with them. Jim Adamson and members of his top management team also spoke in Toronto, and I was pleased in listening to their presentations that they were beginning to acknowledge the problems and mistakes of the past. I thought that it was very therapeutic to hear management talk so openly and frankly about their past mistakes in the context of planning for the future and coming up with strategies aimed at restoring restaurant sales. In discussing possible solutions, management presented their initial ideas for implementing a value menu, which in my judgment, was the first and most important step. I thought their initial proposals were a little weak as far as the value issue was concerned, but it did represent a good start. I was beginning to feel that Jim Adamson might be just the right person to get

Burger King back on the rails. I liked his decisiveness, candor, and straightforward approach in talking to the franchisees. He was obviously serious about attacking the problems and issues we had spoken about.

After leaving Toronto I met Nancy in Chicago, where she had been visiting her mother. We flew from there to Denver and then on to our home at Old Baldy in Wyoming. Burger King had recently canceled plans to hold a national convention in San Francisco in the fall, where at management's request, I had planned to address the gathering. There had been an expected attendance of over 4000 members and participants of the franchisee community. The cancellation of this convention was very disappointing to the franchisees who had been looking forward to an opportunity to get together and hear some encouraging news about future plans. Conventions of this kind enabled management to outline their marketing plans for the future and present their ideas for building the business.

After learning about the cancellation, the NFA decided to hold their own convention in October and asked me to attend and be their featured speaker. I accepted this invitation and between my occasional trips to Miami during the summer, I spent a considerable amount of time talking with franchisees and management about the current situation. It was time to fix the business, so it was important for me to get a more accurate understanding of what was going on in the marketplace. I wanted to help unite management and the franchisees in the hope that by building bridges of understanding the parties would develop a feeling of confidence in each other. Tension was still running deep, and in this hostile environment many unresolved issues continued to exist. I hoped that my remarks to the NFA convention would help to heal some wounds and assist in the recovery process. This would start to happen when franchisees had evidence that business was on the rebound.

The main concern of the franchisees was how well they were doing in terms of sales and profits. Most of them had been looking at negative results for years, and at this point they needed to be encouraged that things were going to improve. It was important for them to see that something was being done to get Burger King back in the "win" column again. The challenge before management was to come up with plans and ideas which would stimulate sales and restore our battered image. At this point having been asked by both management and the franchisees to come back and get involved again was a challenging invitation which I couldn't resist. I had confidence that I could contribute in important ways to the recovery process, and I hoped that my remarks to the NFA convention would be a step in that direction.

My relationship with Barry Gibbons had certainly been a cordial one during the four and a half years he had served as Burger King's chief executive officer. He was an intelligent and forceful leader with strong opinions on marketing, restaurant operations, and franchising. Although I did not agree with him on many of these important matters, we were able to communicate freely and easily with each other on those rare occasions when we got together. Barry had a number of confrontations with franchisees, and on some occasions, he spoke rather sharply to them in expressing views about franchisees' responsibility under their contractual relationships with the company. I had never been asked to take an active role in the company, and I really never expected to be asked. Barry was well-received by the business community in Miami. He was an excellent speaker, able to deliver his remarks with great charm, and he had earned a reputation as an effective corporate executive. The sales and profit figures he delivered and reported on indicated that Burger King Corporation itself was doing very well. It is difficult to say how much of the reported profitability came from recurring operations and how much came from the sale of assets or cutbacks in personnel, although it is generally conceded that there had been substantial sales of company-owned restaurants and corporate real estate along with major reductions in staff.

On July 21, 1993, Barry Gibbons announced the appointment of Jim Adamson as the company's new chief executive officer. For the past several months I had been in close contact with Jim, sharing with him my ideas about problem areas in the restaurants. What was unique in our relationship was that Adamson was willing to listen to me and even go so far as to ask me to elaborate on my ideas for improving the situation. Jim and I were getting along very well. We both felt that my personal relationship with the franchisee community was an advantage that could be used to close ranks and work more closely together in the pursuit of revitalizing the business. Both of us began to feel the benefit that could be derived from our building a good working relationship. Jim continued to encourage me to speak to franchisee groups and restaurant managers as frankly and candidly as I had done before, even though he knew that I would be critical of much that had gone on in the past. We both felt that the ultimate result of my constructive criticisms would lead to finding solutions to the company's problems. Adamson's position seemed to be that he was prepared to make any changes that would help restore the business to higher levels of sales and profitability, and he was inviting me to be as actively engaged in that process as I had time for. I thought to myself that this fellow had a lot of confidence in himself and if he had any ego at all, he wasn't going to let it get in the way of making good decisions. I wondered how many CEOs in his position would have invited a founder and former CEO of the company to come back and work side by side with him in the process of healing the business. I admired this unique quality very much and felt that I could work quite successfully with a man of his character, mind-set, and temperament.

As the summer of 1993 came to a close at Old Baldy, I accepted invitations to address several restaurant managers' conferences which were scheduled for the early part of the fall, but during the summer months I was focused on the message I intended to bring to the NFA convention, which was scheduled to be held in San Francisco during early October. This would be the "first annual" convention of the NFA, and I viewed it as a fine opportunity to outline an approach to the recovery and revitalization of the system. I also saw it as my opportunity to make clear to everyone connected with Burger King that I was willing to help in any way that I could.

My talk at the NFA convention was well-received. I was given another warm reception by the franchisees who seemed to be encouraged by my recent involvement and visibility. I hammered away with many of the same messages I had delivered in Tampa and Toronto, but I touched much more heavily on the value issue, stressing the importance of meeting our competition head-on and suggesting that the Whopper should be the vehicle to deliver the message of price and value. I expressed a feeling of optimism that our business could surely get a lot better if we returned to the basic fundamentals which had built the business. We had neglected these principles in recent years, and it was time to refocus on them again. The important issues of quality, speed, simplicity, cleanliness, and customer service needed to be stressed before we could expect our customers to return.

What I felt was particularly therapeutic about my message was the fact that I was still hammering away at management about their past mistakes, inadequacies, and inept leadership. Jim and members of his top management team were in the audiences listening to my description of what had gone wrong and what needed fixing. I had warned Jim that I would continue "throwing harpoons at him" to make the point that Burger King had a lot to do before we could get the system back on track. I had no end of admiration and respect for someone who was so willing to welcome such challenges as a means of restoring vitality to a business which had suffered so much in recent years.

Adamson's own remarks to the franchisees were also well-received. He and his management team had recently introduced a value-oriented menu which seemed to be producing favorable results at the time. He established the fact that he recognized the importance of menu simplification and product improvements and stated that he expected to introduce such innovations in the near future. He committed himself to a thorough review of the advertising and marketing situation, which he acknowledged was in need of a major overhaul. He was candid in stating which franchisee demands he would support and which ones he would reject. His integrity and forthright expression earned him a great deal of respect. The parties seemed to be reaching a common ground. I knew that they could never expect to agree on all the issues, but the important message that came out of the San Francisco meeting was that mutual confidence was being restored.

After the San Francisco meeting I received a flood of invitations from regional franchisee associations asking me to speak at their meetings, which were usually structured in the form of restaurant managers' training conferences. I planned to accept as many of these invitations as I could possibly fit into my schedule, because of the belief that my presence and comments would contribute to the revitalization of the system.

I accepted invitations to address multistate gatherings of franchisees and restaurant managers in Chicago, Myrtle Beach, Cincinnati, Boston, Buffalo, and Tampa. Most of these gatherings hosted up to 400 restaurant managers, and I had a strong feeling that speaking to these managers was one of the most important contributions I could make toward improving our business. These managers have the responsibility to see that our customers are greeted and served in the proper manner. Each manager has an opportunity to influence 50 or more employees at each Burger King restaurant, which meant that my message at each conference could influence 20,000 employees, each one of whom could help to make a customer's visit more satisfactory.

By the early fall of 1993 the Burger King management team was working on a number of strategies that looked very promising, although a number of them were still very much in need of sharpening. Jim and I were spending more and more time together, with healthy exchanges of ideas on the subject of improving our business. One of our important communication projects involved sending videotape messages to the 1500 franchisees and management people on a variety of subjects of current interest. These half-hour tapes featured Jim and me exchanging comments and observations about operational and marketing issues. This provided Adamson with the opportunity to respond to questions as to how he proposed to address these issues. The discussions were direct, challenging, and sometimes heated, but the message came through that we were acting as an effective team in formulating a plan to build business up to levels we had enjoyed in the past.

By this time the financial and trade press had picked up the magic of the transformation Jim Adamson was working on Burger King. *Business Week* magazine ran a story about the current turnaround and focused on my becoming more involved in the business. *Florida Trend* magazine did an interesting story which pictured Jim and me on the cover with the caption "Burger King Goes Back To Basics—And Listens To An Old Pro." *Advertising Age* and *Brand Week* ran similar stories, citing changes and our new direction. Burger King was waking up and people were beginning to catch the significance of the great potential that still remained in the sleeping giant.

Looking Back

The benefit of hindsight is wonderful. In 1994 when I was approaching my 68th birthday, and was busily engaged in writing this book, I asked myself, If I had to do it over again, what would I do differently? I think the question breaks down into two parts: business and personal.

First, what would I have done differently about charting the course of Burger King during the 13-year period from 1954 to 1967 when Dave and I were in control of its destiny? I would have built the small hamburger to sell for 15 cents rather than the 18 cents we started with. The originators of the Insta Burger King system thought there was a marketing advantage in offering a 2-ounce meat patty over McDonald's 1.6-ounce patty, even though we would have to sell it at a higher price. I think they were wrong about that. The 15-cent price was a compelling issue with consumers at the time, and we failed to fully recognize the importance of it. I would have given serious thought to grilling our hamburgers rather than broiling them the way we did, simply because we could have delivered the product hotter, faster, and perhaps better-flavored. We should have insisted on getting rid of the Insta machines much sooner than we did. Clearly they were part of the production problems we faced during the early years. These cantankerous machines were slow and unreliable, and we contended with their inconsistent performance much longer than we should have. A 15-cent hamburger properly prepared, coupled with the important introduction we made in 1957 of a 39-cent Whopper, would have better-positioned us in the marketplace during the early years.

I would have sought a different level of professional advice concerning financial strategy and real estate development, and I would have taken more risks than we did following our expansion outside of Florida in 1961. We should have signed more leases and bought more real estate than we did. It would have been very advantageous to have done as Harry Sonneborn and McDonald's did in developing a more profitable and workable real estate development plan. Sonneborn's masterful real estate financing formula provided the real foundation for the McDonald's success story. Perhaps if we had sought more sophisticated and professional financial counseling on this important aspect of our business much earlier, we could have positioned Burger King as a much more profitable company.

After McDonald's and Kentucky Fried Chicken went public in 1965 and 1966, I should have been more aggressive in seeking out an investment banker who would have helped us in building a more effective corporate financial strategy. I believe we made a mistake in going to Blyth and Company. I should have challenged their statement that Burger King was not ready to become a public company and gone to a more venturesome banker who was willing to take some risk and provide some leadership in this regard. Of course it is easy to find fault with yourself when you realize 30 years later that Burger King Corporation as a public company might have had a market capitalization of $3 billion or more.

Had we gone public in 1965 or 1966, it would have been unlikely that we would have given any serious consideration to a merger proposal from The Pillsbury Company. If such a proposal had been made, I doubt that we would have had any interest in considering it. Had we been an independent public company, Dave, Harvey Fruehauf, and I probably would never have considered a merger with anyone. Our merger with The Pillsbury Company was a disappointing strategic decision. Burger King suffered the loss of forward momentum because of Pillsbury's mandated cutbacks. The consequence of cutting back on franchising and real estate development meant that we were never again in a position to seriously challenge

McDonald's for the lead. At the time of the merger in 1967 I felt that we were only 40 months behind our competition in terms of growth and profitability, and it was my sense that we were in a relatively good position to close the gap. A quick glance at the size and earning capacity of the two companies in the nineties tells the story. As far as growth and profitability are concerned, we were beaten quite soundly.

There were also a lot of things I would never have changed. First of all, I made a good decision in picking Dave Edgerton as a partner. Dave was a decent, thoughtful, considerate person, and he was my friend. He worked hard. He was intelligent, creative, and devoted to the business. We worked well together as a team. We rarely disagreed or had any confrontational difficulties. We enjoyed a solid personal and business relationship that worked well in the formative years of building the business. Dave was a great contributor to our growth and success.

I would never have deviated from our insistence on forging a contractual relationship that required franchisees to support a cooperative advertising program. This was an "industry first," containing a firm stipulation that helped us grow the business. It remains the basic foundation of the business. The creation and positioning of the Whopper as our signature product was the most important decision we ever made and the one thing that was most responsible for our success. As far as growth and expansion are concerned, I think we were right in entering as quickly as possible into every state in the country. Gaining national stature as rapidly as we did gave us the advantage of using the efficiency of mass media and network television advertising when most of our competition had to wait years to reach the same level of national awareness. Rapid, profitable, and large-scale franchising came on the heels of this positioning. We were right to plunge into as much real estate development as our limited resources would permit during those early years. We should have done more, but what we did do proved to be enormously profitable to the company. Our determination to enforce quality standards in the four fundamental areas of good restaurant operations paid the ultimate dividend. We were uncompromising in demanding quality in food, service, cleanliness, and courtesy, which are the four basic ingredients of success. Finally, we were right in seeing to it that our franchisees were successful. We worked hard to ensure that. Putting the franchisees' interests ahead of our own paved the way to our own success.

It was a rocky road, full of bumps and potholes, and it wasn't always easy, but the point is that although we did a lot of things that were not particularly well-conceived, and oftentimes not too smart, we did exercise good judgment most of the time and did a lot more things that were right than were wrong. The success of Burger King Corporation makes the point better than I can.

This brings me to the second part of the question, which involves Jim McLamore in a much more personal way. Would I have done anything differently concerning my service to the company?

Taking stock of myself now, I feel grateful for all the many good things that have happened to me in the past. A great marriage, a wonderful family, good health, financial security, and the sense that I have been using my life in what I consider to be a useful and constructive fashion. That last part is important to me simply because I derive such pleasure and satisfaction from my involvement in community service and philanthropy. I have learned important lessons as a result of doing this. I feel comfortable with life in the nineties. I am under no stress, and I am fascinated with all the activities in which I have become so deeply involved.

Would I have been quite as comfortable today if Burger King had gone public instead of becoming a part of Pillsbury? That is very hard to say, but I suspect that had we gone public, my deep sense of commitment to building and managing the company would have resulted in my staying on much longer than I did. When it might have come time to change the top leadership of the company, I may not have been the best person to evaluate my effectiveness as the chief executive officer of Burger King or make a judgment about my stepping down. It is very difficult to make such a decision in an objective and unbiased way. I believe that I have strong leadership skills, and I enjoy exercising that kind of responsibility. I have been in leadership positions during most of my professional career and in my community service. Having a thorough understanding of the Burger King business and the marketplace we were competing in made me very comfortable and confident about my ability to serve Burger King as the CEO. However, that same feeling of confidence might have led me to believe that my service to the company was indispensable. It would have been unfortunate if I had stayed too long and failed to realize it. Getting optimum corporate results is the real test of effective leadership and if I had failed in that regard, I would have been deeply disappointed.

Many questions come to mind. Would I have been qualified to run a large public company and if so, for how long? What kind of an organization and what kind of competent professional management would I have been able to attract and develop? What about my willingness to delegate authority to other executives? Would the additional pressures of the job have had a negative effect on my attitude, disposition, and leadership ability? What about my health? How would this have been affected? I was smoking three packs of Lucky Strike cigarettes a day, which wasn't a very intelligent way to ensure longevity and good health. When would I have had the good sense to quit? And what about the stress factor—how would I have been able to cope with the increased burdens of leadership?

How could I tell whether I was the right person for the job, and how could I evaluate my effectiveness as a leader? The one thing that is certain is that if Burger King Corporation had been a public company in 1972, I would have been very reluctant to step down when I did at the age of 46. The fact that I did step down and "retire" at that point was a very important decision in my life. I'm very pleased with the way things turned out for me, even though I had difficulty in accepting the idea of retirement at the time. With the benefit of hindsight, I recognize that stepping down when I did under the prevailing circumstances was the right thing for me to have done, notwithstanding my passionate interest in the company and its future.

Whether it was the best thing for Burger King at that time, I will leave to the judgment of others.

I have no doubt that I would have been a more effective leader as the CEO of a publicly owned Burger King Corporation than I was as a "hired gun" for Pillsbury. The principal reason centered on matters involving the company's strategic direction. I would have energized the company's momentum as to growth rather than pulling back on it. There is no question in my mind that I would have seen to it that Burger King grew much more rapidly than it did during those important formative years. I'm not sure what I would have been able to accomplish for the company over a longer period of time. I doubt, for instance, that I would have been smart enough to hire Don Smith, who did a lot to increase the company's momentum at a critical time. It might have been too difficult for me to let go. How many mistakes and miscalculations I might have made are probably not worthy of conjecture.

The bottom line to the question "Would I have done anything differently?" boils down to this: Burger King should have remained independent until it was the right moment to go public, and I probably should have been smart enough to see this and insist upon it.

My confidence that Pillsbury was the right company to help us grow and keep pace was clearly misplaced. If I had known that they would abandon our growth strategy, there would have been no doubt about the direction we would have taken. We would have waited and remained independent hoping to take the company public whenever we could have arranged it.

In retrospect it would have been in our best interests to become a public company. Being in that position we would have been able to acquire franchisees for stock, and having gained access to the capital markets, we could have reaped the rewards which over so many years have been so clearly abundant in the real estate market. I expect that as an independent public company with an entrepreneurial style of management, we would have grown more rapidly and at a higher level of profitability. Certainly our management team would have been more highly motivated.

Although it is likely that I would have stayed on as CEO longer than I did, it is difficult to say for how long. As we entered the 1970s the company was reaching a size which demanded a more professional and sophisticated style of management. There comes a point in such situations when the service of a founder-entrepreneur has run its course. The trick is in knowing when that point has been reached.

Certainly I'm deeply grateful for all the wonderful things that have happened to me and become a part of my life since 1972. I could hardly have asked for more than I have received, and I am comfortable to leave it at that.

What's Next?

Burger King restaurant sales were growing at a brisk pace as calendar year 1994 began. The value menu was in place, and it was receiving broad customer approval. Close to 25 percent of our restaurants were offering the Whopper for 99 cents, and this was producing double-digit sales increases along with greatly improved profitability. Average customer traffic was up over 20 percent in the restaurants offering this program, and because of this we were beginning to substantially add to our share of the market. This is not to single out the restaurants serving the 99-cent Whopper as the only success story in the Burger King system. The rest of the restaurants had all adopted variations on the value-menu theme and they, too, seemed to be enjoying great success. The healing process had begun, traffic had picked up dramatically, and optimism began to fill the air. The future began to look much more promising than it had in many years. I was pleased to have been able to contribute something to help bring this about and even more pleased that Jim Adamson was asking me to continue staying involved. The company and its franchisees were beginning to enjoy their first taste of renewal and prosperity in years. It was fun to be part of that.

There was still much more to do. The marketing problems remained largely unanswered, but when Paul Clayton was selected to step in as the new chief marketing officer, things started to improve quite noticeably. Following his appointment, he led Adamson's search for new advertising agencies to take over the lucrative Burger King account. As a result of the search D'Arcy Masius Benton & Bowles was selected as the agency to handle media planning and buying. A small but highly innovative agency, Ammirati and Puris, was selected to handle the creative side. I spent several days in New York with Burger King management and franchisees on the marketing Advisory Committee in this selection process. Our advertising in recent years had lost much of its impact and focus, and had produced little, if any, tangible results. It was obvious to me that we needed not only smart new advertising and a new, revitalized, and innovative marketing approach, but to sharpen the quality of our restaurant services. With these factors fully implemented, and boosted by an advertising expenditure which could easily exceed $200 million a year, the promise of significant increases in sales was clearly in the cards. This was part of the excitement and anticipation felt by management and franchisees as a newly charged Burger King Corporation entered mid-year 1994.

A sharp new marketing strategy could give us a boost, but there was still the thorny problem of dealing with the many restaurants which were not measuring up to acceptable operating standards. This matter was in need of a considerable amount of attention.

When Burger King was compared to Wendy's and McDonald's on the National Adult Tracking study, we were ranked third as being a "pleasant place," third in offering "value for the money," third in consistency, third in cleanliness, and third in exterior appearance. This was a humiliating and alarming report about our restaurant operations. It would be pointless to launch a hard-hitting advertising campaign if we were unable to deliver the promise our advertising would be making. In all the meetings I addressed, I tried to drive home the urgency of correcting these weaknesses. We knew what was going on. The consumer attitudes were right in front of us for everyone to see and read, but up to this point we had been very slow in responding.

At this very same time, management was attempting to introduce a number of promising improvements to our product line. I had always been concerned about the size of our small hamburger. It weighed 1.8 ounces against our major competitor's 1.6 ounces, and there were two things wrong with that. First of all, we were not getting any credit for being "just a little bit bigger." The difference in size was hardly noticeable. Secondly, we charged a higher price which, as far as consumers were concerned, offered very little in exchange. I thought management's response to this situation was right on the money. They decided to introduce a 2.8-ounce product to replace the 1.8-ounce patty we had been using for the regular hamburger, cheeseburger, and the Whopper, Jr. Using two of these significantly larger patties of beef, they introduced the new "mega double cheeseburger," which created a bit of a sensation. Even with the competition able to challenge us on price, we believed that consumers would buy on the basis of quality. This was no longer the 15-cent burger war that had been the basis upon which the hamburger fast-food business had been built. This was a matter of a good hamburger beating out a rather ordinary hamburger. Price would be immaterial. Our advertising would soon be able to convey the message that our regular hamburgers were 75 percent larger than our competition's. Having built their business on a small hamburger, this would present them with another major challenge inasmuch as we would again be presenting a critical distinction between ourselves and our major competitor. We hadn't done that since 1973 when we told the world to "Have it your way."

There was still much to do so far as service was concerned and much more was needed in terms of employee training and operational support at the restaurant level. Many of our restaurants were in great need of physical upgrading and reinvestment. These deficiencies had come about largely as the result of the inability of franchisees to generate adequate cash flows in recent years. Our company-operated restaurants had fallen into a state of disrepair because of the reluctance of management to adequately reinvest in the business. An improved marketing approach was certainly important, but the first order of business would be to improve the quality of our restaurant operations. If we couldn't satisfy the public that our restaurants were in excellent physical condition and well-run, the success of even the finest marketing program would be seriously compromised. I had been stressing the importance of this with top management, and I was pleased to see that considerable progress was being made in this regard.

Entering the fall of 1994, we had made a good start toward rebuilding the business, and it was evident that we had some very powerful forces to draw upon in our quest for increased sales and profitability. The first factor was the Whopper itself, which was unquestionably the most preferred sandwich in the United States. Consumer attitude surveys clearly verified the fact that the Whopper was preferred by 2 to 1 over any other sandwich being offered by our principal competitors. We had built a reputation for flame-broiling and having it "your way," and these were very important consumer issues. According to the National Adult Tracking study, consumers were giving us high marks on both accounts. The second factor was our strong physical presence in the marketplace. We had over 7000 restaurants in operation, and most of them were located on major pieces of commercial real estate throughout the country. With such gigantic size, excellent locations, and the very strong image that this projected on a national scale, we were enjoying a significant marketing advantage.

The third factor was the commitment of the Burger King system to spend a minimum of 4 percent of sales to promote the business. By 1994 we projected an annual marketing budget in excess of $275 million, $200 million of which was planned to be spent on advertising alone. With such powerful advantages and a commitment by management to improve restaurant operations and customer service, we could expect to be able to significantly increase restaurant sales. The only question that remained was how well Burger King management and our franchisees could execute the strategy. The full support of the franchisees would be critical to our success. Jim Adamson's main challenge at that particular moment was to put it all together and make this new strategy work. I felt confident that he was the one person who had the ability to do that.

This was all taking place in 1994. Burger King at the time was definitely on a roll having only recently come out of the doldrums. This was in contrast to conditions in the restaurant marketplace where competition was heating up. Many companies were experiencing declining sales, numerous cost pressures, and in many cases sharply reduced earnings. There was mounting evidence that the supply of restaurants was now exceeding the demand for these services. "Saturation" was the buzzword that financial analysts, restaurateurs, and chain executives used with a growing concern about its many implications.

At this point I wasn't concerned about Burger King's ability to grow and prosper in this competitive arena. We had made some smart changes, and we were getting high marks from a rapidly expanding customer base. I had no doubt that we were on the right track and well positioned to accept the challenges that would come in the future. I expected to see a continuation and buildup of price discounting coming from our major competitors. Everyone was battling for a share of a market that was getting squeezed. It would be quite natural for participants to return to their original roots, which involved the delivery of good food at the lowest possible cost in the marketplace.

As to the future, I couldn't see many fundamental changes in the way the domestic food-service industry would continue to function. The American people will not deviate in their demand for quality food, clean restaurants, efficient and courteous service, and "value," which is a term I use to describe a variety of offerings. Value certainly suggests price yet it stands for much more than that. Consumers will continue to reward the deliverer of low prices and high economic value, but they expect more than that, demanding a variety of services and personal attention in addition to price. Fast, courteous service is just one example. These very simple yet fundamental issues will continue to be the foundation upon which successful businesses will be built and continue to grow into the future. Certain things never change.

Another important key to the success of restaurant operations in the future will be the ability of food-service operators to adjust to changing consumer tastes and demands. In recent years consumers have focused on nutritional and health concerns. This has had a significant impact on bringing about changes in menu offerings in the nation's restaurants. The preference for beef is gradually losing ground to chicken, fish, and other items which contain less fat. Fried foods are being looked upon with increasing disfavor. Consumers and governmental agencies are demanding that nutritional labeling be placed on packaged consumer products sold in grocery stores, and this will dictate changes in the way food is sold in restaurants. Consumers want to know facts concerning the amounts of fat, protein, cholesterol, vitamins, minerals, carbohydrates, sodium, and calories present in the foods they eat. People are conscious about their weight and physical fitness and how the food they eat affects their personal health. As these and other related matters become more important to consumers, restaurateurs will either recognize their significance and adapt or become a casualty in a changing marketplace.

During the 1940s when I began my career in the foodservice industry, I couldn't possibly have imagined that such things as smoking in public places would someday be outlawed. I could not have predicted that consumers would develop such radically different attitudes about the foods we eat. Changes such as these, along with the public's increased focus on physical fitness, health care, and nutritional issues, have already resulted in extending the life expectancy of the American people. We should expect that these issues will come into much sharper focus in the future and that the nation's restaurants will need to address these concerns by providing the kind of service a changing customer base will demand.

This invites speculation as to how the restaurants of tomorrow, particularly those operated by the large chains, will react and respond to changing consumer demands. The most noticeable changes in the marketplace will occur in the demographic profile of the American people. As the baby boomers grow older and senior citizens live longer, consumer profiles, attitudes, and preferences will shift quite noticeably. The senior-citizen category will increase as a percentage of the total, while the teenaged and 18- to 24-year-old youth categories, although growing in number, will decline as a percentage of the overall total. This will have significant implications in terms of consumer demands and the future styling of the nation's restaurants.

Fast-food restaurants deserve the credit for bringing about the phenomenal increase in the incidence of "eating out" in America. The baby boomers were nurtured and brought up on hamburgers, hot dogs, chicken, pizza, and tacos. As they reach ever-increasing levels of maturity and economic status, they will continue to enjoy fast-food, but they will also demand an upgrade in their dining experiences. This shift in demand and preference has already resulted in the establishment of many casual and theme dinner houses, which are proving to be quite successful. Among the leaders in this field are such participants as TGI Friday's, Chili's, Applebee's, Longhorn and Outback steak houses, Steak and Ale, Bennigan's Tavern, Olive Garden, Red Lobster, Chart House, and many others. The fast-changing food-service marketplace has also made it possible for many new small and innovative restaurant concepts to succeed along with these large multiunit chains. Consumers welcome change and tend to reward innovation and unique expression in choosing their dining experience. This poses a certain threat to the huge multiunit chains which offer what can be best described as a uniform and highly predictable consistency. Restaurant customers will always be looking for more than that, and they are willing to experiment while they search. These multiunit chains, including Burger King, will be constantly challenged to provide the kind of ambiance and quality of food and service which attract and reward a more choosy and demanding customer.

I believe the real challenge for the fast-food chains will be to address the needs and demands of the rapidly growing ranks of senior citizens. I would target this group as the most promising of them all. Older people are more willing to accept a service which is familiar to them, and being more set in their ways, they are less interested in looking for new and innovative concepts. That turf, they believe, belongs to the young. Accordingly, I tend to think that the big restaurant chains will align themselves with the needs and preferences of an aging population. This is not to suggest that large chains won't target kids, families, and young people. They may find it quite frustrating to come up with an efficient and productive way to serve the younger generation's preferences, but this market is far too big and important to ignore.

I believe there are endless opportunities available to the management and franchisees of Burger King Corporation. There continues to be a growing domestic opportunity, and there is a huge potential for growth in the international markets. American expertise in restaurant operations is light years ahead of our international food-servicing counterparts. People in foreign lands have welcomed American food-service innovations, and they will continue to do so. To be sure, foreign markets are complex and very complicated, but they nonetheless offer a bonanza of opportunity.

As far as the U.S. market is concerned, I seriously doubt that many new or existing multiunit restaurant chains will ever succeed in developing a full-scale national presence. Strong regional and local chains will offer far too much in the way of stiff competition and so will the established national chains that already exist. It should be remembered that most of the major markets are already heavily saturated. The financial, marketing, and operational risks are just too great to overcome at this point. Because of its size and presence in the marketplace, Burger King still has a domestic growth potential which should help ensure the continuation of its strong and relatively unassailable position.

In recent years Burger King management has gone "back to basics" which is another way of saying that it has reemphasized the principles upon which the business was originally built. In essence these basics involve quick, courteous service, a simple and easy to understand menu, clean restaurants, low and affordable prices, and top-quality food. We got away from some of that for a while, but we are back on course and the results indicate that the basic fundamentals still work quite well. Proper execution is all that is needed now to elevate the business to the next level of success. What Dave Edgerton and I envisioned back in the 1950s has become reality. In the beginning we set out to build a successful chain of restaurants wherever we could establish them, and we attempted to accomplish that by enlisting the help and support of many people who would become our franchisees. Part of our vision was to pool our combined resources in an attempt to build a brand awareness in every one of the markets we entered. The company has grown dramatically as a result of this. I am often asked if we could ever have envisioned creating such a huge success. The quick and easy answer is that it is beyond anything we could possibly have imagined so many years ago. We owe a debt of gratitude to the thousands of people who played such important roles in bringing all this about. The Burger King story is already over 40 years old, but this could be just the beginning because our world of opportunity is still unfolding.

Burger King has the luxury of resting on a solid foundation, and this is reinforced by strong consumer acceptance and approval of the way we conduct our business. Burger King management will be challenged to strengthen this base in a constantly changing marketplace. During my more than 50 years of experience in the food-service and hospitality field, I have witnessed many companies reaching pinnacles of great success only to stumble and fall as the result of an inability to recognize and deal with change.

Burger King has been at the crossroads of making important strategic decisions in the past, and the company has made its share of mistakes in determining direction. These occasional errors in corporate judgment have derailed opportunity and threatened business survival as this historical account has pointed out. As strong as the company may be at any point in the future business cycle, it would be a great mistake to assume that it can survive the inadequacies of inept management or decision making that fails to meet the needs, demands, and preferences of restaurant customers.

My business experience has taught me that very few managers really know how to *listen*. I have always thought of myself as a good listener, and I believe that this is the quality that a leader must have in order to be effective. I have very little patience with people in leadership positions who are unable to control their egos. People with huge egos might climb on the rungs of the management ladder for a while, but ultimately their performance is negatively affected by an inability to listen to few people other than themselves. Egos can act as ear plugs, and I have witnessed too many situations where this has interfered with good executive decision making.

Jim Adamson has a rare and unique quality as a leader and as a chief executive. Not only does he invite the opinions of others, but he listens to them. He surrounds himself with intelligent, knowledgeable people who can offer valuable advice and insight. I was impressed by the fact that Jim has always been willing to acknowledge that he didn't have all the answers. He was willing to admit this to his own management team and the entire franchisee community.

Shortly after becoming the CEO, Jim invited me to join him for breakfast at the Grand Bay Hotel in nearby Coconut Grove. My February 1993 address to the franchisees in Tampa had impressed him on two counts. The first was that the franchisees seemed to be very pleased that I was taking an interest in the affairs of the company again. Second and more important was that they felt what I had said had put a finger on the problems that were facing the company. I had outlined exactly what I thought was wrong with the business and the franchisees who attended that meeting seemed pleased that finally someone had called attention to them. I was highly critical about the company's handling of matters in the past. Normally, this kind of criticism would have turned off a CEO. I had put my own personal observations on the table, citing a thoughtless array of too many marginal menu items, customer reactions to a confusing menu board, product quality and pricing issues, an unfocused marketing strategy, bad advertising, and slow service in unclean restaurants, all of which led to discouraged employees and franchisees who were losing faith in the system. These things needed to be said, and Jim was smart enough to recognize that this discussion could help in the recovery process he envisioned.

I had a distinct advantage as a spokesperson because of my unique position. I was not a member of management, but the franchisees seemed to appreciate the fact that because of my background experience and long-standing interest in the business, I new what worked and what didn't work. I was an unbiased and highly objective independent with no ties or obligations to either management or the franchisees. I was free to say what I thought, and both management and franchisees were willing to listen.

Perhaps as a result of the discouragement that had set in by that time, many franchisees had quit carrying their share of the load. I could challenge them on that issue and get away with it because it was an honest and fair-minded expression of concern on my part. They were willing to accept it on that basis. I could challenge them on that while mentioning all of the things which the franchisees themselves needed to address. I could do this much in the manner that I could chastise management for their lack of effective leadership, with nothing to lose and nothing to gain and the credibility to go along with it. I could be totally honest and forthright in stating what I believed to be the problem and what I believed needed immediate fixing.

Jim Adamson, at the time, was a 45-year-old executive with no previous experience of any kind in the restaurant business. He was candid with everyone about that, acknowledging that although he was not a restaurateur, he was "a darned good retailer." His admission told me quite a bit about the man, and that level of honesty and candor was well received by our franchisees.

First of all, Jim knew that the fundamental issue confronting Burger King involved the marketing of our food and restaurant services. He obviously understood the importance of building brand awareness, a key factor which would be so important in restoring the business to health and profitability. Second, I couldn't help but be impressed by the fact that this man's ego wasn't going to interfere with his getting the best advice he could obtain. He quickly recognized the importance of seeing to it that our customers received the very best in terms of restaurant services. He would find the people in the organization who could deliver on this important commitment. Meanwhile, he would stay focused on building the brand.

During our breakfast meeting, Jim asked me to become more actively involved in the business. I was impressed, particularly in light of the fact that I was continuing to call attention to management's previous lack of leadership. I accepted his suggestion, which I viewed as a great compliment, and I told him that I would do whatever I could to help. I cautioned him, however, that until he got the defects in the system ironed out that I would be constantly challenging him and his management people to get it right. This understanding formed the basis of a working relationship which has been a matter of great personal satisfaction to me. I have not been the architect of the new strategic direction of Burger King. That credit belongs to Adamson and his management team. I did play a role in calling attention to the problems we were facing, and I did suggest many of the things which needed to be done to correct these problems, but that is all.

I had a history of making a lot of mistakes during my business career, and many of them were made during the fifties, sixties, and early seventies when I was the CEO of the company. Sometimes I think that it is a small wonder that I survived at all. I often look back to the period of 1949 to 1951 and the opening of my first two restaurants. Mistakes in judgment forced me to cope with many disappointments, which on several different occasions put me on the verge of failure and personal bankruptcy. Perhaps the only benefit that can be derived from defeat and near failure is the recognition that adversity is such a great teacher. I was taught some harsh lessons enroute to building the business. Each bump in the road was a learning experience, helping me prepare for the next challenge. When I was down in the dumps and suffering from the humiliation of making a mess of a business career which meant so much to me, I learned how to listen and reflect on how to steer a better course into the future. I guess my advice to young people would include not being afraid to make mistakes.

What attracted me to Jim Adamson was his intelligent approach to studying past mistakes, his willingness to listen to people who could give him good advice, and his ability to put it all together and chart a new strategic direction that made sense and was appropriate for the company's future.

This is by no means to suggest that I thought the company was home free in 1994. The resurgence in sales and profitability that came as the result of Jim's leadership was impressive to be sure, but there were also roadblocks in the way. Burger King still had to contend with the concerns of the NFA and franchisees who remained unconvinced that their interests were receiving adequate consideration. Proposed franchising legislation and regulation at the national and state level were posing a threat to the continuation of mutually productive business relationships between franchisors and franchisees. My advice to franchisees was to avoid, at all costs, inviting government into the picture. There were complex organizational issues to deal with, much of which came about as the result of corporate reengineering, which involved cutbacks in personnel and the realignment of job responsibilities. This was a painful and difficult process for Burger King to have undergone, and there was still much healing to be done. The intricacies of expansion into so many international markets posed many challenging questions about structure, control, and operations. The opportunity was huge, but so were the risks.

By 1994 ominous signs had appeared which indicated that the restaurant industry was becoming overly saturated. Although the chains which made up the major share of the market were still adding units, they were being forced to fight for an increasing share of a market that was no longer expanding as rapidly as it had done in the past. The proliferation of chain restaurants was growing faster than the market itself, and it was doing so with predictable results. Casualty reports began to flood the business and trade press. By 1994 the industry was well into the "value decade," with discounting being the order of the day. All of this had the effect of squeezing margins and putting pressure on profits. In many cases, returns on invested capital failed to meet the expectations of the financial community, and this only aggravated the situation. For many years Wall Street viewed the restaurant industry as a field ripe with promise and opportunity and with good reason. There had been many examples of extraordinary successes in the restaurant business.

However, as saturation and discounting reared their ugly heads, a lot of things began to unravel. Management and personnel cutbacks predictably led to inferior restaurant operations. Customers began to experience poor service and complain about it, restaurants were often not as clean as they should be, and different managements, often in desperation, began to "short term" the business in order to focus more on cash flows and less on operations. They began to lose sight of the importance of the quality of the customers' experience in the restaurant. This was hardly the way to increase sales and profits. My prediction was that a shakeout could be right around the corner. There were too many players in an overcrowded market, and with some of them pursuing quick fixes and short-term objectives, there were bound to be some casualties and disappointments.

Within the industry there had been many instances of leveraged buyouts and ill-conceived financing schemes. Many of these overleveraged situations ultimately were forced to seek the protection of the bankruptcy courts in order to continue. During 1994 in particular, changes in the ranks of top management and news of disappointing earnings were regularly reported in the trade press. Investors began to look at the restaurant industry with renewed caution and a keener investment approach. Meanwhile, as competition continued to grow, the strongest players began to beat up on the weaker ones. An extraordinarily high turnover in the ranks of top management was witnessed in 1994, as bankers, investors, and directors tried to restore the beleaguered and downtrodden chains back to financial health. Every segment of the industry was affected. There were serious problems in steak houses, the pizza business, sub shops, casual-theme restaurants, coffee shops, cafeterias, the chicken business, double-drive-thru restaurants, and a number of fast-food hamburger operations. Consumers were being bombarded by "deals" and price discounting, which were causing disruption and a lowering of profit margins. More and more it appeared that survival of the fittest would be the governing rule in these situations. Weak players in tough markets are forced to expect such treatment when competition heats up. With so many inexperienced and undercapitalized participants in an already crowded and highly competitive field, some of the weaker players dropped by the wayside. It seemed almost a certainty that many more would follow.

The year 1994 marked a point of beginning when good management, sound restaurant and marketing operations, and adequate capitalizations came forth to bring some long-overdue sanity to an industry which, in too many cases, had overextended its limits. This was the prevalent economic situation in the food-service business as we entered 1995. As far as Burger King was concerned, I remained involved, at least to the extent that I could contribute in a constructive way to the benefit of the company, but the real leadership responsibility would remain with a much younger management team. I had no interest in assuming an active role in day-to-day management, but I was very willing to counsel and advise when called upon to do so.

My career in the food-service industry had lasted over 50 years, ever since 1943 when I hitchhiked to Cornell as a 17-year-old with no money, but with an acceptance to the university in my pocket. As I approach the age of 70, I am constantly reminded that this is a time when most business people are already retired. Fortunately, at least for the time being, I do not belong in that category, and I am happy to be able to say that. I don't know where the road of life will lead me, but I am enjoying the experience of walking it. I am busy and very much stimulated by all the many things that I am doing. I feel as though I am contributing something of value to society and the world around me. I have a wonderful family, a good many valued friends, a great marriage to an extraordinarily special woman, our good health, and a mind which continues to function reasonably well. As far as my mind is concerned, I like to think that "the marbles" are still all there. For this and all the rest, I feel very fortunate and grateful. My personal life has been very good to me.

My professional life and business career has been, to a large extent, dominated and influenced by my involvement with Burger King Corporation. I have had the pleasure and satisfaction of playing a role in elevating the company into the enviable position of being the world's second largest restaurant chain, which is something I could never have imagined so many years ago. This accomplishment is a matter of considerable personal pride and satisfaction, which I would have enjoyed sharing with my parents and grandparents, all of whom passed away when I was very young. This book attempts to tell the story of how all this happened and how the company reached its pinnacle of success, but the story itself will probably never end, nor will a final chapter ever be written. I expect that this history will continue to be written and that it will record the pride of many people, including me, who were there and helped make it happen.

Index

About the Author

Jim McLamore (1926–1996) started his first fast-food restaurant at the age of 23. Within five years, he helped form the corporation Burger King of Miami, Inc., which grew to become the world's second-largest fast-food chain. He remained as CEO of Burger King until 1972, later becoming president of the National Restaurant Association and serving on seven corporate boards. He helped create The Nightly Business Report, *which is now broadcast worldwide.*